Windows on the World

Windows on the World

International Books for Elementary and Middle Grade Readers

Rosanne Blass

LIBRARIES UNLIMITED

An Imprint of ABC-CLIO, LLC

A B C CLIO

Santa Barbara, California • Denver, Colorado • Oxford, England

Library of Congress Cataloging-in-Publication Data

Blass, Rosanne J., 1937-
  Windows on the world : international books for elementary and middle grade readers / Rosanne Blass.
      p. cm.
  ISBN 978-1-59158-830-6 (alk. paper) -- ISBN 978-1-59158-831-3 (ebook)
1. Children's literature--Study and teaching (Primary)--United States. 2.
Children's literature--Study and teaching (Middle school)--United States. 3.
Children--Books and reading--English-speaking countries. 4. Children--Books
and reading--United States. 5. Multiculturalism in literature. I. Title.
  LB1527.B56 2010
    372.64'044--dc22   2009042251

14 13 12 11 10   1 2 3 4 5

This book is also available on the World Wide Web as an eBook.
Visit www.abc-clio.com for details.

ABC-CLIO, LLC
130 Cremona Drive, P.O. Box 1911
Santa Barbara, California 93116-1911

This book is printed on acid-free paper ∞
Manufactured in the United States of America

Copyright Acknowledgments

American Association of School Librarians: Standards for the Twenty-First Century Learner were developed by the American Library Association in 2007. They can be downloaded at http://www.ala.org/aasl/standards. Used with permission.

Contents

Acknowledgment and Dedication

I wish to thank my editor, Sharon Coatney, for suggesting the idea of developing this book that focuses on international books for elementary and middle grade readers, and for her continued support and encouragement during the writing process. I also want to thank my granddaughter, Maria Glenski, an avid young reader, for our many conversations about "good books that kids really like," and for her recommended list of titles.

This book is dedicated to media specialists, teachers, parents, and others who open the world of books to young readers. Hopefully, this book will be an aid to all of you as you pass on the joy of reading.

Introduction

Interest in books that provide an international perspective is an emerging trend in literature for children and young adults. An increasing number of foreign titles are coming from U.S. publishers as well as from foreign publishers who have distributors in the United States. Many of these books are translations from other languages into English. Others are written and or illustrated by authors and illustrators who are from countries other than the United States, or who have lived extensively in other countries.

The purpose of this book is to introduce teachers and librarians who work with elementary and middle grade readers to international points of view and perspectives presented by authors and illustrators from countries and cultures outside of the United States. Hopefully this book will open windows that will enable readers to see themselves reflected in the books they read and to discover worlds other than their own.

Titles include books published within the last ten years that are translations from languages other than English, books by authors and illustrators from countries and cultures outside the United States, books by authors and illustrators born outside of but now living in the United States, books by Americans living in other countries and cultures, and reissues of books by authors such as Jules Verne and C. S. Lewis. A few titles by American authors and illustrators that provide authentic representations of other cultures and that fit appropriately are included with the related books.

Books that have won international awards, as well as works written and/ or illustrated by authors and illustrators who are recognized and recommended by professional organizations such as the United States Board on Books for Young People (USBBY), International Reading Association, National Council of Social Studies, National Science Teachers Association, American Library Association, National Council of Teachers of English, and Children's Book Council were selected for inclusion. Publications such as *Booklist, Book Report, Book Talk, Bulletin of the Center for Children's Books, JOYS, School Library Journal, VOYA-Voices of Young Advocates, Multicultural Review, Instructor, Teaching K–12, Reading Teacher*, and *Language Arts* were consulted for reviews and recommendations.

Three international book awards are featured in this book: the Batchelder Award, the BolognaRagazzi Award, and the Hans Christian Andersen Prize. The Batchelder Award is granted annually to the publisher of the most outstanding translated book published in the United States. The BolognaRagazzi Award is granted annually for fiction and nonfiction at the Bologna Book Fair. The Hans Christian Andersen Prize is granted biennially to honor a living author and a living illustrator. In addition, this book features the Outstanding International Books selected annually by the United States Board on Books for Young People (USBBY). Finally, books by Rudyard Kipling, the first Englishman to receive the Nobel Prize for literature, and by Michael Morpurgo, the Children's Laureate of Britain are included.

Titles consist of fiction, nonfiction, and poetry, with over 100 lead books and over 350 related books for a total of about 475 titles. The book is organized by age levels 4–8 and 8–12. Within age levels the book is organized by countries and cultures. Entries consist of bibliographic data, information about the author and illustrator, identification of genre and recommended age level, a summary of the book, suggested curriculum responses correlated with national curriculum standards, and related books. Age levels are suggested as a general guide. Those who use this book are urged to use their own judgment in selecting and using titles with their children.

Curriculum responses are intended to stimulate ideas rather than provide detailed lesson activities. They are natural rather than artificial responses to books, in that they are directly related to and flow from the books. The purpose of the curriculum responses is to make connections between books and children's lives, and between books and school studies. Curriculum responses relate to language arts, social studies, science, and the arts, and they are correlated with national curriculum standards. The curriculum responses are designed to stimulate language, literacy, and cognitive development through oral language use, conversations, and discussions; through art, music, and drama; through inquiry, research, and critical thinking. Those who use this book will want to adapt activities to the needs and interests of their children. In doing so, let the book be your guide!

The primary audiences for this book are media specialists, school librarians, and teachers, as well as children's librarians, church and synagogue librarians, parents, and others who work with elementary and middle-grade children. Media specialists, school librarians, and church and synagogue librarians will find this book helpful in selecting and promoting books in media centers, classrooms, and in church and synagogue programs. Teachers can use this book to promote books with related instructional activities in their classrooms. Public children's librarians who serve young students in the library, or who make school visits, can use this book to promote their collections and services. Hopefully, parents, especially those who home-school, and others who work with young readers will also find this book useful.

Books chosen for inclusion represent only a sampling of books available in the United States from English and non–English-speaking countries of the world. Although there are far more books available from English than from non–English-speaking countries, more books available from Asia than from the Middle East, and many books available from Europe, an attempt has been made to provide a balanced selection of books from various countries.

Readers will have the opportunity to explore regions of the world, step into fantasy worlds, travel back in time, meet real people, and engage in nature study. They will experience issues of social justice and of children in crisis; they will learn about war and the struggle to survive, and death and the mourning process. They will meet young people who are caught between two cultures and who are attempting to resolve their identities. Fun and humor also await, along with an abundance of information about space, the ocean, dinosaurs, robots, and pyramids. Folktales, fairy tales, and poetry; interactive books and graphic novels; an introduction to artists and their paintings; music, classic stories, and outstanding illustrations are all part of the offerings. Selections offer many choices with which to learn, share, and enjoy.

Ages 4–8

AFRICA

Book selections give readers a view of contemporary life and of the cultural heritage of Africa through realistic fiction from South Africa and through folklore and mythology from West Africa and Egypt. Related books include folklore and mythology from Ghana and Nigeria. In addition, South African authors and illustrators Barry Downard, Diane Hofmeyr, and Jude Daly treat readers to retellings of traditional folktales from the English-speaking world, from Persia, and from China. An illustrated book of prayers and an illustrated version of Ecclesiastes 3:1–8, by Jude Daly, can be found in related books. Finally, South African illustrator Joan Rankin offers an assortment of books written by American authors, and one that she authored, as well as illustrated. The United States Board on Books for Young People (USBBY) selected books by three authors as Outstanding International Books. In addition to being recognized by USBBY, author and illustrator Niki Daly was nominated for the Hans Christian Andersen Prize. Curriculum Responses include map work, poetry reading, art, and other activities.

Beake, Lesley. *Home Now*. Waterton, MA: Charlesbridge, 2007. Unpaged. Illustrated by Karin Littlewood. $16.95. ISBN 978-1-58089-162-2.

Author and Illustrator

Author Lesley Beake was born in Scotland and moved to South Africa where she now lives in Tamboerskloof. Illustrator Karin Littlewood lives in England. The United States Board on Books for Young People listed this book as a 2008 Outstanding International Book. South Africa is the setting for this book.

📖 Realistic Fiction, Picture Book, Ages 5–7

Summary

Sieta now lives with Aunty. She remembers her real home in the mountains, the geraniums outside the front door, going to church with Ma and Pa, and then Ma and Pa getting sicker and sicker until they're not there anymore. Satara is also an orphan just like Sieta. She is the smallest elephant who lives at the elephant park with other elephants who have lost their families. Sieta returns to the elephant park to visit Satara. She also begins to pay attention to the people in her new village, some happy, some sad, some frightened— and she even makes a new friend. Vibrant watercolor and gauche illustrations enhance this gentle tale of death, mourning, and new life. A note prior to the title page locates the village and Knysna Elephant Park on the Western Cape of South Africa. An ending Note About the Story tells of the plight of AIDS in Africa and lists Web sites for more information.

Curriculum Responses with Curriculum Standards

1. After reading, find Africa on a world map, and locate the Western Cape of South Africa. (American Association of School Librarians Standards 1.1.6, 2.3.1, 2.4.3, 4.1.1, 4.1.2; English Language Arts Standards 1, 3; Social Studies Standards III)
2. Sieta looks at the pictures in her head. After reading, ask children whether they have pictures in their heads about happy times with people they love. Encourage discussion. (American Association of School Librarians Standards 1.1.2, 1.1.6, 1.3.4, 2.3.1, 3.1.2, 3.1.3, 3.2.1, 3.2.2, 3.3.1, 3.3.2, 3.3.5, 4.1.1, 4.1.2, 4.1.3, 4.1.5, 4.3.1; English Language Arts Standards 1, 3, 4, 6, 11, 12)
3. Sieta misses her home in the mountains and her parents. After she meets Satara, she begins to pay attention to life in her new home, and she makes a new friend. Discuss with children, then have them make pictures of Sieta, first missing her home and parents, then giving attention to Satara and her new home. (American Association of School Librarians Standards 1.2.3, 1.3.4, 2.1.6, 2.2.4, 3.1.2, 3.1.3, 3.2.1, 3.2.2, 3.3.4, 3.3.5, 4.1.3, 4.1.8, 4.3.1; English Language Arts Standards 4, 6, 11, 12; Visual Arts Content Standards 1, 3)

Related Books

1. Nivola, Claire A. *Planting the Trees of Kenya: The Story of Wangari Maathai.* New York: Frances Foster Books, 2008. Unpaged. $16.95. ISBN 0-374-39918-2.

Wangari Maathai, recipient of the Nobel Peace Prize and founder of the Green Belt Movement, returned to Kenya after studying in the United

States. In Kenya she taught the women and children to replant the trees that had been cut down.

Daly, Niki. *Happy Birthday, Jamela!* New York: Farrar, Straus & Giroux, 2006. Unpaged. $16.00. ISBN 0-374-32842-0.

Author and Illustrator

Author and illustrator Niki Daly lives in Cape Town, South Africa which is the setting for his books about Jamela. Three of Niki Daly's books (*Happy Birthday, Jamela; Pretty Selma: A Little Red Riding Hood Story from Africa*; and *Ruby Sings the Blues)* were listed by the United States Board on Books for Young People (USBBY) as Outstanding International Books. Daly was also nominated for the Hans Christian Andersen Prize.

📖 Realistic Fiction, Picture Book, Ages 4–8

Summary

It's almost Jamela's birthday. Mama takes her shopping for birthday clothes—a dress and shoes. Jamela wants the white sparkly Princess Shoes, but Mama buys black shoes that Jamela can wear to school. Jamela is ready to cry. Then she has an idea! She creates her own Princess Shoes by gluing sparkles all over her new black shoes. What do you suppose Mama says when she sees Jamela's Princess Shoes? It's Lily the artist who lives down the road who has an idea! What might that be? What do you suppose Jamela finds in her birthday bag?

Curriculum Responses with Curriculum Standards

1. After reading, have children either draw princess shoes or fold and make princess shoes using butcher paper or newspaper and decorate using sparkles and glue. (American Association of School Librarians Standards 1.1.6, 2.1.6, 2.2.4, 4.1.3, 4.1.8; English Language Arts Standard 1, 3, 4, 6; Visual Arts Content Standard 1, 2)
2. After reading, discuss with children how Jamela felt when her mother bought the black school shoes instead of the white sparkly Princess Shoes. How did Jamela feel when she received the Princess Shoes for her birthday? Ask children what their birthday wishes are or have been. Did they get their wish? How did they feel? (American Association of School Librarians Standards 1.1.2, 1.1.3, 1.1.6, 1.1.9, 1.3.4, 2.1.1, 2.3.1, 2.4.3, 3.1.2, 3.1.3, 3.2.1, 3.2.2, 3.2.3, 3.3.1, 3.3.2, 3.3.5, 4.1.1, 4.1.2, 4.1.3, 4.1.4, 4.1.5, 4.3.1; English Language Arts Standards 1, 3, 4, 6, 11, 12; Social Studies Standard IV)

3. Extend the activity by exploring and sharing with classmates birthday celebrations around the world. (American Association of School Librarians Standards 1.1.1, 1.1.2; 1.1.3, 1.1.4, 1.1.6, 1.1.9, 1.2.2, 1.2.3, 1.2.5, 1.3.4, 2.1.1, 2.1.5, 2.1.6, 2.2.1, 2.2.4, 2.4.3, 3.1.1, 3.1.2, 3.2.1, 3.2.2, 3.2.3, 3.3.5, 4.1.1, 4.1.2, 4.1.3, 4.1.6, 4.1.7, 4.2.1, 4.2.2, 4.3.1, 4.4.1, 4.4.3; English Language Arts Standards 1, 3, 4, 6, 11, 12; Social Studies Standard I)

4. Have the children find Cape Town, South Africa, on the globe. Point out that South Africa is in the Southern Hemisphere, and that we live in the Northern Hemisphere. Have children discuss how the two hemispheres are alike and how they are different. (American Association of School Librarians Standards 1.1.1, 1.1.2, 1.1.3, 1.1.9, 1.2.1, 1.3.4, 2.1.1, 2.3.1, 3.1.1, 3.1.2, 3.1.3, 3.2.1, 3.2,2, 3.3.1, 3.3.2, 3.3.3, 3.3.5, 4.1.2, 4.1.3, 4.3.1; English Language Arts Standards 1, 3, 4, 5, 11, 12; Social Studies Standard III)

5. Find the latitude of Cape Town, South Africa. Explain latitude. Locate and identify other cities in the Southern Hemisphere at about the same latitude (Buenos Aires, Argentina; Sydney, Australia; Auckland, New Zealand). Locate and identify cities in the Northern Hemisphere at about the same latitude as Cape Town, South Africa (Atlanta, GA.; Dallas/Fort Worth, TX; Phoenix, AZ.; Los Angeles, CA). How are these cities in the Northern and Southern Hemispheres alike and different? (American Association of School Librarians Standards 1.1.1, 1.1.3, 1.1.6, 1.3.4, 2.1.1, 2.1.3, 2.1.5, 2.3.1, 3.1.1, 3.1.2, 3.1.3, 3.2.1, 3.2.2, 3.3.3, 3.3.5, 4.1.2, 4.1.3, 4.1.4, 4.3.1; English Language Arts Standards 1, 3, 4, 6, 11, 12; Social Studies Standards I, III)

Related Books

1. Daly, Niki. *Pretty Salma: A Little Red Riding Hood Story from Africa.* New York: Clarion Books, 2006. 29p. $16.00. ISBN 9-780-618723454.

Meet Pretty Salma, Mr. Dog, and Granny in this African version of *Little Red Riding Hood.*

2. Daly, Niki. *Ruby Sings the Blues.* New York: Bloomsbury USA Children's Books, 2005. 32p. $16.95. ISBN 1-58234-995-9.

The kids at school won't play with Ruby, and her neighbors call her "loud-mouth," until some the neighbors teach Ruby to use her voice to sing the blues.

3. Daly, Niki. *Welcome to Zanzibar Road.* New York: Clarion Books, 2006. 31p. $16.00. ISBN 0780618649266.

Five short stories introduce readers to neighbors and life on Zanzibar Road.

4. Daly, Niki. *What's Cooking, Jamela?* New York: Farrar, Straus & Giroux, 2001. Unpaged. $16.00. ISBN 0-374-35602-5.

Jamela loses the chicken that her mother bought to fatten for Christmas dinner.

5. Daly, Niki. *Where's Jamela?* New York: Farrar, Straus & Giroux, 2004. Unpaged. $16.00. ISBN 0-374-38324-3.

Jamela is unhappy because she and Mama are moving to a different house.

Diakite, Baba Wague. *The Magic Gourd.* New York: Scholastic Press, 2003. Unpaged. $16.95. ISBN 0-439-43960-4.

Author and Illustrator

Author and illustrator Baba Wague Diakite is from Mali, West Africa. His illustrations are characterized by his use of traditional West African patterns. The United States Board on Books for Young People (USBBY) listed Baba Wague Diakite's book *Mee-An and the Magic Serpent: A Folktale from Mali,* as a 2008 Outstanding International Book.

📖 Folktale, Picture Book, Ages 4–8

Summary

Chameleon rewards Brother Rabbit for rescuing him from a thorn bush with the gift of his gourd. The magic gourd provides food and drink for Brother Rabbit, his family, and their hungry neighbors. Trouble starts when word of the magic gourd reaches the greedy king. Chameleon has a second gift for Rabbit. With the second gift, the greedy king learns to appreciate what he has and "learns the importance of generosity and friendship."

This retelling of the West African folktale derives from the oral tradition and finds variants across European, Asian, North and South American, and African cultures. Hand-painted ceramics and West African mud cloth patterns illustrate every page. A Song of Praise, an author's note, a description of the meanings of mud cloth patterns, a glossary, and a brief explanation of the folktale are included at the back of the book. The richness of this book lends itself to use with children across all ages.

Curriculum Responses with Curriculum Standards

1. After reading, encourage children to write their own variations of the folktale. (American Association of School Librarians Standards 1.1.6, 2.1.6, 2.2.4, 3.1.3, 4.1.3, English Language Arts Standards 4, 5, 12)
2. Use the glossary in the back of the book for pronunciations and meanings of the Bambara (national language of Mali) words used in the text. (English Language Arts Standards 1, 9)

3. Have children show and then tell the meanings of the mud cloth patterns shown in the illustrations. Use the meanings given in the back of the book. (American Association of School Librarians Standards 1.3.4, 2.1.5, 3.1.3, 3.2.1, 3.2.2, 3.3.5, 4.1.3, 4.3.1; English Language Arts Standards 1, 3, 4, 6, 11, 12; Visual Arts Content Standard 4)

4. Using the designs in the books as models, have children create designs using repetitive patterns. (American Association of School Librarians Standards 2.1.6, 2.2.4, 4.1.3, 4.1.8; English Language Arts Standards 4, 6, 12; Visual Arts Content Standard 1; English Language Arts Standard 4, 12)

5. See Folkloric Cousins of *The Magic Gourd* in the back of the book for references to other variations of this folktale. Have children read and compare variations of the tale. (American Association of School Librarians Standards 1.1.6, 4.1.1, 4.1.2; English Language Arts Standards 1, 2, 3, 4, 6, 11, 12)

Related Books

1. Diakite, Penda. *I Lost My Tooth in Africa*. New York: Scholastic Press, 2006. Unpaged. Illustrated by Baba Wague Diakite. $16.99. ISBN 0-439-66226-5.

The illustrator's daughter tells the story of how her little sister, Amina, loses a tooth in Africa. Amina puts her tooth under a calabash gourd, where the African tooth fairy finds it and replaces it with a chicken.

2. Diakite, Baba Wague. *Mee-An and the Magic Serpent: A Folktale from Mali*. Groundwood, 2007. 32p. $16.96. ISBN 978-0-88899-719-7.

Mee-An, who believes that she deserves a perfect husband, is tricked into marrying a serpent disguised as a handsome young man, but is rescued by her younger and wiser sister, Assa, who turns herself into a fly.

3. Musgrove, Margaret. *The Spider Weaver: A Legend of Kente Cloth*. New York: Scholastic Inc., 2001. Unpaged. Illustrated by Julia Cairns. $16.96. ISBN 0-590-98787-9.

Bold and colorful illustrations that reflect the African landscape enliven the Ghanaian legend of the spider weaver who taught Ameyaw and Kragu to weave intricate designs into a new fabric called Kente cloth.

4. Olaleye, Isaac O. *In the Rainfield Who Is the Greatest?* New York: Blue Sky Press, 2000. Unpaged. Illustrated by Ann Grifalconi. $16.96. ISBN 0-590-48363-3.

In this Nigerian folktale, Wind, Fire, and Rain hold a contest to determine which one is the greatest.

5. Williams, Sheron. *Imani's Music*. New York: Atheneum Books for Young Readers, 2002. Unpaged. Illustrated by Jude Daly. $17.00. ISBN 0-689-82254-5.

In the days of Used-to-Be, when there is no music, Imani the grasshopper discovers his gift for music, prays to the Ancestors to give the gift of music to the world, and carries his music from Africa to the New World aboard a slave ship.

Downard, Barry. *The Race of the Century.* New York: Simon & Schuster Books for Young Readers, 2008. Unpaged. $15.99. ISBN 1-4169-2509-0.

Author and Illustrator

Author and illustrator Barry Downard lives in the KwaZulu-Natal Midlands in South Africa.

📖 Fiction, Retelling, Ages 4–8

Summary

Everyone in Critterville is talking about it! The news is on TV and in the paper. The race of the century between Twinkle Toes (Tom Tortoise) and Flash Harry Hare is about to begin. Computer-generated photo-collages illustrate the lively text that retells the classic folktale about the tortoise and the hare.

Curriculum Responses with Curriculum Standards

1. After reading, have children write a script and act out the lively text. (American Association of School Librarians Standards 1.1.6, 1.1.9, 1.3.4, 2.1.5, 2.1.6, 2.2.4, 3.1.2, 3.1.3, 3.2.1, 3.2.3, 3.3.1, 3.3.2, 3.3.5, 4.1.1, 4.1.3, 4.1.8, 4.3.1; English Language Arts Standards 1, 3, 4, 5, 6, 11, 12; Theater Content Standards 1, 2)
2. After reading, have children retell the story by writing newspaper articles giving details about the race. (American Association of School Librarians Standards 1.1.6, 2.1.6, 2.2.4, 3.1.3, 3.3.5, 4.1.1, 4.1.3, 4.1.8, 4.3.1; English Language Arts Standards 1, 3, 4, 5, 6, 11, 12)
3. After reading, have children create collages based on the story. (American Association of School Librarians Standards 1.1.6, 1.2.3, 2.1.6, 2.2.4, 4.1.1, 4.1.3, 4.1.8; English Language Arts Standards 1, 3, 4, 6, 11, 12; Visual Arts Content Standards 1, 2, 3)

Related Books

1. Brooks, Jeremy. *Let There Be Peace: Prayers from Around the World.* London: Frances Lincoln Children's Books, 2009. Illustrated by Jude Daly. $16.95. ISBN 1-845-07530-7.

The author has compiled a collection of prayers for young people from the Christian, Shinto, B'hai, Native American, Taoist, Hindu, Buddhist, and Muslim traditions.

2. Daly, Jude. *The Little Blue Slipper: An Irish Cinderella Story.* London: Frances Lincoln Children's Books, 2008. 32p. $16.95. ISBN 1-845-07815-2.

Trembling is the beautiful Irish girl left at home by her sisters, who are afraid that she will marry before they do.

3. Daly, Jude. *To Everything There Is a Season.* Grand Rapids, MI: Wm. B. Eerdmans Publishing Co., 2006. 32p. $16.00. ISBN 0-828-5286-6.

A rural South African landscape illustrates the words of Ecclesiastes 3:1–8.

4. Downard, Barry. *Carla's Famous Traveling Feather and Fur Show.* New York: Milk & Cookies Press, 2006. 32p. $16.95. ISBN 1-596-87171-7.

Carla is one chick who's not satisfied with life in the barnyard or in the coop!

5. Downard. Barry. *The Little Red Hen.* New York: Simon & Schuster Children's Publishing, 2004. 32p. $16.95. ISBN 1-689-85962-7.

Full-color, computer-generated photo-collages illustrate this contemporary retelling of the story of the little red hen.

Hofmeyr, Dianne. *The Star-Bearer: A Creation Myth from Ancient Egypt.* New York: Farrar Straus Giroux, 2001. Unpaged. Illustrated by Jude Daly. $16.00. ISBN 0-374-37181-4.

Author and Illustrator

Author Dianne Hofmeyr was born and raised in South Africa, traveled throughout Thailand, Hong Kong, Australia, Canada, the United States, Europe, and Africa, and now lives in London. Illustrator Jude Daly was born in London, immigrated with her family to South Africa at the age of two, where she was raised and educated, returned to London, and now lives in Cape Town, South Africa, with her husband, Niki Daly, who is also a children's author and illustrator.

📖 Fiction, Mythology, Picture Book, Ages 4–8

Summary

Atum rises from the deep waters, breathes air and rain across the waters, and produces Shu and Tefnut, who have two children, Geb, the god of earth, and Nut, the goddess of the sky. When Atun separates Geb and Nut,

Geb's grief gives rise to the mountains and volcanoes, while his mother Tefnut creates the rivers and valleys with her tears. In his pity for Geb, Atun sprinkles Nut with the stars, the planets, and the moon so Geb can see her. But Atun's work is not yet done. Nut will bear children, and Atun will join her in the sky.

Curriculum Responses with Curriculum Standards

1. Have children read, then search for, read, compare, and contrast other creation myths. (American Association of School Librarians Standards 1.1.1, 1.1.2, 1.1.3, 1.1.4, 1.1.6, 1.1.9, 1.2.2, 1.2.3, 1.3.4, 2.1.1, 2.1.3, 2.1.5, 3.1.1, 3.1.2, 3.1.3, 3.2.1, 3.2.2, 3.3.2, 3.3.3, 3.3.5, 4.1.1, 4.1.2, 4.1.3, 4.1.4, 4.1.7, 4.3.1; English Language Arts Standards 1, 2, 3, 4, 6, 7, 11, 12)

2. What role do Nut's children Osiris, Horus, Set, Isis, and Nephthys play in Egyptian mythology? Have children research and report their findings to their classmates. (American Association of School Librarians Standards 1.1.1, 1.1.2, 1.1.3, 1.1.4, 1.1.5, 1.1.6, 1.1.7., 1.1.8, 1.1.9, 1.2.1, 1.2.2, 1.2.3, 1.2.6, 1.2.7, 1.3.1, 1.3.2, 1.3.3, 1.3.4, 1.4.1, 1.4.2, 1.4.3, 1.4.4, 2.1.1, 2.1.2, 2.1.3, 2.1.5, 2.2.1, 2.4.3, 2.4.4, 3.1.1, 3.1.2, 3.1.3, 3.2.1, 3.2.2, 3.2.3, 3.3.1, 3.3.3, 3.3.5, 4.1.1, 4.1.2, 4.1.3, 4.1.4, 4.1.7, 4.2.1, 4.2.2, 4.2.3, 4.3.1; English Language Arts Standards 4, 6, 7, 8, 11, 12)

3. Use this book in conjunction with a study of Egypt. Set up a display of books about Egypt. Have children read and give oral book talks about their favorite books to encourage their classmates to expand their reading. (American Association of School Librarians Standards 1.1.6, 1.1.9, 1.2.2, 1.3.4, 2.1.5, 3.1.2, 3.1.3, 3.2.1, 3.2.2, 3.2.3, 3.3.2, 3.3.3, 3.3.5, 4.1.1, 4.1.2, 4.1.3, 4.1.4, 4.1.5, 4.1.7, 4.1.8, 4.2.1, 4.2.2, 4.2.4, 4.3.1, 4.3.3, 4.4.1, 4.4.2; English Language Arts Standards 1, 2, 4, 6, 11, 12)

Related Books

1. Bower, Tamara. *The Shipwrecked Sailor: An Egyptian Tale with Hieroglyphs.* New York: Atheneum Books for Young Readers, 2000. 32p. $17.00. ISBN 0-689-83046-7.

A Note About This Story, Explanation of Symbols, About Hieroglyphs, and Further Reading complete the story of an ancient voyage to a land of riches south of Egypt retold from a nineteenth century BC papyrus scroll of hieroglyphs.

2. Hofmeyr, Dianne. *The Stone: A Persian Legend of the Magi.* London: Frances Lincoln Children's Books, 2005. Unpaged. Illustrated by Jude Daly. $7.95. ISBN 1-845-07446-7.

In this story of the three wise men, based on the story that Marco Polo heard and recorded in his journals, the child gives the wise men the gift of a stone that bursts into flames when it is tossed into a well.

3. Roome, Diana Reynolds. *The Elephant's Pillow.* London: Frances Lincoln Children's Books, 2007. 32p. Illustrated by Jude Daly. $7.95. ISBN 1-845-07798-3.

Sing Lo, a Chinese boy, is determined to cure the Imperial Elephant of his insomnia when the elephant can't sleep after the Emperor dies.

4. Rumford, James. *Seeker of Knowledge: The Man Who Deciphered Egyptian Hieroglyphs.* New York: Houghton Mifflin Company, 2000. Unpaged. $15.00. ISBN 0-395-97934-X.

Examples of Egyptian hieroglyphs, words, and translations are included in this picture biography of the father of Egyptology, Jean-Francois Champollion, the Frenchman who deciphered hieroglyphic writing and proved that some hieroglyphs were sounds and that royal names were inscribed on cartouches.

5. Stewart, Dianne. *Gift of the Sun: A Tale from South Africa.* London: Frances Lincoln Children's Books, 2007. 32p Illustrated by Jude Daly. $7.95. ISBN 1-845-07787-3.

In this South African variation on the story of "Lazy Jack," similar to the Puerto Rican folktale about Juan Bobo, Thulani, who loves sitting in the sun and hates doing chores, stumbles onto a way to make his life easy and keep his wife happy.

Ruddell, Deborah. *A Whiff of Pine, a Hint of Skunk: A Forest of Poems.* New York: Margaret K. McElderry Books, 2009. Unpaged. Illustrated by Joan Rankin. $16.99. ISBN 1-4169-4211-4.

Author and Illustrator

Author Deborah Ruddell is an American art teacher who lives in Illinois. Illustrator Joan Rankin is an award-winning South African artist.

📖 Poetry, Picture Book, Ages 4–8

Summary

Twenty-two woodland poems introduce young readers to a snail, a salamander, a wild turkey, and other woodland creatures across the four seasons. Soft, full-page illustrations show the creatures in their habitats. Short, rhythmic poems lend themselves to reading aloud.

Curriculum Responses with Curriculum Standards

1. Read aloud to your students. Encourage children to listen, reread, and select a favorite poem, practice with expression, then read aloud or recite for classmates. (American Association of School Librarians Standards 1.1.6, 1.3.4, 2.2.4, 3.1.2, 3.1.3, 3.2.2, 3.3.5, 4.1.1, 4.1.3; English Language Arts Standards 1, 4, 11, 12)

2. Identify and discuss woodland creatures that are depicted. Which creatures live in your community, and what do their habitats look like? Have children draw and color pictures of the woodland creatures in their habitats that can be found in your community. (American Association of School Librarians Standards 1.1.1, 1.1.2, 1.1.6, 1.3.4, 2.1.1, 2.1.3, 2.1.6, 2.2.3, 2.2.4, 2.3.1, 3.1.1, 3.1.2, 3.1.3, 3.1.5, 3.2.1, 3.2.2, 3.2.3, 3.3.4, 3.3.5, 4.1.2, 4.1.3, 4.1.4, 4.1.5, 4.1.8, 4.3.1; English Language Arts Standards 3, 4, 6, 11, 12; Life Science Standards: Organisms and environments; Visual Arts Content Standard 1)

3. Call attention to illustrations. Ask children which seasons the illustrations portray and have them explain how they recognize the seasons. (American Association of School Librarians Standards 1.1.1, 1.1.2, 1.1.6, 1.3.4, 2.1.1, 2.1.3, 2.1.5, 2.3.1, 3.1.1, 3.1.2, 3.1.3, 3.2.1, 3.2.2, 3.3.5, 4.1.5, 4.3.1; English Language Arts Standards 4, 11, 12; Visual Arts Content Standard 4)

Related Books

1. Borden, Louise. *Off to First Grade*. New York: Margaret K. McElderry, 2008. 40p. Illustrated by Joan Rankin. $16.99. ISBN 0-689-87395-6.

In this alphabet book, each of the children from Anna to Yoshi, the teacher Mrs. Miller, the school bus driver Xavier, and the principal Mr. Zimmerman have something to say about starting first grade.

2. Capucilli, Alyssa Satin. *Mrs. McTats and Her Houseful of Cats*. New York: Aladdin Books, 2004. 32p. Illustrated by Joan Rankin. $6.99. ISBN 0-689-86991-6.

Mrs. McTats takes in stray cats, has twenty-six of them, and names them alphabetically from Abner to Zoom.

3. Rankin, Joan. *First Day*. New York: Aladdin Books, 2007. 32p. $10.99. ISBN 1-146-96848-2.

Haybillybun is filled with worries as he sets off for his first day at Yappy Puppy Play School.

4. Ruddell, Deborah. *Today at the Bluebird Café*. New York: Margaret K. McElderry, 2007. 40p. Illustrated by Joan Rankin. $15.99. ISBN 0-689-97153-8.

Twenty-one poems about birds and children, with each placed on an illustrated two-page spread provide a mix of humor, fancy, and realism.

5. Wilson, Karma. *A Frog in the Bog.* New York: Margaret K. McElderry, 2007. 32p. Illustrated by Joan Rankin. $6.99. ISBN 1-416-92727-1.

Similar to "There Was an Old Lady Who Swallowed a Fly," this counting book enumerates all of the many things that the frog eats.

ASIA

Readers will sample folktales, poetry, and realistic fiction, including Asian American experiences in the following selections. Folktales such as *The Hunter* and *The Lost Horse: A Chinese Legend,* may be new to readers, whereas other stories such as *The Runaway Rice Cake* and *Stone Soup* are likely to be familiar. Note in particular the illustrations of Ed Young, which reflect a philosophy of Chinese painting, in which the painting is accompanied by words, whereas Jon Muth incorporates aspects of Zen Buddhism in his books. Haiku written by the eighteenth-century Japanese poet Kobayashi Issa is illustrated by Brian Karas in *Today and Today.*

Related books of haiku include some written by Kobayashi Issa. Mari Takabayashi takes readers on a tour of Tokyo, and Eun-hee Chung provides readers with a glimpse of contemporary Korean life. Milly Lee and Lenore Look share with readers the experience of being Asian American. Three books were selected by the United States Board on Books for Young People (USBBY) as Outstanding International Books. Curriculum Responses include repeated readings, retellings, compilation of class book, and other activities.

Casanova, Mary. *The Hunter.* New York: Atheneum Books for Young Readers, 2000. Unpaged. Illustrated by Ed Young. $16.95. ISBN 0-689-82906-X.

Author and Illustrator

Author Mary Casanova is an American known for her environmentally themed picture books. Illustrator Ed Young was born in China, grew up in Shanghai, moved to Hong Kong, then came to the United States as a young man, where he now lives. His illustrations are inspired by a philosophy of Chinese painting in which the painting is accompanied by complementary words.

📖 Folktale, Picture Book, Ages 5–8

Summary

In this retelling of a Chinese folktale, the Dragon King rewards Hai Li Bu for saving the life of his daughter. Hai Li Bu's only request is to understand the language of animals in order to be a better hunter and to provide food for the hungry people of his village. Hai Li Bu's wish is granted, with the stipulation that he never reveal his secret. When the animals warn Hai Li Bu that rains will destroy his village, the villagers demand to know how they can know that Hai Li Bu speaks the truth. Hai Li Bu must decide whether to risk his own death by revealing his secret or risk the death of his villagers. What will his decision be?

Curriculum Responses with Curriculum Standards

1. Use the illustrations and colors in the book as a model. After reading, have children draw scenes from the book using orange paper or brown paper bags and black crayons. Have the children add their own words to their drawings. (American Association of School Librarians Standards 1.1.6, 2.1.6, 2.2.4, 3.1.3, 4.1.1, 4.1.3, 4.1.8; English Language Arts Standards 1, 3, 4, 5, 6, 12; Visual Arts Content Standard 1)

2. Call students' attention to the chop mark in the lower right corner of each two-page spread. Chop marks are interpreted in the front of the book. Suggest that students select the appropriate chop marks to add to their illustrations of scenes from the book. (English Language Arts Standards 3, 4, 6, 12; Visual Arts Content Standard 4).

3. Have students compare the Dragon King in this story with the Dragon King in Ed Young's *The Sons of the Dragon King.* (American Association of School Librarians Standards 1.1.2, 1.1.6, 1.1.9, 1.3.4, 2.1.1, 2.1.3, 2.1.5, 3.1.1, 3.1.2, 3.1.3, 3.2.1, 3.2.2, 3.3.5, 4.1.2, 4.3.1; English Language Arts Standards 1, 4, 11, 12)

Related Books

1. Young, Ed. *Beyond the Great Mountains.* Chronicle Books, 2005. 36p. $17.95. 0-811-84343-0.

Read from top to bottom, this illustrated poem is a magnificent work of art!

2. Young, Ed. *Cat and Rat: The Legend of the Chinese Zodiac.* New York: Henry Holt and Co., 1998. 32p. $17.95. ISBN 0-805-06049-9.

The Emperor promises to name the twelve years of the Chinese zodiac after the first twelve creatures who win the race through the forest and across the river.

3. Young, Ed. *Seven Blind Mice.* New York: Putnam Juvenile, 2002. 40p. $7.95. ISBN 0-698-11895-2.

In this retelling of the fable about the blind men and the elephant, seven blind mice experience different parts of an elephant.

4. Young, Ed. *The Lost Horse: A Chinese Folktale.* Voyager Books, 2004. 32p. $17.00. ISBN 0-152-05023-X.

Why does this wise man say that it might not be so bad when his horse runs away, and it might not be so good when his horse returns with a mare?

5. Young, Ed. *The Sons of the Dragon King: A Chinese Legend.* New York: Atheneum Books for Young Readers, 2004. Unpaged. $16.95. ISBN 0-689-85184-7.

The Dragon King learns to appreciate and use the talents of each of his seven sons.

Chung, Eun-hee. *Minji's Salon.* La Jolla, CA: Kane/Miller, 2008. Unpaged. $15.95. ISBN 978-1-933605-67-8.

Author

Author Eun-hee Chung lives in South Korea. She received the grand prize in the Korean Published Arts Contest in 2005. In 2009, the United States Board on Books for Young People (USBBY) listed her book, *Minji's Salon,* as an Outstanding International Book. The book is set in contemporary South Korea. Two Related Books, *New Clothes for New Year's Day,* and *My Cat Copies Me,* were also listed as Outstanding International Books in 2008.

📖 Realistic Fiction, Picture Book, Ages 5–7

Summary

Contemporary Korea is the setting for this book. Simple text and two-page spreads tell the parallel stories with parallel illustrations of Minji giving the dog a shampoo, a set, and a color treatment at home, while her mother is having a shampoo, set, and color treatment at the hair salon.

Responses with Curriculum Standards

1. Simple illustrations and text lend themselves to repeated readings. Read aloud to your children; then reread and encourage children to chime in with you on the simple text. On the third reading, have children take the lead in telling the story and reading the text.

(American Association of School Librarians Standards 1.1.6, 3.1.3, 3.2.2, 4.1.1, 4.1.3; English Language Arts Standards 1, 3, 4, 6, 11, 12)

2. What did Minji's mother say when she saw what Minji had done while she was at the beauty shop? Ask the children what they think their mothers would have said if they had done what Minji did. (American Association of School Librarians Standards 1.3.4, 2.1.5, 2.3.1, 3.1.2, 3.1.3, 3.2.1, 3.2.2, 3.3.2, 3.3.5, 4.1.3, 4.1.5, 4.3.1; English Language Arts Standards 3, 4, 6, 11, 12)

3. Have children create a new hairdo for Minji, her mother, or the dog, for themselves, their mothers, or their pets, by painting pictures. (American Association of School Librarians Standards 2.1.6, 2.2.4, 4.1.3, 4.1.8; English Language Arts Standards 4, 6, 11, 12; Visual Arts Content Standards 1)

Related Books

1. Bae, Hyun-Joo. *New Clothes for New Year's Day.* La Jolla, CA: Kane/Miller, 2007. 32p. $15.95. ISBN 978-1-9336-5-29-6.

Because it is the Lunar New Year, also known as Chinese New Year, a young Korean girl celebrates the holiday by carefully dressing in traditional clothes, beginning with a white under-robe, over which she layers a fancy red silk skirt and a rainbow striped jacket. She then adds colorful ribbons to her hair, and puts on socks and embroidered shoes.

2. Choi, Yangsook. *Behind the Mask.* New York: Frances Foster Books, 2006. Unpaged. $16.00. ISBN 0-374-30522-6.

Kimin dresses up for Halloween in his grandfather's Korean Mask Dancer costume.

3. Choi, Yangsook. *Peach Heaven.* New York: Frances Foster Books, 2005. Unpaged. $16.00. ISBN 0-374-35761-7.

The rains come down, and so do the peaches from the orchards in the mountains above Puchon, Korea.

4. Kwon, Yoon-duck. *My Cat Copies Me.* La Jolla, CA: Kane/Miller, 2007. Unpaged. $15.95. ISBN 978-1-933605-26-5.

A little girl and her cat play together in the house, with the cat following the girl, then the girl following the cat, until finally both the little girl and cat join the children outside to play.

5. Pak, Soyung. *A Place to Grow.* New York: Arthur A. Levine Books, 2002. Unpaged. Illustrated by Marcelino Truong. $16.95. ISBN 0-439-13015-8.

In a conversation between a father and daughter, the father tells his daughter that seeds need good soil, rain, and sunshine to grow. The illustrations show that people also need a nourishing environment in which to grow.

Compestine, Ying Chang. *The Runaway Rice Cake.* New York: Dutton Children's Books, 2001. Unpaged. Illustrated by Tungwai Chau. $16.95. ISBN 0-689-82972- 8.

Author and Illustrator

Author Ying Chang Compestine grew up in China during the Cultural Revolution and now lives in the United States. Illustrator Tungwai Chau was born in Hong Kong and now lives in the United States.

📖 Folktale, Picture Book, Ages 5–8

Summary

It's Chinese New Year, and Momma Chang has only enough rice flour to make one Nian-Gao (rice cake). As Momma takes the Nian-Gao out of the steamer and is about to cut it, the rice cake leaps out of the pan, rolls out of the kitchen into the courtyard and through the village. The Changs and the villagers chase the rice cake until it collides with a hungry little old woman, who eats the rice cake, leaving nothing for the Changs' New Year's meal. Yet the Changs celebrate their happiest New Year ever! How does that happen?

Curriculum Responses with Standards

1. After reading the book, read "Celebrating Chinese New Year" in the back of the book. Engage children in a discussion. Do you have a Chinese population in your community or in a nearby community who celebrate Chinese New Year? How do they celebrate? (American Association of School Librarians Standards 1.1.1, 1.1.2, 1.1.3, 1.1.4, 1.1.5, 1.1.6, 1.1.7, 1.1.9, 1.2.6, 1.3.4, 2.1.5, 2.3.1, 3.1.1, 3.1.2, 3.1.3, 3.1.5, 3.2.1, 3.2.2, 3.3.2, 3.3.5, 4.1.4, 4.3.1; English Language Arts Standards 1, 2, 3, 4, 6, 11, 12; Social Studies Standard I)
2. With the children, plan a Chinese New Year's celebration. Chinese New Year falls between January 20 and February 20. Use the recipe in the back of the book to bake or steam Nan-Gao. Serve for your Chinese New Year's celebration. (American Association of School Librarians Standards 1.1.1, 1.1.2, 1.1.3, 1.1.4, 1.1.5, 1.1.6, 1.1.9,

1.3.4, 2.1.5, 2.2.4, 2.3.1, 3.1.2, 3.1.3, 3.2.2, 3.2.3, 3.3.4, 3.3.5, 4.1.2, 4.1.3, 4.1.4, 4.1.7, 4.1.8, 4.3.1; English Language Arts Standards 1, 3, 11: Social Studies Standard I)

3. Compare the story of *The Runaway Rice Cake* with stories of the Gingerbread Man. (American Association of School Librarians Standards 1.1.1, 1.1.2, 1.1.3, 1.1.4, 1.1.6, 1.1.9, 1.3.4, 2.1.5, 3.1.2, 3.1.3, 3.2.1, 3.2.2, 3.3.5, 4.1.1, 4.1.2, 4.2.4, 4.3.1; English Language Arts Standards 1, 2, 3)

Related Books

1. Chan, Hingman. *Celebrating Chinese New Year: An Activity Book.* Asia for Kids, 2004. 32p. $8.95. ISBN 1-932-45704-6.

Usable instructions and templates for crafts and activities, plus basic information about the Chinese New Year and the Chinese zodiac signs, make this book a valuable resource for teachers, librarians, and parents.

2. Demi. *Happy, Happy Chinese New Year!* New York: Crown Books for Young Readers, 2003. 24p. $8.95. ISBN 0-375-82642-4.

Readers learn about celebrating Chinese New Year with preparations, symbols, and food.

3. Holub, Joan. *Dragon Dance: A Chinese New Year LTF: A Lift-the-FlapBook.* New York: Puffin Books, 2003. 16p. Illustrated by Benrei Huang. $16.99. ISBN 0-142-40000-9.

Lift the flap and discover the fun of the Chinese New Year.

4. Jango-Cohen, Judith and Jason Chin. *Chinese New Year (On My Own, Holidays).* Minneapolis, MN: Carolrhoda Books, Inc., 2004. 48p. $6.95. ISBN 1-575-05763-8.

Easily readable and informative text explains the Chinese zodiac, traditions, symbols, feasts, and activities that accompany the celebration of the Chinese New Year.

5. Wong, Janet S. *This Next New Year.* New York: Frances Foster Books, 2000. Unpaged. Illustrated by Yangsook Choi. $16.00. ISBN 0-374-35503-7.

A Chinese-Korean boy prepares to celebrate Chinese New Year with his friends, who are French and German, and Hopi and Mexican.

Issa, Kobayashi. *Today and Today.* New York: Scholastic Press, 2007. Unpaged. Illustrated by G. Brian Karas. $16.99. ISBN 0-439-59-78-7.

Author and Illustrator

Author Kobayashi Issa is a beloved Japanese poet who was born in 1763. Illustrator G. Brian Karas is an American artist who selected and arranged the haiku verse.

📖 Poetry, Picture Book, Ages 4–8

Summary

Delicate illustrations enhance classic, traditional haiku verse of a Japanese master, which are organized according to the seasons. Illustrations and verses depict a family's experiences with nature. "A Word from the Artist" at the beginning of the book talks about Issa, haiku, and what the artist hopes to convey with his illustrations.

Curriculum Responses with Curriculum Standards

1. Introduce the book and haiku by reading aloud to your children and showing the illustrations. Explain that haiku consists of three lines, with five syllables in the first and third lines, and seven syllables in the second line. The haiku poem usually makes reference to nature. Because haiku is highly abstract and difficult for young children to write, it is better to familiarize them with the verse form by reading aloud, reciting, and copying, than by having them create their own haiku. (American Association of School Librarians Standards 1.1.6, 4.1.1; English Language Arts Standards 1, 2).

2. Develop an ongoing unit of study of haiku. Add related books of haiku to your classroom library corner. Read aloud, and encourage children to recite the verse after you. Encourage children to read and recite their favorites to classmates. (American Association of School Librarians Standards 1.1.6, 1.2.2, 1.3.4, 3.1.2, 3.1.3, 3.2.1, 3.2.2, 3.3.5, 4.1.1, 4.1.2, 4.1.3, 4.2.4, 4.3.1, English Language Arts Standards 1, 3, 4, 11, 12)

3. Compile a class book of children's favorite haiku verses. Be sure to ascribe sources to verses. (American Association of School Librarians Standards 1.3.1, 1.3.3, 1.3.4, 2.1.2, 2.1.6, 3.1.2, 3.1.3, 3.2.1, 3.2.2, 3.2.3, 3.3.2, 3.3.4, 4.1.3, 4.1.6, 4.1.8, 4.3.1, English Language Arts Standards 4, 5, 6, 11, 12)

Related Books

1. Gollub, Matthew. *Cool Melons—Turn to Frogs! The Life and Poems of Issa.* New York: Lee & Low Books, 2004. 40p. Illustrated by Kazuko G. Stone. $7.95. ISBN 1-584-30241-0.

A brief biography of Issa's life, coupled with his haiku poems, enhanced by illustrations and calligraphy.

2. Janeczko, Paul. *Stone Bench in an Empty Park.* New York: Scholastic, 2000. 40p. Illustrated by Henri Silberman. ISBN 0-531-30259-8.

A collection of haiku poems, including some by Issa, depict an urban rather than rural landscape, and many depart from the traditional haiku pattern, but maintain the spirit of haiku.

3. Mannis, Celeste. *One Leaf Rides the Wind.* New York: Puffin, 2005. 32p. Illustrated by Susan Kathleen Hartung. $6.99. ISBN 0-142-40195-1.

This counting book written in haiku verse takes a Japanese girl on a visit to a temple garden.

4. Prelutsky, Jack. *If Not for the Cat.* New York: New York: Greenwillow, 2004. 40p. Illustrated by Ted Rand. $16.95. ISBN 0-060-59677-5.

Seventeen haiku verses are written from the point of view of an animal.

5. Spivak, Dawnine. *Grass Sandals: The Travels of Basho.* New York: Atheneum, 40p. Illustrations by Demi. $18.99. ISBN 0-689-80776-7.

This story of Basho, the seventeenth-century Japanese poet viewed as the father of haiku, includes stories of his travels across Japan, with translations of his haiku verses, Japanese words with English translations, and paintings by Demi inspired by Japanese art.

Lee, Milly. *Nim and the War Effort*. Il. Yangsook Choi. NY: Farrar, Straus, Giroux, 2002. Unpaged. $5.95. ISBN 0-374-45506-6.

Author and Illustrator

Author Milly Lee was born and raised in San Francisco's Chinatown. Illustrator Yangsook Choi was born and raised in Korea, and now lives in New York.

📖 Realistic Fiction, Picture Book, Ages 6–9.

Summary

It is 1943 in San Francisco's Chinatown. Nim is collecting newspapers for the war effort and wants to win the prize for collecting the most newspapers. Garland Stephenson also wants to win the prize. He taunts Nim by saying that an American will win the prize for the American war effort. At the last minute, Nim does something that brings both disgrace and honor to her family.

Curriculum Responses with Curriculum Standards

1. While reading, encourage discussion. Nim is an American girl. She is also a Chinese girl. How do you know that she is American? How do you know that she is Chinese? (American Association of School Librarians Standards 1.1.6, 1.3.4, 3.1.3, 3.2.1, 3.2.2, 3.3.5, 4.3.1; English Language Arts Standards 1, 2, 3, 4, 6, 9, 11, 12; Social Studies Standards I, IV)
2. After reading, continue discussion. How did Nim disgrace her family? How did Nim honor her family? (American Association of School Librarians Standards 1.1.6, 1.3.4, 3.1.3, 3.2.1, 3.2.2, 3.3.5, 4.3.1; English Language Arts Standards 1, 2, 3, 4, 6, 9, 11, 12; Social Studies Standards I, IV)
3. After reading, encourage children to put themselves in Nim's place, to imagine and share with classmates what they would have done had they been Nim. (American Association of School Librarians Standards 1.1.6, 1.3.4, 2.3.1, 3.1.3, 3.2.1, 3.2.2, 3.3.5, 4.3.1; English Language Arts Standards 1, 2, 3, 4, 6, 9, 11, 12; Social Studies Standards IV)

Related Books

1. Lee, Milly. *Earthquake.* New York: Frances Foster, 2001. Unpaged. Illustrated by Yangsook Choi. $6.95. ISBN 0-374-39964-6.

Text and illustrations tell the story of the 1906 San Francisco earthquake.

2. Lee, Milly. *Landed.* New York: Frances Foster, 2006. Unpaged. Illustrated by Yangsook Choi. $16.00. ISBN 0-374-34314-4.

Based on her father-in-law's experiences, the author tells the story of Chinese immigrants who arrive in San Francisco and wait in a detainment camp on Angel Island, fearing that they will be turned back to China.

3. Thong, Roseanne. *Gai See: What You Can See in Chinatown.* New York: Abrams Books for Young Readers, 2007. Illustrated by Yangsook Choi. $16.95. ISBN 0-810-99337-67.

A little boy and his family visit the street market in Chinatown during the different seasons of the year.

Look, Lenore. *Uncle Peter's Amazing Chinese Wedding.* New York: Atheneum Books for Young Readers, 2006. 40p. Illustrated by Yumi Heo. $16.95. ISBN 0-689-84458-1.

Author and Illustrator

Author Lenore Look is Chinese American. Illustrator Yumi Heo was born in Korea and now lives in the United States.

📖 Realistic Fiction, Picture Book, Ages 4–8

Summary

Uncle Peter is getting married, and Jenny doesn't like it. She has always been Uncle Peter's special girl, and she is feeling slighted. While the family prepares for a traditional Chinese wedding complete with gifts for the groom, bargaining for the bride, a tea ceremony, and Hungbau (red packets of lucky money) for the bride and groom, Jenny sulks, but her new Aunt Stella wins her over.

Curriculum Responses with Curriculum Standards

1. Encourage discussion. Uncle Peter is getting married, and Jenny feels that she is no longer special to him. Ask children whether they have ever felt that they were no longer special to someone. Did their feelings change? What made their feelings change? (American Association of School Librarians Standards 1.1.6, 1.3.4, 3.1.2, 3.1.3, 3.2.1, 3.2.2, 3.3.5, 4.1.2, 4.1.3, 4.1.5, 4.3.1; English Language Arts Standards 1, 2, 4, 11, 12)
2. Continue the discussion. How did Aunt Stella win Jenny over? Ask children whether there is someone in their lives who needs to feel special. How can they help that person to feel special? (American Association of School Librarians Standards 1.1.6, 1.3.4, 3.1.2, 3.1.3, 3.2.1, 3.2.2, 3.3.5, 4.1.2, 4.1.3, 4.1.5, 4.3.1; English Language Arts Standards 1, 2, 4, 11, 12)
3. How do you know this is a Chinese American family celebrating a wedding? Have the children make a chart identifying the Chinese practices that the family observes. Add a second column to the chart identifying how you know this family is American as well as Chinese. (American Association of School Librarians Standards 1.1.6, 1.1.9, 1.3.4, 2.1.2, 2.1.5, 3.1.2, 3.1.3, 3.2.1, 3.2.2, 3.2.3, 3.3.5, 4.1.2, 4.1.3, 4.1.6, 4.1.7, 4.1.8, 4.3.1; English Language Arts Standards 1, 4, 5, 6, 9, 11, 12; Social Studies Standards 1, IV)

Related Books

1. Look, Lenore. *Alvin Ho: Allergic to Girls, School, and Other Scary Things*. Schwartz & Wade, 2008. 176p. Illustrated by LeUyen Pham. $15.99. ISBN 0-375-83914-3.

Alvin Ho is a Chinese American second grader who loves superheroes, but is afraid of everything.

2. Look, Lenore. *Alvin Ho: Allergic to Camping, Hiking, and Other Natural Disasters.* Schwartz & Wade, 2009. 176p. Illustrated by LeUyen Pham. $15.99 ISBN 0-375-85705-2.

As if school isn't scary enough, now Alvin has to go camping!

3. Look, Lenore. *Henry's First Moon Birthday.* New York: Atheneum Books for Young Readers, 2001. 40p. Illustrated by Yumi Heo. $16.96. ISBN 0-689-82294-4.

Jenny's Chinese American family prepares to celebrate baby Henry's first month birthday.

4. Look, Lenore. *Ruby Lu: Brave and True.* New York: Aladdin, 2006. 112p. Illustrated by Anne Wilsdorf. $3.99 ISBN 1-416-91389-0.

Nine humorous short chapters relate the antics of eight-year old Ruby Lu, a Chinese American girl, and her friends.

5. Look, Lenore. *Ruby Lu: Empress of Everything.* New York: Atheneum, 2006. 164p. Illustrated by Anne Wilsdorf. $15.95. ISBN 0-689-86560-4.

Learning Chinese sign language is only one of the changes in Ruby Lu's life, when her deaf cousin Flying Duck immigrates from China.

Muth, Jon J. *Stone Soup.* New York: Scholastic Press 2003. Unpaged. $16.99. ISBN 0-439-33909-X.

Author and Illustrator

Author Jon Muth is an American who studied art in Japan, Austria, Germany, and England. His picture books have been published in more than ten languages.

📖 Folktale, Picture Book, Ages 4–8

Summary

Muth incorporates aspects of Zen Buddhism and Eastern culture into his variation of this European folk tale, which he has set in China. Three Zen monks named Hok, Lok, and Lieu, stop to make stone soup as they pass through a village, where the people know no happiness and are experiencing hard times. A little girl dressed in yellow asks them what they are doing. They tell her that they are making stone soup, and that they need three stones and a larger pot. When the little girl asks her mother for a pot, the mother wants to know how to make soup from stones.

The little girls and curious neighbors gather. Little by little, the villagers offer seasonings, then vegetables. As one person gives a little, the next gives a little more. The soup grows richer and more delicious. The simple meal turns into a feast. The feast becomes a celebration. The villagers learn that they will always have plenty by sharing, and that happiness "is as simple as making stone soup!" The Author's Note explains Muth's incorporation of the Buddhist story tradition, names of deities prominent in Chinese folklore, and symbols from Eastern culture that have specific meaning.

Curriculum Responses with Curriculum Standards

1. After reading, have children retell the story by acting out, using a flannel board or creating reader's theater. (American Association of School Librarians Standards 1.1.6, 1.1.9, 1.2.2, 1.3.4, 2.1.2, 2.1.5, 2.1.6, 2.2.4, 2.3.1, 3.1.2, 3.1.3, 3.2.1, 3.2.2, 3.2.3, 3.3.1, 3.3.2, 3.3.5, 4.1.3, 4.1.1, 4.1.3, 4.1.8, 4.3.1; English Language Arts Standard 1, 3, 4, 5, 6, 11, 12; Theater Content Standards 1, 2)

2. Encourage students to compare and discuss variants of the stone soup story that can be found in folklore from Europe, Jamaica, Korea, and the Philippines. (American Association of School Librarians Standards 1.1.6, 1.1.9, 1.3.4, 3.1.2, 3.1.3, 3.2.1, 3.2.2, 4.1.1, 4.1.2, 4.1.7, 4.2.4, 4.3.1; English Language Arts Standard 1, 3, 4, 6, 11, 12)

3. After reading, make stone soup with your children. (American Association of School Librarians Standards 1.1.6, 2.2.4, 2.3.1, 3.2.3, 3.3.4, 4.1.1, 4.1.3, 4.1.8; English Language Arts Standard 1, 3, 11)

4. The villagers learn that happiness "is as simple as making stone soup." After reading, ask the children what that means. What happened as the villagers began to give? How did sharing make them richer? Ask the children, "What makes you happy? What might make you happier?" (American Association of School Librarians Standards 1.1.6, 1.3.4, 2.1.5, 2.3.1, 3.1.2, 3.1.3, 3.2.1, 3.2.2, 3.3.1, 3.3.2, 3.3.5, 4.1.1, 4.1.2, 4.1.3, 4.1.5, 4.3.1; English Language Arts Standards 1, 3, 4, 6, 11, 12; Social Studies Standard IV)

5. Encourage children to read the Author's Note, and to identify and discuss the elements of Zen Buddhism and Eastern culture that Muth used. (American Association of School Librarians Standards 1.1.6, 1.3.1, 1.3.4, 2.1.5, 2.4.3, 3.1.1, 3.1.2, 3.1.3, 3.2.1, 3.2.2, 3.3.5, 4.1.1, 4.1.2, 4.1.3, 4.3.1, 4.4.4; English Language Arts Standards 1, 2, 3, 4, 6, 11, 12; Social Studies Standards I, III)

Related Books

1. Compestine, Ying Chang. *The Real Story of Stone Soup*. New York: Dutton Children's Books, 2001. Unpaged. $12.75. ISBN 0-525047493-5.

Also set in China, this version of Stone Soup is the story of a fisherman and three brothers.

2. Muth, Jon J. *The Three Questions.* New York: Scholastic Press, 2002. Unpaged. $16.95. ISBN 0-439-19996-4.

This retelling of Tolstoy's short story reflects Muth's studies of Zen.

3. Muth, Jon J. *Zen Shorts.* New York: Scholastic Press, 2005. Unpaged. $16.95. ISBN 0-439-33911-1.

Stillwater, the panda bear, tells three short Zen stories to Karl, Michael, and Addy.

Say, Allen. *Home of the Brave.* Boston: Houghton Mifflin, 2002. 30p $17.00 ISBN 0-618-21223-X.

Author and Illustrator

Author and illustrator Allen Say was born in Japan and came to the United States at the age of 16.

 📖 Fiction, Picture Book, Ages 6–10

Summary

In this mystical fantasy, the narrator is wrenched from his kayak and swept away by the churning of an underground river. He finds himself in a cave with a ladder to a sunlit opening. At the top of the ladder is the hot, dry desert, with two young children waiting to go home. Where are they? "In camp," the children say, "a camp with many children, blinding searchlights, and loud-speakers." And so the author relates a dreamlike vignette of the experience of the World War II Japanese Internment Camps in the Western United States.

Curriculum Responses with Curriculum Standards

1. Before reading, page through the book with children and focus only on the illustrations. Ask what they see. What stories do the pictures tell? How do the pictures feel? What do they think the book is about? (American Association of School Librarians Standards 1.1.6, 1.3.4, 3.1.3, 3.2.1, 3.2.2, 3.3.1, 3.3.5, 4.1.1, 4.1.2, 4.1.3, 4.3.1, 4.4.4; English Language Arts Standards 1, 2, 3, 4, 6, 11, 12; Visual Arts Content Standards 3, 5)
2. Young readers may not know about the Japanese internment camps in the United States during World War II. Plan to explain this history to your children before they read the book. Encourage children to ask questions as they read, or after reading. Discuss their questions with them. (American Association of School Librarians Standards 1.1.6, 1.3.4, 2.3.1, 3.1.3, 3.2.1, 3.2.2, 3.3.1, 3.3.5, 4.1.1, 4.1.2, 4.1.3, 4.3.1, 4.4.4; English Language Arts Standards 1, 2, 3, 4, 6, 11, 12; Social Studies Standards V)

3. Consider focusing on Allen Say as author and illustrator. Set up a display of his books in your library or your classroom library corner. Encourage children to read, compare, discuss, and share favorites. (American Association of School Librarians Standards 1.1.6, 1.1.9, 1.3.4, 2.1.5, 3.1.2, 3.1.3, 3.2.1, 3.2.2, 3.3.5, 4.1.1, 4.1.2, 4.2.4, 4.3.1; English Language Arts Standards 1, 4, 6, 11, 12)

Related Books

1. Say, Allen. *Emma's Rug.* Boston: Houghton Mifflin Company, 1996. 32p. $6.95. ISBN 0-618-33523-4.

Emma draws the pictures she sees in her rug until her mother washes the rug. Then the pictures are gone—or are they?

2. Say, Allen. *The Sign Painter.* Boston: Houghton Mifflin Company, 2000. 32p. $17.00 ISBN 0-395-97974-9.

A young boy helps a painter paint billboards in the desert—for what?

3. Say, Allen. *Under the Cherry Blossom Tree: An Old Japanese Tale.* New York: Houghton Mifflin Company, 1974. 32p. $5.95. ISBN 0-618-55615-X.

Black and white ink drawings illustrate this retelling of an old Japanese folktale about the miserly landlord whose troubles begin with the cherry tree growing out of the top of his head.

Takabayashi, Mari. *I Live in Tokyo.* Boston: Houghton Mifflin Company, 2001. Unpaged. $16.00. ISBN 0-618-07702-2.

Author and Illustrator

Author and illustrator Mari Takabayashi was born in Tokyo, raised and educated in Japan, and now lives in New York.

📖 Realistic Fiction, Picture Book, Ages 5–10

Summary

Holidays and celebrations, family and friends, home, school, and play are all part of seven-year-old Mimiko's life in Tokyo. She leads readers through a calendar year and introduces them to foods, customs, and practices. The final page lists Months of the Year, A Few Words, Numbers, and Japanese phrases.

Curriculum Responses with Curriculum Standards

1. Have children use information in the back of the book to learn Japanese names for months of the year, Japanese words and phrases, and how to count in Japanese. (American Association of School Librarians

Standards 1.1.2, 2.3.1, 2.4.3, 4.1.3, 4.4.4, English Language Arts Standards 1, 3, 4, 6, 9, 11, 12; Social Studies Standards I)

2. Have children use the map on the second two-page spread to find Tokyo and Mimiko's grandparents' home in Kobe. Then have children find Japan, Tokyo, and Kobe on a world map. (American Association of School Librarians Standards 1.1.2, 2.3.1, 4.1.3, English Language Arts Standards 1, 3, 4, 6, 11, 12; Social Studies Standards III)

3. After reading, discuss with your children how Mimiko's life in Tokyo is similar to and how it is different from their lives in the United States. Make a Venn diagram showing likenesses and differences between Mimiko's life and your children's lives. (American Association of School Librarians Standards 1.1.6, 1.1.9, 1.2.1, 1.3.4, 2.1.1, 2.1.2, 2.1.5, 2.1.6, 2.3.1, 3.1.2, 3.1.3, 3.2.1, 3.2.2, 3.2.3, 3.3.5, 4.1.1, 4.1.2, 4.1.3, 4.1.5, 4.3.1; English Language Arts Standards 1, 3, 4, 6, 11, 12; Social Studies Standards I, IV)

Related Books

1. Iijima, Geneva Cobb. *The Way We Do It in Japan.* Morton Grove, IL: Albert Whitman & Co., 2002. 32p. Illustrated by Paige Bilbin-Frye $16.99. ISBN 0-807-57822-3.

When Gregory moves from California to Tokyo with his American mother and Japanese father, he discovers differences in culture and lifestyle such as language, foods, traffic patterns, and others, some of which tend to be stereotypical.

2. Reynolds, Betty. *Japanese Celebrations: Cherry Blossoms, Lanterns, and Stars!* Tuttle Publishing, 2006. 48p. $16.95. ISBN 0-804-83658-2.

Each two-page spread features the celebration of a holiday such as New Year, Children's Day, Festival of Sails, and others.

AUSTRALIA AND NEW ZEALAND

Authors from Australia and New Zealand, Belgian author Laurence Bourguignon and illustrator Valerie d'Heur introduce readers to the natural environment, take them on a tour of Australia, touch the heart, and entertain with light-hearted and realistic fiction. Australian author Dyan Blacklock and illustrator David Kennet tell the story of the Olympic Games, beginning with their origins dating from the eighth century B.C. Curriculum Responses include the recreation of a nature reserve, retelling, art and other activities.

Bishop, Nic. *Backyard Detective: Critters Up Close.* New York: Scholastic Press, 2002. 48p. $16.95. ISBN 0-439-17478-3.

Author and Illustrator

Author Nic Bishop is an award-winning science writer and photographer from New Zealand, who now lives in the United States.

📖 Nonfiction, Picture Book, Ages 5 up

Summary

Computer-generated illustrations provide close-up views of backyard flowers, vegetables, weeds, leaves, and tiny critters. Seven two-page spreads feature photographs, each followed by a two-page spread of text describing what is seen in the photographs. Two introductory pages suggest that readers use a magnifying glass to explore their backyards. The last sections of the book offer suggestions for nature investigations and projects. Finally, an eight-page, alphabetized picture index identifies critters that children are likely to find.

Curriculum Responses and Curriculum Standards

1. Follow up by using suggestions in the back of the book, such as creating a nature reserve by leaving a small weed patch for critters to live in, planting a butterfly garden, putting up a bird feeder, or following one of the many other suggestions. (American Association of School Librarians Standards 1.1.1, 1.1.2, 1.1.3, 1.1.9, 1.2.1, 1.2.3, 1.2.4, 1.2.5, 1.2.6, 1.3.4, 1.4.2, 1.4.3, 1.4.4, 2.1.1, 2.1.2, 2.1.3, 2.1.5, 2.1.6, 2.2.2, 2.2.3, 2.2.4, 2.3.1, 2.4.1, 2.4.2, 2.4.3, 2.4.4, 3.1.1, 3.1.2, 3.2.1, 3.2.2, 3.2.3, 3.3.4, 4.1.3, 4.1.4, 4.1.7, 4.1.8, 4.3.1; Life Science Standards)

2. Select a small outdoor area (3 or 4 feet square). Have children observe and record what they see in that area over a period of time (a week or a month) and make a chart identifying what they observed. Encourage children to extend their observations over several months and record the changes that they see. (American Association of School Librarians Standards 1.1.1, 1.1.2, 1.1.3, 1.1.9, 1.2.5, 1.3.3, 1.3.4, 1.4.1, 1.4.2, 1.4.3, 1.4.4, 2.1.1, 2.1.2, 2.1.3, 2.1.5, 2.1.6, 2.2.2, 2.3.4, 2.3.1, 2.4.1, 2.4.2, .2.4.3, 2.4.4, 3.1.1, 3.1.2, 3.1.3, 3.2.2, 3.2.3, 3.3.1, 3.3.2, 3.3.4, 3.3.5, 3.4.1, 3.4.3, 4.1.6. 4.1.7, 4.3.1; English Language Arts Standards 4, 5, 7, 11, 12; Science As Inquiry Standards; Life Science Standards)

3. Encourage children to talk about what they see in their outdoor nature areas. Create an idea bank, develop vocabulary, and expand sentences using prepositional phrases and subordinate clauses. Use alliteration and active verbs, write poetic chants and patterns, or develop rhyme and poetry, using patterns. Create similes, idioms,

and metaphors. Engage in word play with jokes, riddles, and puns. (American Association of School Librarians Standards 3.1.3, 4.3.1; English Language Arts Standards 4, 5, 6, 11, 12)

4. Encourage children to make a collage or shoebox diorama of what they see in their outdoor nature areas. (American Association of School Librarians Standards 1.2.1, 2.1.6, 2.2.4, 2.3.1, 3.3.4, 4.1.3; Visual Arts Content Standards 1, 3, 6)

5. Have children study the relationship between the plants and wildlife that they observe and their local environment. How do plants and wildlife affect the environment? How does the environment affect plants and wildlife? Encourage children to extend their research by using print and nonprint sources and to share their findings with their classmates. (American Association of School Librarians Standards 1.1.1, 1.1.2, 1.1.3, 1.1.4, 1.1.5, 1.1.6, 1.1.8, 1.1.9, 1.2.1, 1.2.2, 1.2.3, 1.2.4, 1.2.5, 1.2.6, 1.2.7, 1.3.1, 1.3.4, 1.3.5, 1.4.1, 1.4.2, 1.4.3, 1.4.4, 2.1.1, 2.1.2, 2.1.3, 2.1.4, 2.1.5, 2.2.1, 2.2.2, 2.2.3, 2.3.1, 2.4.1, 2.4.3, 3.1.1, 3.1.2, 3.1.3, 3.1.6, 3.2.1, 3.2.2, 3.2.3, 3.3.5, 4.1.2, 4.1.5, 4.1.7, 4.3.1 4.4.3; English Language Arts Standards 7, 8, 11, 12; Science As Inquiry Standards, Life Science Standards)

Related Books

1. Bishop, Nic. *Butterflies and Moths.* New York: Scholastic Press, 2004. 48p. $15.99. ISBN 0-439-87757-1.

Colored photographs and simple text provide basic information about butterflies and moths including their likenesses and differences and their life cycles.

2. Bishop, Nic. *Forest Explorer: A Life-Size Field Guide.* New York: Scholastic Press, 2004. 48p. $17.95. ISBN 0-439-17480-5.

Using the same format as *Backyard Detective: Critters Up Close,* Nic Bishop introduces readers to the forest habitat and critters who live there.

3. Bishop, Nic. *Frogs.* New York: Scholastic Press, 2008. 48p $16.99. ISBN 0-439-87755-5.

Close-up photographs and informative, fact-filled text introduce readers to frogs around the world.

4. Cowley, Joy. *Red-Eyed Tree Frog.* New York: Scholastic Press, 1999 Unpaged. Photographs by Nic Bishop. $16.95. ISBN 0-590-87175-7.

Colored photos and sparse text depict a day in the life of a red-eyed tree frog as it searches for food and escapes the danger of predators in the rain forest.

5. Cowley, Joy. *Chameleon, Chameleon,* New York: Scholastic Press, 2005. Unpaged. Photographs by Nic Bishop. $16.95. ISBN 0-439-66653-8.

Young readers will enjoy the simple text and colored photos depicting panther chameleons from the island of Madagascar.

Blacklock, Dyan. *Olympia: Warrior Athletes of Ancient Greece.* New York: Walker & Company, 2000. 48p. Illustrated by David Kennett. $17.95. ISBN 0-8027-8790-8.

Author and Illustrator

Author Dyan Blacklock and illustrator David Kennett are Australians who live in Adelaide.

📖 Nonfiction, Picture Book, Ages 6–10

Summary

Intricately detailed illustrations, some in bold color, and others in black and white, with two or three sentences of informative text on each page, tell the story of the Olympic Games, beginning with their origins dating from the eighth century B.C. A map of Greece and Asia Minor, a map of Olympia dating from 1776, and a diagram of the temple of Zeus built in the fifth century B.C. enrich the text. A glossary at the back of the book defines terms used.

Curriculum Responses with Curriculum Standards

1. Consider reading this book when the Olympic Games are being held. After reading, have students use the book to create a roll movie showing the history and events of the Olympic Games. (American Association of School Librarians Standards 1.1.6, 1.1.9, 1.3.4, 2.1.2, 2.1.6, 2.2.4, 2.3.1, 3.1.2, 3.2.2, 3.2.3, 3.3.4, 3.3.5, 4.1.1, 4.1.2, 4.1.3, 4.1.8, 4.3.1; English Language Arts Standards 1, 2, 3, 4, 6, 11; Social Studies Standards I, II; Visual Arts Content Standards 1, 2, 3)
2. Extend the activity by having students explain the roll movie to another class or group of students. (American Association of School Librarians Standards 1.3.4, 2.3.1, 3.1.3, 3.2.1, 3.2.2, 3.2.3, 3.3.5, 4.1.3, 4.3.1; English Language Arts Standards 3, 4, 6, 11, 12; Social Studies Standards I, II; Visual Arts Content Standards 3)
3. Have students use the pictures in the book to demonstrate movements such as the javelin throwing, jumping, racing and others. (American Association of School Librarians Standards 1.3.4, 2.2.4, 2.3.1, 3.1.2, 3.2.1, 3.2.2, 3.3.5, 4.1.3, 4.1.8, 4.3.1; English Language Arts Standards 3, 4, 11, 12)

Related Books

1. Blacklock, Dyan. *The Roman Army: The Legendary Soldiers Who Created an Empire.* New York: Walker Books for Young Readers, 2004. 48p. Illustrated by David Kennett. $17.95. ISBN 0-802-78896-3.

Illustrations and text provide information about the powerful Roman army, such as who they were, what they used, and how they treated conquered people.

2. Kennett, David. *Pharaoh.* New York: Walker Books for Young Readers, 2008. 48p. $17.95. ISBN 0-802-79567-6.

Bold illustrations and informative text describe life in Ancient Egypt, the roles of the Pharaoh, the lives of Seti I and his son Rameses II, and their preoccupation with the afterlife.

Bourguignon, Laurence. *Heart in the Pocket.* Grand Rapids, Michigan: Eerdmans Books for Young Readers, 2008. 26p. Illustrated by Valerie d'Heur. $16.50. ISBN 978-0-8028-5343-1.

Author and Illustrator

Author Laurence Bourguignon is an author and editor in Belgium, whose books have been translated into several languages. Illustrator Valerie d'Heur is a graphic designer, writer, and illustrator whose books have been published in Belgium.

📖 Fiction, Picture Book, Ages 4–7

Summary

Jo-Jo, a baby kangaroo, lives happily in his mama's pocket and doesn't want to leave. Mama Kangaroo loves her baby. She tells him and shows him the wonderful things that the big world has to offer. Still Jo-Jo doesn't want to leave Mama's pocket until she tells him that her heart is not in her pocket, but somewhere else.

Curriculum Responses with Curriculum Standards

1. Before reading, have children draw pictures of Mama Kangaroo and Jo-Jo. (American Association of School Librarians Standards 2.1.6, 2.2.4, 4.1.3, 4.1.8; English Language Arts Standards 4, 12; Visual Arts Content Standard 1)
2. Read aloud to your children. Then have children retell the story using a flannel board. (American Association of School Librarians Standards 1.1.6, 1.3.4, 2.1.2, 2.1.6, 4.1.1, 4.1.3; English Language Arts Standards 1, 3, 4, 11, 12)

3. After reading, engage children in a discussion of safe places where they like to be. (American Association of School Librarians Standards 1.1.6, 1.3.4, 2.3.1, 3.1.3, 3.2.1, 3.3.5, 4.1.1, 4.1.5, 4.3.1; English Language Arts Standards 1, 4, 11, 12)

Related Books

1. Doyle, Roddy. *Her Mother's Face.* New York: Arthur A. Levine Books, 2008. Unpaged. Illustrated by Freya Blackwood. $16.99. ISBN 0-439-81501-0.

Siobhan cannot remember the face of her mother, who died when Siobhan was only three until a beautiful lady tells her to look in the mirror.

Bunting, Eve. *Whales Passing.* New York: The Blue Sky Press, 2003. Unpaged. Illustrated by Lambert Davis. $15.95. ISBN 0-590-60358-2.

Author and Illustrator

Author Eve Bunting is an American and a winner of the Caldecott Medal and many other awards. Illustrator Lambert Davis was born in Hawaii and now lives in Australia.

📖 Fiction, Picture Book, Ages 4–8

Summary

As a boy and his dad watch a pod of killer whales pass by, the killer whales watch the boy and his dad. As the boy and his dad talk about the whales passing by, the whales talk about the boy and the dad they are passing. A full-page narrative at the back of the book gives information about the killer whales. Killer whales, also known as Orcas, are not actually whales, but are very large dolphins. Full-page illustrations and simple text provide readers with a realistic experience of Orcas.

Curriculum Responses with Curriculum Standards

1. After reading, use the narrative dialog as a model. Encourage children to elaborate on the conversations between the boy and his dad, the conversations between the boy and his mom, and the conversations among the dolphins. Ask the children what else they might say to the dad and what else they might want to tell the mom if they were the little boy. Ask the children what else the dolphins might say to each other. (American Association of School Librarians Standards 1.1.6, 1.3.1, 2.1.5, 2.3.1, 3.1.2, 3.1.3, 3.2.1, 3.2.2, 3.2.1, 3.2.2, 3.3.5, 4.1.1, 4.1.2, 4.1.3, 4.1.5, 4.3.1; English Language Arts Standards 1, 3, 4, 6, 11, 12)
2. Extend the activity by encouraging children to write and illustrate their conversations. (American Association of School Librarians

Standards 2.1.6, 2.2.4, 3.1.3, 3.3.4, 4.1.3; English Language Arts Standards 3, 4, 6, 12; Visual Arts Content Standards 1, 2)

3. Encourage children who are interested to begin with the information about Orcas in the back of the book, generate questions, do research, and report their findings to their classmates. (American Association of School Librarians Standards 1.1.1, 1.1.2, 1.1.3, 1.1.4, 1.1.5, 1.1.6, 1.1.8, 1.1.9, 1.2.1, 1.2.2, 1.2.3, 1.2.5, 1.2.6, 1.2.7, 1.3.1, 1.3.3, 1.3.4, 1.3.5, 1.4.1, 1.4.2, 1.4.3, 1.4.4, 2.1.1, 2.1.2, 2.1.5, 2.1.6, 2.2.1, 2.2.4, 2.3.1, 2.4.1, 2.4.3, 3.1.1, 3.1.2, 3.1.3, 3.2.1, 3.2.2, 3.3.5, 4.1.2, 4.1.3, 4.1.4, 4.1.5, 4.3.1; English Language Arts Standards 1, 3, 4, 7, 8, 11, 12; Life Science Standards)

Related Books

1. Buffett, Jimmy and Savannah Jane Buffett. *The Jolly Mon.* New York: Harcourt Children's Books, 2006. 32p. Illustrated by Lambert Davis. $17.95. ISBN 0-152-05786-2.

Based on the Jimmy Buffett song, "The Jolly Mon," a singing Caribbean fisherman with a magic guitar is rescued by a dolphin.

2. Davis, Lambert. *Swimming with Dolphins.* New York: Blue Sky Press, 2004. 32p. $15.95. ISBN 0-439-47257-1.

Kookaburra watches while a little girl and her mother wait for and then swim with a pod of dolphins.

3. Rylant, Cynthia. *The Journey: Stories of Migration.* New York: Blue Sky Press, 2006. 48p. Illustrated by Lambert Davis. $15.95. ISBN 0-590-3717-7.

Photorealistic paintings and clear text tell about the migration of six species: the desert locust, the blue whale, the American silver eel, the monarch butterfly, the caribou, and the Arctic tern.

Cowley, Joy. *The Wishing of Biddy Malone.* New York: Philomel Books, 2004. Unpaged. Illustrated by Christopher Denise. $15.99. ISBN 0-399-23404-7.

Author and Illustrator

Author Joy Cowley is a well-known, prolific New Zealand writer. Illustrator Christopher Denise is an American.

📖 Fiction, Fantasy, Ages 4–8

Summary

Biddy Malone stumbles over her feet when she dances and has a raspy singing voice and a quick temper. In a fit of temper one night, she storms out of her cottage, slams the door, and runs to the edge of the river, where she hears the music and sees the little houses of a fairy village. Biddy's feet dance her right through the doorway, where a beautiful boy greets her and asks her for three wishes. Biddy wishes to be light on her feet with the voice of a bird and to have a loving heart. As she dances with the boy, Biddy's feet are light, her voice is sweet, and her heart is happy. Then the dance ends. Biddy is alone by the river in the dark of night. When she returns home, Biddy still stumbles when she dances, sings with a raspy voice, and has a temper. But with the fairy music inside of her, she practices dancing and singing, and develops a loving heart. Biddy wonders why she must work so hard to get her wishes. She wonders what is the point of having a loving heart, when she can love only the beautiful boy and none of her suitors. And then her questions are answered.

Curriculum Responses with Curriculum Standards

1. Introduce the book by reading aloud. The lyrical text is written with an Irish lilt. Although the book is a bit long, the language deserves to be heard. After reading aloud, place the book where children can select it for independent reading. (American Association of School Librarians Standards 1.1.6, 4.1.1, 4.2.4; English Language Arts Standards 1)

2. After reading, discuss with your children why Biddy had to work so hard to get her wishes and why she could love only the beautiful boy. Ask the children whether there is anything that they have to work hard for.(American Association of School Librarians Standards 1.1.2, 1.1.6, 1.1.9, 1.3.4, 2.1.5, 2.3.1, 2.4.3, 3.1.2, 3.1.3, 3.2.1, 3.2.2, 3.3.1, 3.3.2, 3.3.5, 4.1.1, 4.1.2, 4.1.3, 4.1.4, 4.1.5, 4.3.1; English Language Arts Standards 1, 3, 4, 6, 11, 12; Social Studies Standards IV)

3. Biddy had a temper. Sometimes her heart was filled with anger. She developed a loving heart. After reading, discuss with children what it feels like to have a heart filled with anger and a heart filled with love. (American Association of School Librarians Standards 1.1.2, 1.1.6, 1.1.9, 1.3.4, 2.1.5, 2.3.1, 2.4.3, 3.1.2, 3.1.3, 3.2.1, 3.2.2, 3.3.1, 3.3.2, 3.3.5, 4.1.1, 4.1.2, 4.1.3, 4.1.4, 4.1.5, 4.3.1; English Language Arts Standards 1, 3, 4, 6, 11, 12; Social Studies Standards IV)

Related Books

1. Cowley, Joy. *Agapanthus Hum and the Eyeglasses.* New York: Putnam Juvenile, 2001. 48p. Illustrated by Jennifer Plecas. $12.76. ISBN 0-698-11883-9.

This humorous beginning chapter book features Agapanthus Hum, who is full of music, motion, and accidents.

2. Cowley, Joy. *Mrs. Wishy-Washy's Farm.* New York: Philomel Books, 2003. Unpaged. Illustrated by Elizabeth Fuller. $15.99. ISBN 0-399-23872-7.

Because Mrs.Wishy-Washy scrubs them in her tub, the cow, the pig, and the duck run away from the farm to the city, only to end up in jail, after finding that there is no place for them to rest or to feed.

3. Cowley, Joy. *The Rusty, Trusty Tractor.* Honesdale, PA: Boyds Mills Press, 2000. 32p. $9.95. ISBN 1-563-97873-3.

The little boy wonders, and finds out, why Grandpa loves his old tractor with its worn-out seat cushion, cracked tires, and no cab enclosure.

4. Mahy, Margaret. *Down the Back of the Chair.* New York: Clarion Books, 2006. 32p. Illustrated by Polly Dunbar. $16.00 ISBN 0-618-69395-5.

Rhyming text with watercolor and cut-paper illustrations reveal what Dad pulls out from the back of the chair when he goes looking for his car keys.

5. Mahy, Margaret. *Simply Delicious!* London: Frances Lincoln Children's Books, 2000. 32p. Illustrator Jonathan Allen. $16.00. ISBN 0-711-21441-7.

Children will want to chime in as they listen to the rhythm and alliteration of this story about Mr. Minky and all that he has to do to protect the ice cream cone that he bought for his son from the animals along the jungle track.

Fox, Mem. *Hattie the Hen.* New York: Aladdin Books, 2005. 32p. Illustrated by Patricia Mullins. $16.95. ISBN 1-416-90308-9.

Author and Illustrator

Author Mem Fox was born in Australia, grew up in South Africa, was educated in England, and now lives in Australia, where she is an author and teacher educator. Illustrator Patricia Mullins is an Australian author and illustrator.

📖 Fiction, Picture Book, Ages 3–6

Summary

The farm animals ignore Hattie the Hen as she warns them about a mysterious nose in the bushes. They continue to ignore her as she continues to warn them about the two eyes, followed by two ears, then a body, four legs, and a tail that appear. But when Hattie screams "It's a fox!" the animals are shocked into silence, while the cow's MOO scares the fox away. This cumulative tale with repetitive phrases and animal noises is illustrated with tissue paper collage and crayon.

Curriculum Responses with Curriculum Standards

1. Read aloud and encourage children to listen and chime in with the repetitive phrases and noises that the animals make. After reading, place the book where children can select it and read it independently. (American Association of School Librarians Standards 1.1.6, 3.1.3, 4.1.1, 4.1.3; English Language Arts Standards 1, 3, 4, 11, 12)

2. After reading, encourage children to retell the story by acting out, with individual children taking the parts of each of the animals. (American Association of School Librarians Standards 1.1.6, 1.1.9, 1.2.3, 2.2.4, 3.1.2, 3.1.3, 3.2.2, 3.2.3, 4.1.3, 4.1.8; English Language Arts Standards 1, 3, 4, 11, 12; Theater Content Standards 2)

3. Follow up with an art activity using tissue paper collage and crayon. (American Association of School Librarians Standards 1.2.3, 2.1.6, 2.2.4, 4.1.3, 4.1.8; English Language Arts Standards 3, 4, 6; Visual Arts Content Standards 1)

4. Visit Mem Fox's website at http://memfox.net/welcome for information about the author and her books. (American Association of School Librarians Standards 1.1.1, 1.1.2, 1.1.6, 1.1.8, 1.1.5, 2.1.1, 2.1.4, 2.1.6, 3.1.6, 4.1.4; English Language Arts Standards 1, 8, 12)

5. Feature Mem Fox as author of the week or month. Display a collection of her books, and encourage your children to read them. (American Association of School Librarians Standards 1.1.6, 4.1.1, 4.1.2, 4.2.4; English Language Arts Standards 1)

Related Books

1. Fox, Mem. *A Particular Cow.* San Diego, CA: Harcourt Children's Books, 2006. 32p. Illustrated by Terry Denton. $16.00. ISBN 0-152-00250-2.

Cartoon-like illustrations enliven the humorous cumulative tale of the cow, who runs through a clothes line, snags her head into a pair of bloomers, and causes one accident after another.

2. Fox, Mem. *Harriet, You'll Drive Me Wild!* Australia: Sandpiper, 2003. 32p. Illustrated by Marla Frazee. $7.00. ISBN 0-152-04598-2.

Harriet doesn't mean to be naughty or to get into mischief, and her mother doesn't want to yell at her, but she does—and she does!

3. Fox, Mem. *Feathers and Fools.* Australia: Voyager Books, 2000. 36p. Illustrated by Nicholas Wilton. $7.00. ISBN 0-152-02365-8.

In this antiwar allegory, the peacocks gather arms out of fear that the swans will attack, them, until the war they fear actually occurs.

4. Fox, Mem. *Hunwick's Egg.* San Diego, CA: Harcourt Children's Books, 2005. 32p. Illustrated by Pamela Lofts. $16.00 ISBN 0-152-16318-2.

Animals and plants of Australia adorn the story of Hunwick, a bandicoot, who finds an egg—an egg that doesn't hatch—an egg that is not an egg, but a stone.

5. Fox, Mem. *The Magic Hat.* Australia: Voyager Books, 2006. 32p. Illustrated by Tricia Tusa. ISBN 0-152-05715-3.

Repetitive rhymes tell the predictable story of the magic hat that changes each person it lands on into an animal.

Graham, Bob. *How to Heal a Broken Wing.* Cambridge, MA: Candlewick Press, 2008. Unpaged. $16.99. ISBN 978-0-7636-3903-7.

Author

Author Bob Graham is Australian. His book *How to Heal a Broken Wing* was selected by the United States Board on Books for Young People (USBBY) as an Outstanding International Book.

📖 Fiction, Picture Book, Ages 4–8

Summary

In this almost wordless book, cartoon-like illustrations and sparse text tell the story of the bird that flew into the window of a skyscraper, fell to the sidewalk, was found, rescued, and nursed back to health by a small boy and his parents. This is a book that must be seen. It is the pictures that tell the gentle story. Some illustrations are greatly detailed; others are not. One two-page spread is similar to a page from *Where's Waldo,* with many details and no text.

Curriculum Standards with Curriculum Responses

1. Introduce the book by reading aloud, showing the pictures, and focusing attention to the details of the pictures. Encourage questions and discussion. After reading aloud, place the book where children can read it independently. (American Association of School Librarians Standards 1.1.6, 1.1.9, 1.3.4, 2.1.5, 2.3.1, 3.1.2, 3.1.3, 3.2.1, 3.2.2, 3.3.1, 3.3.2, 3.3.5, 4.1.1, 4.1.3, 4.3.1; English Language Arts Standards 1, 3, 4, 6, 11, 12)

2. After reading, ask children if they have ever found an injured bird or animal or had an injured pet. Encourage discussion. What did they do? What happened? (American Association of School Librarians

Standards 1.1.6, 1.1.9, 1.3.4, 2.1.5, 2.3.1, 3.1.2, 3.1.3, 3.2.1, 3.2.2, 4.1.1, 4.3.1; English Language Arts Standards 1, 3, 6, 1, 12)

3. Take advantage of the discussions to develop children's oral language. Encourage children to expand on what they are thinking and saying, with probing questions such as "Tell us more." "Then what happened?" "What did you think?" "How did you feel?" (American Association of School Librarians Standards 1.1.2, 1.1.3, 1.3.4, 2.1.5, 2.3.1, 3.1.2, 3.1.3, 3.2.2, 3.3.5, 4.1.3, 4.1.5, 4.3.1; English Language Arts Standard 3, 4, 6, 11, 12)

Related Books

1. Graham, Bob. *Benny: An Adventure Story.* Cambridge, MA: Candlewick Press, 2003. 32p. $6.99. ISBN 0-763-61703-2.

Benny is a down-and-out show dog, hopping the trains and looking for a new home after he loses his job with Brillo the Magician.

2. Graham, Bob. *Jethro Byrd, Fairy Child.* Cambridge, MA: Candlewick Press, 2005. 32p. $6.99. ISBN 0-763-62697-X.

After she sees him hit the fence, bounce off the driveway, and fly onto a leaf, Annabelle invites Jethro, the finger-sized fairy child and his family for tea and cakes.

3. Graham, Bob. *The Trouble with Dogs.* Cambridge, MA: Candlewick Press, 2007. 32p. $12.99. ISBN 0-763-63316-X.

In this sequel to *Let's Get a Pup*, little dog Dave needs training, and his trainer, the Brigadier, learns that a softer voice is better than firm and harsh voice.

Lester, Alison. *Ernie Dances to the Didgeridoo.* Boston: Houghton Mifflin Company, 2000. Unpaged. $15.00. ISBN 0-618-10442-9.

Author and Illustrator

Alison Lester is an Australian children's author and illustrator. In 2005 she initiated the Kids Antarctic Art Project when she sailed to Antarctica.

📖 Realistic Fiction, Picture Book, Ages 4–8

Summary

Ernie writes letters to his friends, one letter for each of the six seasons, when he visits Gungalanya in Arnhem Land, a land belonging to Australia's Aboriginal people for over 40,000 years. An informative introductory page tells readers about Arnhem Land and names the six seasons with a pronunciation guide. The final page is a glossary of names used throughout the book.

Curriculum Responses with Curriculum Standards

1. Have students find Australia, Northern Territory, and Darwin on a map. Look for Arnhem Land, which is the northern portion of the Northern Territory. (American Association of School Librarians Standards 1.1.1, 1.1.2, 1.1.6, 1.1.9, 1.2.2, 1.3.4, 2.1.1, 2.3.1, 3.1.2, 4.1.2, 4.3.1; English Language Arts Standards 1, 11; Social Studies Standard III)

2. After reading, have the children create collages showing each season. (American Association of School Librarians Standards 1.1.6, 2.1.2, 2.1.6, 2.2.1, 4.1.1, 4.1.3, 4.1.8; English Language Arts Standards 1, 3, 4, 6, 11, 12; Visual Arts Content Standard 1)

3. Google Alison Lester to learn more about her books, her home in Australia, her voyage to Antarctica, and the Kids Antarctic Art Project. You can view her diary, interactive maps, photos, e-mails and children's pictures related to Antarctica. Encourage children to develop questions and share their findings. (American Association of School Librarians Standards 1.1.1, 1.1.3, 1.1.4, 1.1.5, 1.1.6, 1.1.8, 1.3.4, 1.3.5, 1.4.1, 1.4.2, 1.4.4, 3.1.1, 3.1.3, English Language Arts Standards 1, 3, 4, 6, 7, 8, 11, 12)

Related Books

1. Lester, Alison. *Are We There Yet?* La Jolla, CA: Kane Miller Book Publishers, 2005. 32p. $16.95. ISBN 1-929-13273-5.

Grace and her family tour Australia, with small maps and detailed illustrations showing the family's travels.

2. Ormerod, Jan. *Lizzie Nonsense: A Story of Pioneer Days.* New York: Clarion Books, 2005. 49p. $15.00. ISBN 0-618-57493-X

Lizzie, an imaginative Australian pioneer girl who lives in the Australian bush with her mother, father, and baby brother, daydreams of better times and places, while she stays alone with her mother and baby brother when her father takes a long trip to town to sell his sandalwood.

CANADA

Authors Ruth Ashby and Kalli Dakos offer readers a retelling of an Old English tale and a collection of poetry. Curriculum responses provide opportunities for students to read aloud and to write their own poetry.

Canadian illustrators Krysten Brooker and Rob Gomsalves offer fun and imaginative stories about a prince who won't go to bed, a talking cat, an urban angel, and dream-like places. Curriculum Responses include poetry writing, choral reading, and the creation of M. C. Escher–like drawings.

Ashby, Ruth. *Caedmon's Song*. Grand Rapids, Michigan: Wm B. Eerdmans Publishing Co. 2006. Unpaged. Illustrated by Bill Shavin. $16.00 ISBN 0-8028-5241-6.

Author and Illustrator

Author Ruth Ashby is an American whose writing focuses on nonfiction and biographies. Illustrator Bill Slavin is Canadian and lives in Ontario. The story is a retelling of the Old English version of "Caedmon's Hymn," a tale from Bede, England's earliest historian.

📖 Retelling, Picture Book, Ages 5 and up

Summary

The story of Caedmon is the true story of a 7th-century cowherd who is considered to be the first English poet. Caedmon was a real person who worked as a cowherd at the monastery of Whitby in Yorkshire in 660 AD. He hated poetry and said, "There is no poetry in me. . . . " He was told, "There is poetry in everyone. . . . Sing about the things you know." He became a monk and composed the "1st Hymn of Praise." The Biographical Note at the end of the book includes "Caedmon's Hymn," written in Old English.

Curriculum Responses with Curriculum Standards

1. After reading engage children in a discussion. Is there poetry in everyone? What does that mean? What does it mean to "Sing about the things you know."? (American Association of School Librarians Standards 1.1.6, 1.1.9, 1.2.1, 1.3.4, 2.1.1, 2.1.3, 2.3.1, 3.1.2, 3.1.3, 3.2.1, 3.2.2, 3.3.1, 3.3.2, 3.3.5, 4.1.1, 4.1.2, 4.1.3, 4.1.5, 4.3.1; English Language Arts Standards 1, 2, 3, 4, 6, 11, 12)
2. After reading, have children create and share their own poems about things they know. Introduce the activity with a whole class or as a small-group language experience activity using the cinquain format. Follow up by encouraging children to write their own poems, individually, in pairs, or in small groups. (American Association of School Librarians Standards 1.1.2, 1.1.6, 1.3.4, 2.1.6, 2.2.4, 3.1.3, 3.3.2, 3.3.4, 3.3.5, 4.1.8, 4.1.3, 4.1.5, 4.1.8, 4.3.1; English Language Arts Standards 1, 4, 5, 6, 11, 12)

3. After reading, have children read "Caedmon's Song" as a choral reading activity. (American Association of School Librarians Standards 1.1.6, 1.1.9, 2.1.5, 3.1.2, 3.1.3, 3.2.2, 3.2.3, 4.1.1, 4.1.3, 4.1.8; English Language Arts Standards 1, 3, 4, 11, 12)

Related Books

Cowling, Douglas. *Hallelujah Handel.* New York: Scholastic Press, 2002. Unpaged. Illustrated by Jason Walker. $16.95. ISBN 0-439-05850-3.

Older children will enjoy the story of Handel's *Messiah* and the "Hallelujah Chorus," given for the benefit of orphaned children at London's Foundling Hospital to Thomas, the boy who could not speak, but who sang like an angel.

Dakos, Kalli. *Put Your Eyes Up Here and Other School Poems.* New York: Simon & Schuster Books for Young Readers, 2003. 64p. Illustrated by G. Brian Karas. $16.95. ISBN 0-689-8117-9.

Author and Illustrator

Author Kalli Dallos is Canadian and lives in Ottawa. Illustrator G. Brian Karas is American.

📖 Poetry, Ages 7–11

Summary

Black and white cartoon-like illustrations and text that wander and dance on the pages enhance this humorous collection of school poems about life in Ms. Roy's classroom. Poems for two or more voices, couplets, free verse, rhyming verse, and other poems introduce children to a wide range of poetic formats.

Curriculum Responses and Curriculum Standards

1. Select poems to read aloud and encourage children to read their favorite poems aloud. Listen, enjoy, and have fun. Incorporate a "poetry break" into your classroom or library program. (American Association of School Librarians Standards 3.1.2, 3.1.3, 4.1.1, 4.1.2, 4.2.4, 4.4.1; English Language Arts Standards 1, 3, 4)
2. Select poems such as "Excerpts from Dead Pencils," or "Why We're Sitting at Our Desks Wearing Raincoats and Holding Umbrellas," as models for student writing. Encourage students to write their own poems. Have students compile a book of poems that they have written and illustrated. (American Association of School Librarians

Standards 2.1.6, 2.2.4, 3.1.2, 3.1.3, 3.2.1, 3.2.2, 3.2.3, 3.3.4, 3.1.2, 3.1.3, 3.2.3, 3.3.4, 4.1.3, 4.1.8, 4.4.1; English Language Arts Standards 4, 5, 6, 12)

3. Encourage children to select and prepare poems such as "I Don't Believe in Ghosts," or "A Gift for Ms. Roys," to read aloud and perform as poems for two voices or as choral reading experiences. (American Association of School Librarians Standards 1.1.6, 3.1.2, 3.1.3, 3.2.2, 3.2.3, 4.1.1, 4.1.7, 4.1.8; English Language Arts Standards 4, 12)

Related Books

1. Dakos, Kalli. *Don't Read This Book, Whatever You DO! More Poems about School.* New York: Four Winds Press, 1998. 60p. Illustrated by G. Brian Karas. $13.95. ISBN 0-689-82132-8.

More fun, interactive poems enliven the elementary school classroom.

2. Dakos, Kalli. *If You're Not Here, Please Raise Your Hand: Poems about School.* New York: Four Winds Press, 1995. 60p. Illustrated by G. Brian Karas. $12.95. ISBN 0-689-80116-5.

Humorous poems about school will tickle young readers' funny bones.

3. Dakos, Kalli. *Greatest Magic: Poems for Teachers.* New York: Scholastic Inc, 2000. 28p. $10.95. ISBN 0-439-20181-0.

Add humor and poetry to your classroom and library programs with more poems from Kalli Dakos.

4. Dakos, Kalli. *Mrs. Cole on an Onion Roll.* New York: Simon and Schuster Books for Young Readers, 1999. 40p. Illustrated by JoAnn Adinolfi. $16.45. ISBN 0-613-15913-6.

Lively poems entertain young readers.

5. Dakos, Kalli. *The Bug in Teacher's Coffee and Other School Poems.* New York: Harper Trophy, 2002. 38p. Illustrated by Mike Reed. $10.95. ISBN 0-064-44305-1.

More humorous poems appeal to young readers.

Dodds, Dayle Ann. *The Prince Won't Go to Bed.* New York: Farrar, Straus and Giroux, 2007. 32p. Illustrated by Kyrsten Brooker. $16.00. ISBN 0-374-36108-8.

Author and Illustrator

Author Dayle Ann Dodds is American. Illustrator Krysten Brooker is Canadian.

📖 Fiction, Picture Books, Ages 4–8

Summary

Nanny, the squire, the cook, and other members of the royal household try to put the prince to bed. Pillows, pudding, and a warm bath are not what the prince wants. Finally his big sister, the Princess Kate, comes running. She asks what the trouble is. The prince whispers in her ear. What do you think he asks for? Each group of four pages follows the same format. The first two-page spread puts the prince to bed and ends with "But then . . ." The second two-page spread begins with a crying wail, followed by a repetitive line.

Curriculum Responses with Curriculum Standards

1. Introduce the book by reading aloud and showing the pictures. After reading the first seven pages, encourage children to chime in with the crying wail and repetitive line. (American Association of School Librarians Standards 1.1.6, 3.1.2, 3.1.3, 3.2.2, 4.1.1, 4.1.3; English Language Arts Standards 1,3, 4, 6, 11, 12)

2. Extend the activity by asking children what they think the prince wants. After children make their predictions, turn the page and read to find out. (American Association of School Librarians Standards 1.1.2, 1.1.3, 1.1.6, 1.1.9, 1.3.4, 2.1.5, 3.1.3, 3.2.1, 3.2.2, 3.2.3, 3.3.1, 3.3.2, 3.3.3, 3.3.5, 4.1.1, 4.1.3, 4.1.8, 4.3.1; English Language Arts Standards 1, 3, 4, 6, 11, 12)

3. Continue the activity by asking children what they think the prince whispered in his sister's ear. (American Association of School Librarians Standards 1.1.2, 1.1.3, 1.1.9, 1.3.4, 2.1.5, 3.1.2, 3.2.2, 3.2.3, 3.3.1, 3.3.2, 3.3.3, 3.3.5, 4.1.3, 4.3.1; English Language Arts Standards 1, 3, 4, 6, 11, 12)

Related Books

1. Dodds, Dayle Ann. *Henry's Amazing Machine.* New York: Farrar, Straus, and Giroux, 2004. 32p. Illustrated by Krysten Brooker. $16.00. ISBN 0-374-32953-2.

   Henry must find a new home for his machine when it fills the house, and his parents move into a tree.

2. Lazo, Caroline. *Someday When My Cat Can Talk.* New York: Schwartz and Wade, 2008. 32p. Illustrated by Kyrsten Brooker. $16.99. ISBN 0-375-83754-X.

   A little girl imagines the adventures her cat has when he sails off to Europe, and all that he will tell her when he can talk.

3. Spinelli, Eileen. *City Angels.* New York: Dial, 2004. 32p. Illustrated by Rob Gonsalves. $16.00. ISBN 803-72821-2.

Short, rhyming stanzas, and photographic images with artistic embellishments depict a day in the life of an urban angel who rides a skate board, plays basketball, and helps those in need.

Thomson, Sarah L. *Imagine a Place.* New York: Atheneum Books for Young Readers, 2008. Unpaged. Illustrated by Rob Gonsalves. $17.99. ISBN 1-4169-6802-4.

Author and Illustrator

Author Sarah Thomson is American. Rob Gonsalves is an award winning Canadian illustrator.

📖 Fiction, Picture Book, All Ages

Summary

Written in lyrical prose, each two-page spread features a few lines beginning with "imagine a place," and an M. C. Escher–like illustration of that place.

Curriculum Responses with Curriculum Standards

1. After reading, use the book as a model by asking students to imagine a place, and then write a few lines and illustrate those lines. Collect and compile a class book. (American Association of School Librarians Standards 1.1.6, 1.3.4, 2.1.6, 2.2.4, 3.1.2, 3.1.3, 3.3.5, 4.1.1, 4.1.3, 4.1.8, 4.3.1; English Language Arts Standards 1, 3, 4, 5, 6, 11, 12; Visual Arts Content Standards 1, 2)
2. After reading, encourage children to look for and find the M. C. Escher–like transformations in the illustrations. Consider introducing older students to the work of M. C. Escher by researching and examining samples of his work. (American Association of School Librarians Standards 1.1.1, 1.1.2, 1.1.3, 1.1.4, 1.1.6, 1.1.8, 1.1.9, 1.2.2, 1.2.3, 2.1.5, 2.3.1, 3.1.2, 4.1.1, 4.1.2, 4.1.3, 4.1.4, 4.2.1; English Language Arts Standards 1, 2, 3, 4, 6, 7; Visual Arts Content Standards 2, 3, 5)
3. Having examined and analyzed M. C. Escher's work, encourage children to create their own M. C. Escher–like drawings and sharing them with classmates. Mount a display for all to see. (American Association of School Librarians Standards 2.1.6, 2.2.4, 3.1.2, 3.3.5, 4.1.3, 4.1.8; English Language Arts Standards 4, 5, 12; Visual Arts Content Standards 1, 2, 3, 5)

Related Books

1. Thomson, Sarah L. *Imagine a Day.* New York: Atheneum, 2005. Unpaged. Illustrated by Rob Gonsalves. $18.99. ISBN 0-689-85219-3.

Surreal illustrations and lyrical text depict daytime images.

2. Thomson, Sarah L. *Imagine a Night.* New York: Atheneum, 2003. Unpaged. Illustrated by Rob Gonsalves. $18.99. ISBN 0-689-85218-5.

Lyrical text and sixteen illustrations invite readers to stretch their imaginations.

CROSS COUNTRIES AND CULTURE

Journey through the deserts of the world, learn to say "hello" in forty-two different languages, and meet Jack, whose stories originated in Great Britain, spread around the world, and became a part of Appalachian Mountain culture. Authors and illustrators are French, Yugoslavian, Japanese, American, Belgian, and English. Curriculum Responses include map work, storytelling, and dramatizations.

Le Rochais, Marie-Ange. *Desert Trek: An Eye-Opening Journey through the World's Driest Places.* New York: Walker & Company, 2001. 40p. Translated from the French by George L. Newman. $17.95. ISBN 0-8027-8765-7.

Author and Illustrator

Author Marie-Ange LeRochais is French and was born in Paris.

📖 Nonfiction, Picture Book, Ages 6–10

Summary

The focus of this nonfiction book is the deserts of the world: Africa, Asia, North and South America, Arabia, Australia, and Antarctica. Each two-page spread uses colorful illustrations and expository text to develop a concept about the desert, such as people, plants and animals, history, and others. Additional information for each two-page spread can be found in To Learn More at the end of the book. A world map at the back of the book shows the locations of the world's deserts. This book is appropriate for use in the middle grades as well as in elementary grades.

Curriculum Responses with Curriculum Standards

1. Have children locate deserts using a world map or globe. (American Association of School Librarians Standards 4.1.4; Social Studies Standard III)
2. Have older children research and report on deserts and their people. Encourage them to organize their research and reports by identifying

and listing what they already know, what they want to know, and what they have learned. (KWL) (American Association of School Librarians Standards 1.1.1, 1.1.2, 1.1.3. 1.1.4. 1.1.8, 1.3.4, 1.3.5, 2.1.2, 2.1.4, 3.1.1, 3.1.3, 3.1.4, 3.2.1, 4.1.2, 4.1.4, 4.1.5, 4.1.4, 4.3.1, 4.4.1, 4.4.2; English Language Arts Standards 1, 3, 4, 6, 7, 8, 11, 12)

3. Have children draw maps of the deserts that they researched and list characteristics of those deserts. (American Association of School Librarians Standards 2.1.2, 2.1.6, 2.2.4, 2.3.1, 3.1.3, 3.3.4, 4.1.3, 4.1.6; English Language Arts Standards 3, 4, 6, 7, 11, 12; Visual Arts Content Standards 1, 2)

Stojic, Manya. *Hello World! Greetings in 42 Languages Around the Globe!* New York: Scholastic, Inc. 2002. 38p. $14.95. ISBN 0-439-36202-4.

Author and Illustrator

Author and illustrator Manya Stojic was born, raised, and educated in Belgrade, Yugoslavia. She lived in the United States and now lives in England.

  📖 Nonfiction, Picture Book, Ages 4–8

Summary

Readers travel around the world from west to east, from Hawaii across North and South America to Europe, Africa, Asia—and on to Australia and New Zealand, learning to say "hello" in 42 languages. Each page features the face of a child and "hello" written in the language of the child's country. The phonetic spelling is written below each translation, and the name of the language of the country is written in the corner.

Curriculum Responses with Curriculum Standards

1. Have children identify the cultural backgrounds of their classmates, of the faculty and staff in their school, and of the residents of their community. Have children learn to say "hello" in the languages of the cultures represented in their community. Extend the activity by encouraging children to learn to say "hello" in the languages of the countries and cultures of the books they read. (American Association of School Librarians Standards 1.1.1, 1.1.2, 1.1.9, 2.1.1, 2.1.2, 2.1.5, 2.3.1, 2.3.2, 3.1.1, 3.1.2, 3.1.3, 3.1.5, 3.2.2, 3.2.3, 3.3.1, 3.3.2, 3.3.5, 3.3.6, 4.1.2, 4.1.3, 4.1.7, 4.3.1, English Language Arts Standards 4, 6, 9, 11, 12; Social Studies Curriculum Standards I, IV, IX)

2. Have children use a map to locate the countries of the languages they are using. List the countries and languages on a chart. (American Association of School Librarians Standards 1.1.1, 1.1.2, 1.1.3, 1.1.9, 1.3.4, 2.1.1, 2.1.2, 2.1.6, 2.2.4, 2.3.1, 2.4.3, 3.1.1, 3.1.2, 3.1.3, 3.1.4, 3.2.2, 3.2.3, 3.3.4, 4.1.6, 4.3.1; English Language Arts Standards 1, 3, 5, 9, 11, 12; Social Studies Standards I, 111)

3. Have children trace and cut out outlines of the countries. On each country write "hello" in the language of the country. Set up a display for all to see. (American Association of School Librarians Standards 1.1.9, 1.3.4, 2.1.6, 2.2.4, 2.3.1, 3.1.2, 3.1.3, 3.2.2, 3.2.3, 3.3.4, 3.3.5, 4.1.3, 4.1.8, 4.3.1; English Language Arts Standards 3, 4, 6, 9, 11, 12; Social Studies Curriculum Standards I, III; Visual Arts Standards 1)

Related Books

Ichikawa, Satomi. *My Father's Shop.* Kane/Miller, 2006. $15.95. ISBN 1-929132-99-9.

As the crowing rooster follows Mustafa, who is draped in one of his father's Moroccan rugs, tourists in the market show how roosters sound in their countries.

Swope, Sam. *Jack and the Seven Deadly Giants.* New York: Farrar Straus Giroux, 2004. 100p. Illustrated by Carll Cneut $16.00. ISBN 0-374-33670-9.

Author and Illustrator

Author Sam Swope is American. Illustrator Carll Cneut is Belgian and lives in Ghent, Belgium. This story is a variation on the Jack Tales that originated in Great Britain and spread to cultures around the world, including the Appalachian Mountain culture in the United States. The setting of the tales in this book is probably England or Europe, rather than the Appalachian Mountains.

📖 Folktale, Ages 4–8

Summary

From the very beginning, Jack was just plain bad. He had no mama and was left on doorstep after doorstep. He cried so much that no one wanted him. He got into trouble in school and even in church. When the village was threatened by the approach of seven deadly giants, the villagers blamed Jack. So Jack ran away with only an apple in his pocket—an apple that he shared with a funny little man who rewarded him with a magic bean seed. Jack made a wish to find his mother, but got a cow. Riding backward on his cow, Jack met the seven deadly giants: first Sloth the Poet, then the Terrible

Glutton, next Mrs. Roth, followed by the Wild Tickler, then Avaritch, after whom came Orgulla the Great. Finally Jack met the Green Queen. What happened when Jack met each of the seven deadly giants? And how did Jack find his mother? For he did, you know.

Curriculum Responses with Curriculum Standards

1. Compare *Jack and the Seven Giants* with other Jack Tales. Explain that the Jack Tales derive from the oral tradition of storytelling. After the children have read other Jack Tales, encourage them to create and tell their own. (American Association of School Librarians Standards 1.1.6, 1.3.4, 2.3.4, 3.1.3, 4.1.1, 4.1.3, 4.1.4, 4.1.8; English Language Arts Standards 1, 4, 6, 11, 12)

2. Each of the seven chapters in which Jack meets a giant is a self-contained story. Divide children into seven small groups and have each group act out a chapter using dramatization, puppetry, or reader's theater. (American Association of School Librarians Standards 1.2.3, 3.1.2, 3.1.3, 3.2,1, 4.1.3, 4.18; English Language Arts Standards 4, 11, 2; Theater Content Standards 1, 2, 4)

3. Select a chapter to read aloud to students. Have them listen, create collages, and retell the chapter from their collages. (American Association of School Librarians Standards 1.1.6, 1.3.4, 2.1.2, 2.1.6, 3.1.3, 3.3.5, 4.1.1, 4.1.3, 4.1.6, 4.1.8, 4.3.1, English Language Arts Standards 4, 6, 11, 12; Visual Arts Content Standards 1, 6)

Related Books

1. Chase, Richard. *The Jack Tales: Folk Tales from the Southern Appalachians.* New York: Houghton Mifflin Company, 1971. 216p. $7.95. ISBN 0-618-34692-9.

Richard Chase collected and retold seventeen Jack Tales from the oral tradition of the Appalachian Mountains of Western Carolina—tales that came to Appalachia from England and were recorded by Joseph Jacobs and Andrew Lang.

2. Johnson, Paul Brett. *Jack Outwits the Giants.* New York: Margaret K. McElderry Books, 2002. Unpaged. $16.00. ISBN 0-689-83902-2.

The story of how the giant woman and the two-headed giant man who lived with her ended up in the bottom of their bottomless well is one of several of Paul Brett Johnson's retellings of the Jack Tales.

3. O'Neal, Shaquille. *Shaq and the Beanstalk and Other Very Tall Tales.* Cartwheel Books, 1999. 80p. Illustrated by Shane Evans. $15.95. ISBN 0-590-91823-0.

This fractured tale features Shaq O'Neal at about the age of seven, climbing the beanstalk, meeting the giant, and delivering cookies to the giant's grandmother, recovering the hen that lays golden basketballs, outwitting the big bad wolf, and hanging out with the Three Bears.

4. Osborne, Mary Pope. *Kate and the Beanstalk.* New York: Atheneum Books for Young Readers, 2000. Unpaged. Illustrated by Giselle Potter. $16.00. ISBN 0-689-82550-1.

A new twist on the traditional story of Jack is the story of plucky Kate, who climbed the beanstalk and slew the giant.

5. Wildsmith, Brian and Rebecca Wildsmith. *Jack and the Meanstalk.* New York: Knopf, 1994. 26p. $13.91. ISBN 0-679-95810-X.

Professor Jack's concoction causes his "meanstalk" to grow into outer space, enabling a space monster to invade earth, only to be thwarted by the root-chewing animals who destroy the "meanstalk."

EUROPE

Americans abroad and Americans at home, German, Russian, Norwegian, and Swedish authors and illustrators present imaginative folktale retellings, humorous fiction, tender fiction, and informative nonfiction. Readers will travel across France with a little gray cat, meet a grandma who embarrasses her grandson, and learn that lots of people are scared. They will get to know Matthew and Anna, whose grim life is changed by Red Bird. They will learn how a mouse becomes a princess, play with the Root children, and identify creatures by their eyes and habitats.

Related Books include Helen Frost's beautifully illustrated explanation of the relationship between the life cycle of the monarch butterfly and the milkweed plant, and Susanne Berner's picture book introducing the seasons with activities related to each season. Four books were selected by the United States Board on Books for Young People (USBBY) as Outstanding International Books. Norwegian author and illustrator Stian Hole received the BolognaRagazzi Award. Swedish author Astrid Lindgren received the Hans Christian Andersen Prize, and her book *Ronia the Robber's Daughter* received the Batchelder Award in 1985. Curriculum Responses include dancing, making puppets, acting out, and other activities.

Banks, Kate. *The Cat Who Walked across France.* New York: Frances Foster Books, 2004. 40p. Illustrated by Georg Hallensleben. $6.95. ISBN 0-374-40000-8.

Author and Illustrator

Author Kate Banks is an American who lives in the South of France. She writes in English, speaks French and Italian, and publishes in France and the United States. Illustrator Georg Hallensleben was born and raised in Germany, lived in Italy for many years, and now lives in Paris.

☐ Fiction, Picture Book, Ages 4–8

Summary

The little gray cat and the little old woman live happily by the sea. One day after the little old woman dies, the little gray cat is packed up with the rest of her belongings and shipped north to her childhood home. Lonely and unhappy, the little gray cat remembers his home by the sea and begins to walk. From Rouen to St. Tropez, through the countryside and cities, past ancient ruins and familiar landmarks, the little gray cat finds his way back to the stone house by the sea, where he had lived happily with the little old woman, and where he now lives happily with a new family. Rich illustrations in the style of French Impressionists and Postimpressionists, lyrical prose, and a map of the cat's journey at the back of the book enhance this story, which is similar to Sheila Burnford's *The Incredible Journey*.

Curriculum Responses with Learning Extensions

1. After reading, have children find France on a world map. Then, using the map in the book as a guide, have children trace the cat's journey from Rousen to St. Tropez on a map of France. (American Association of School Librarians Standards 1.1.6, 1.1.9, 1.2.3, 1.3.4, 2.3.1, 3.1.2, 3.2.2, 3.2.3, 3.3.5, 4.1.2, 4.1.3, 4.1.4, 4.3.1; English Language Arts Standards 1, 3; Social Studies Standards III)

2. After reading, use the illustrations to introduce children to the paintings of French Impressionists and Postimpressionists such as Matisse, Monet, Gaugin, and others. Show scenes of France that these painters have done. Encourage children to look for and discuss similarities between the illustrations in the book and the work of the painters. (American Association of School Librarians Standards 1.3.4, 2.1.1, 2.1.5, 2.3.3, 3.1.1, 3.1.2, 3.1.3, 3.2.2, 3.2.3, 3.3.2, 3.3.3, 3.3.5, 4.1.2, 4.1.3, 4.3.1; English Language Arts Standards 1, 3; Visual Arts Content Standards 4)

3. Extend the activity by encouraging children to use library and internet resources to find additional paintings by the Impressionists and Postimpressionists. Have children gather and exhibit paintings they find. (American Association of School Librarians Standards 1.1.8, 1.1.9, 1.2.2, 1.2.3, 1.2.6, 1.3.4, 2.1.5, 2.1.6, 2.2.4, 2.3.1, 3.1.2, 3.1.4, 3.1.6, 3.2.2, 3.2.3, 3.3.5, 4.1.3, 4.1.6, 4.1.7, 4.3.1; English Language Arts Standards 7, 8, 11, 12; Visual Arts Content Standards 4)

Related Books

1. Banks, Kate. *Monkeys and Dog Days.* New York: Frances Foster Books, 2008. 48p. Illustrated by Tomek Bogacki. $14.95. ISBN 0-374-35028-0.

This is a beginning reader of four chapters, in which Max and his brother Pete discover that having a dog for a pet is far more work than they expected.

2. Banks, Kate. *Max's Words.* New York: Frances Foster Books, 2006. Unpaged. Illustrated by Boris Kulikov. $16.00. ISBN 0-374-9949-2.

One brother collects stamps, and the other collects coins, so Max decides to collect words—big words, small words, strange words, familiar words—words that he can move around, change, rearrange, and even give away!

3. Banks, Kate. *Monkeys and the Universe.* New York: Frances Foster Books, 2009. 48p. Illustrated by Tomek Bogacki. $14.95. ISBN 0-374-35028-0.

In this second book of the *Monkey Reader Series,* Max and his brother Pete learn about the solar system and how to get along with each other.

4. Banks, Kate. *That's Papa's Way.* New York: Frances Foster Books, 2009. Unpaged. Illustrated by Lauren Castillo. $16.95. ISBN 0-374-37445-7.

A little girl and her father go fishing, each doing things in his or her own way.

5. Banks, Kate. *The Night Worker.* New York: Frances Foster Books, 2007. 40p. Illustrated by Georg Hallensleben. $6.95. ISBN 0-374-40000-8.

One night Alex puts on a hard hat, rides in a tractor, and watches a cement mixer and other heavy equipment at the construction site when he goes to work with his dad.

Baryshnikov, Mikhail. *Because . . .* New York: Atheneum Books for Young Readers. 2007. Unpaged. Illustrated by Vladimir Radunsky. $16.99. ISBN 9788-0-689-87582-3.

Author and Illustrator

Author Mikhail Baryshnikov is a Russian ballet dancer. Illustrator Vladimir Radunsky was born and raised in Russia, where he studied art, design, and architecture. He moved to New York and now lives in Rome.

📖 Fiction, Picture Book, Ages 4–8

Summary

In this intergenerational book, Grandma embarrasses her grandson by dancing. Grandma leapfrogs over a neighbor, rolls over with the dog, roller skates without skates, tap dances, turns cartwheels, flaps like a butterfly, swings, gallops, leaps, and flies.

Curriculum Responses with Curriculum Standards

1. Have children act out Grandma's dancing moves. (American Association of School Librarians Standards 2.2.4, 4.1.3; Dance Content Standard 1; Theater Content Standard 2)
2. Engage children in discussion. How did Grandma embarrass her grandson? Ask children whether any of their family members have embarrassed them by doing something. Were they able to resolve their embarrassment? If so, how? If not, how might they be able to? (American Association of School Librarians Standards 1.3.4, 4.1.2, 4.1.8, 4.3.1; Social Studies Standard IV)
3. Find and show a video of the author dancing. (American Association of School Librarians Standard 1.1.6; Dance Content Standard 5)

Related Books

1. Bryan, Ashley. *The Dancing Granny.* New York: Aladdin Books, 1987. Unpaged. $6.95. ISBN 0-689-71149-2.

Another granny loves to dance! In this retelling of a West Indian folktale, Granny Anika sways and dances to the East and to the West, to the North and to the South, while Spider Anansi helps himself to the vegetables in her garden.

2. D'Arc, Karen Scourby. *My Grandmother Is a Singing Yaya.* New York: Orchard Books, 2001. Illustrated by Diane Palmisciano. Unpaged. Illustrated by Diane Palmisciano. $15.95. ISBN 0-439-29309-X.

Yaya sings—walking down the street, at the movies, at the picnic—wherever she goes, and can't be stopped, even though she knows that she embarrasses her granddaughter.

Hole, Stian. *Garmann's Summer.* Grand Rapids, MI: Eerdmans Books, 2008. 42p. $17.50. ISBN 978-0-8028-5339-4.

Author

Author Stian Hole is a Norwegian author and illustrator who won the international 2007 BolognaRagazzi Award for excellence in children's book publishing that is presented annually at the Bologna Children's Book Fair. His book *Garmann's Summer* was listed by the United States Board on Books for Young People (USBBY) as an Outstanding International Book in 2009. Two Related Books—*A Strange Day* and *In the Town All Year 'Round*—were listed by USBBY as Outstanding International Books in 2008 and 2009 respectively.

📖 Fiction, Picture Book, Ages 5–8

Summary

The summer is ending, and school is about to start. Six-year-old Garmann hasn't lost a tooth yet. Each of the neighbor twins has lost two front teeth, and they can do anything. Garmann is scared. His three elderly aunts come to visit. Garmann discovers that they're scared too. Auntie Ruth is scared of winter and of having to use a walker. Auntie Borghild is scared of dying. Auntie Augusta is forgetful and can't remember what being scared feels like. Daddy says that he's scared too—scared of playing his violin just before a concert and of leaving Garmann and Mama when he goes on tour. Daddy says that everyone is scared of something. Even Mama is scared— scared of Garmann crossing the street alone to go to school and of going to the dentist tomorrow. So even though he's scared, Garmann checks his school bag and packs his pencil case to go to school in the morning.

Curriculum Responses with Curriculum Standards

1. Read aloud and show the illustrations to your children. Focus attention on the illustrations on each page with comments and questions such as "how are the tree branches like fingers pointing to the sky?" "where is the ladybug?" and "find the butterflies in Garmann's stomach." Encourage children to respond by showing or talking. (American Association of School Librarians Standards 1.1.6, 1.3.4, 3.1.2, 3.1.3, 3.2.1, 3.2.2, 3.3.5, 4.1.1, 4.1.3, 4.3.1; English Language Arts Standards 1, 3, 4, 6, 11, 12)

2. After reading, engage children in a discussion of being scared. Begin with Garmann, the aunties, Daddy, and Mama. What are they scared of? Extend the discussion by asking students if they are or have been scared. What did they do when they were scared? Did they get over it? Do they know any adults who are or were scared?" (American Association of School Librarians Standards 1.1.6, 1.1.9, 1.2.2, 1.3.4, 2.1.5, 2.3.1, 3.1.2, 3.1.3, 3.2.1, 3.2.2, 3.2.3, 3.3.2, 3.3.3, 3.3.5, 4.1.1, 4.1.2, 4.1.3, 4.1.5, 4.3.1; English Language Arts Standards 1, 3, 4, 5, 6, 11, 12)

3. After reading, have students make pictures about being scared, using pictures cut out of magazines enhanced by their own drawings. Have students write short captions about being scared and then explain their drawings and captions to classmates. (American Association of School Librarians Standards 1.1.6, 1.2.2, 1.2.3, 1.3.4, 2.1.6, 2.2.4, 2.3.1, 3.1.2, 3.1.3, 3.2.1, 3.2.2, 3.3.2, 3.3.4, 3.3.5, 4.1.1, 4.1.3, 4.1.5, 4.1.8, 4.3.1; English Language Arts Standards 1, 4, 5, 6, 11, 12; Visual Arts Content Standards 1, 2, 3)

Related Books

1. Berner, Rotraut Susanne. *In the Town All Year 'Round.* San Francisco, CA: Chronicle Books LLC, 2008. Unpaged. Translated by Neeltje Konings and Nick Elliot. $16.99. ISBN 978-0-8118-6474-9.

This picture book, similar to *Where's Waldo,* introduces each season with a page filled with cartoon-like illustrations of featured characters, followed by seven two-page spreads filled with detailed illustrations that include the featured characters engaged in a variety of activities all around the town.

2. van der Heide, Iris. *A Strange Day.* Honesdale, PA: Lemniscaat/Boyds Mills Press, Inc., 2007. Unpaged. $15.95. ISBN 978-1-932425-94-9.

Be sure to read the illustrations as well as the text in this story about Jack, who is so disappointed not to receive a postcard telling him whether he won the drawing contest that he doesn't notice the postman trying to catch the postcard blown by the wind, or the runaway stroller that he stops from rolling into the river, or the dog that he saves from the colliding bicycles, or the other events in his very strange day.

3. Alsenas, Linas. *Hello My Name Is Bob.* New York: Scholastic Press, 2009. Unpaged. $16.99. ISBN 0-545-05244-0.

Bob is a boring bear who sometimes counts toothpicks or hums, but who mostly just sits, and who is very different from his lively friend Jack, who takes Bob to the ice cream shop, the alligator swamp, and even the amusement park.

4. Alsenas, Linas. *Mrs. Claus Takes A Vacation.* New York: Scholastic Paperbacks, 2008. 32p. $6.99. ISBN 0-439-77979-0.

When Mrs. Claus hitches up Santa's sleigh and flies off on her own world tour, Santa gets worried and lonely, and so does Mrs. Claus.

5. Alsenas, Linas. *Peanut.* New York: Scholastic Press, 2007. 32p. $16.99. ISBN 0-439-7998-4.

A sad little old lady is happy to find a pet puppy in the park, except that Peanut the puppy is an elephant.

Lindgren, Astrid. *The Red Bird.* New York: Arthur A. Levine Books, 2005. Unpaged. Illustrated by Marit Tornqvist. Translated by Patricia Crampton. $16.95. ISBN 0-439-62796-6.

Author, Illustrator, and Translator

Author Astrid Lindgren is a Swedish author and screenwriter who is perhaps best known for her books about Pippi Longstocking. She received the Hans

Christian Andersen Prize in 1958, and her book *Ronia the Robber's Daughter* won the Batchelder Award in 1985. Illustrator Marit Tornqvist was born in Sweden and studied in Amsterdam, where she now lives. Translator Patricia Crampton is an author and translator who lives in England. A Related Book, *Ellen's Apple Tree*, was listed by the United States Board on Books for Young People (USBBY) as a 2009 Outstanding International Book.

📖 Fiction, Picture Book, Ages 4–8

Summary

Lyrical prose, repetitive text, and emotionally moving illustrations tell the touching story of Matthew and Anna, whose grim life with the farmer promises to be brightened by a few weeks of school in the winter. A red bird changes their lives by leading the two young children from the cold, gray, hungry winter through the door in the wall, into the warm, spring sunshine where flowers grow, children play, and Mother feeds all of her children. Must Matthew and Anna continue to return to their stark and austere lives with the farmer? Matthew makes a decision!

Curriculum Responses with Curriculum Standards

1. After reading this book and showing the illustrations, ask your children what the illustrations tell about the story. How does the illustrator use color to depict life with the farmer, winter, school, and spring in Sunnymead? Follow up by asking children to think about, talk about, and then use colors to make pictures showing sad and happy times in their lives. (American Association of School Librarians Standards 1.1.6, 1.2.3, 1.3.4, 2.1.1, 2.1.6, 2.3.4, 3.2.1, 3.2.2, 3.3.4, 3.3.5, 4.1.1, 4.1.3, 4.1.8, 4.3.1; English Language Arts Standards 1, 3, 4, 6, 11, 12; Visual Arts Content Standards 1)

2. Call children's attention to repetitive lines and phrases such as "in the days of poverty," "If only I can live till winter and . . . ," "But God help you if you're not home by . . . ," and "Come, all my children!" Have children retell the story by preparing a reader's theater script using these repetitive lines and phrases. (American Association of School Librarians Standards 1.1.6, 1.3.4, 2.1.5, 2.1.6, 2.3.4, 3.1.2, 3.1.3, 3.2.1, 3.2.2, 3.2.3, 3.3.1, 3.3.4, 3.3.5, 4.1.3, 4.1.8, 4.3.1; English Language Arts Standards 3, 4, 5, 6, 11, 12)

3. Using a two-column chart, have children contrast Matthew and Anna's life with the farmer with their life in Sunnymead. (American Association of School Librarians Standards 1.1.6, 1.1.9, 1.2.2, 1.2.3, 1.3.4, 2.1.1, 2.1.2, 2.1.3, 2.1.4, 2.1.5, 2.1.6, 2.2.4, 3.1.2, 3.1.3, 3.1.4, 3.2.1, 3.2.2, 3.2.3, 3.3.1, 3.3.3, 3.3.4, 3.3.5, 4.1.3, 4.1.6, 4.1.8, 4.3.1; English Language Arts Standards 3, 4, 5, 6, 11, 12)

Related Books

1. Kruusval, Catarina. *Ellen's Apple Tree.* Stockholm: R&S Books, 2008. Unpaged. Translated by Joan Sandin. $16.00 ISBN 978-91-29-66905-3.

When the apple tree that Ellen and her friend Ollie love to play in blows over in a winter storm, Ellen and her family plant a new tree in their yard.

2. Landstrom, Lena. *The Little Hippos' Adventure* Stockholm: R&S Books, 2002. Unpaged. Translated by Joan Sandin. $15.00. ISBN 91-29-65500-5.

The little hippos love swimming and splashing and diving in the river, but they want their diving board to be as high as the tall cliff.

3. Lindenbaum, Pija. *Bridget and the Muttonheads.* Stockholm: R&R Books, 2002. Unpaged. Translated by Kjersti Board. $16.00. ISBN 91-29-65650-8.

While Bridget and her parents vacation at a hotel with a pool, Bridget slips away to dig in the sand and to rescue five small sheep that are stranded on a nearby island.

4. Lindgren. Astrid. *Most Beloved Sister.* Stockholm: R&R Books, 2002. Unpaged. Illustrations by Hans Arnold. Translated by Elisabeth Kallick Dyssegaard. $15.00. ISBN 91-29-65502-1.

Seven-year-old Barbara has an imaginary twin sister named Lalla-Lee, with whom she has wonderful adventures in the Golden Hall, the Great Horrible Forest, and the Most Beautiful Valley in the World.

5. Olaffsson, Helena. *The Little Jester.* Stockholm: R&S Books, 2002. Unpaged. Translated by Kjersti Board. $16.00. ISBN 91-29-65499-8.

Medieval and contemporary illustrations enhance this retelling of the jester who brought a smile to the picture of the Weeping Madonna by hopping onto the high altar in the Cathedral to dance and juggle and do his tricks.

Shepard, Aaron. *The Princess Mouse: A Tale of Finland.* New York: Atheneum Books for Young Readers, 2003. Illustrated by Leonid Gore. $16.95. ISBN 0-689-82912-4.

Author and Illustrator

Aaron Shepard is an American who is known for his retellings based on old books. Illustrator Leonid Gore is a Russian who now lives in the United States.

📖 Fiction, Folktale Retelling, Picture Book, Ages 4–8

Summary

In Mikko's family, the boys must find a wife by cutting down a tree and walking in the direction it points. Mikko's brother has a sweetheart and knows how to cut down trees. His tree points in the direction of his sweetheart. Mikko has no sweetheart and doesn't know how to cut down trees. Once he gets it cut down, Mikko's tree points to the forest. What kind of sweetheart will Mikko find in the forest, asks his brother? A wolf? A fox? No, a mouse. How can a mouse possibly become Mikko's sweetheart?

Curriculum Responses with Curriculum Standards

1. As children read, stop them and ask the questions. What kind of sweetheart will Mikko find in the forest? How can a mouse become Mikko's sweetheart? Engage children in a discussion, and then read on to answer the questions. (American Association of School Librarians Standards 1.1.2, 1.1.6, 1.1.9, 1.3.4, 2.1.5, 3.1.2, 3.1.3, 3.2.1, 3.2.2, 3.3.1, 3.3.2, 3.3.5, 4.1.1, 4.1.3, 4.3.1; English Language Arts Standards 1, 3, 4, 6, 11, 12)
2. After reading, have each child make two masks, one for the mouse, and the other for the beautiful princess. (American Association of School Librarians Standards 1.1.6, 1.2.3, 2.1.6, 2.2.4, 4.1.1, 4.1.3; English Language Arts Standards 1, 3, 4, 6, 12; Visual Arts Content Standards 1, 2)
3. Visit the author's Web site at www.aaronshep.com to download a reader's theater script and a recording of the tune for the Princess Mouse's song. Encourage the children to retell the story using the reader's theater script and to incorporate the Princess Mouse's song. (American Association of School Librarians Standards 1.1.8, 2.1.6, 3.1.2, 3.1.3, 3.2.3, 4.1.3, 4.1.7; English Language Arts Standard 3, 4, 6, 11, 12; Music Content Standard 1; Theater Content Standard 2)

Related Books

1. Shepard, Aaron. *The Sea King's Daughter: A Russian Legend.* New York: Aladdin Paperbacks, 2001. Unpaged. Illustrated by Gennady Spirin. $6.99. ISBN 0-689-84259-7.

In this retelling of the legendary story of Sadko, the merchant-musician, whom Rimsky-Korsakov immortalized in his opera *Sadko,* the Sea King invites Sadko to play his gusli at the palace and offers Sadko one of his daughters in marriage.

2. Burleigh, Robert. *The Secret of the Great Houdini.* New York: Atheneum Books for Young Readers, 2002. Unpaged. Illustrated by Leonid Gore. $16.95. ISBN 0-689-83267-2.

A little boy watches from the pier with his uncle as the great Houdini, the magician who can break free from any bonds, will again mesmerize the crowd as he is wrapped in chains, handcuffed, locked in a trunk, and lowered into the cold waters of the river.

3. Frost, Helen. *Monarch and Milkweed.* New York: Atheneum Books for Young Readers, 2008. Unpaged. Illustrated by Leonid Gore. $17.99. ISBN 1-4169-0085-3.

Lyrical text and full-page illustrations explain the relationship between the life cycle of the monarch butterfly and the milkweed plant.

4. Manushkin, Fran. *The Little Sleepyhead.* New York: Dutton Children's Books, 2004. Unpaged. Illustrated by Leonid Gore. $16.99. ISBN 0-525-46956-7.

He played all day and needs someplace to sleep, someplace soft, cozy, and quiet, with someone to hug.

5. Quattlebaum, Mary. *Sparks Fly High: The Legend of Dancing Point.* New York: Melanie Kroupa Books, 2006. Illustrated by Leonid Gore. $16.00. ISBN 0-374-34452-3.

This is a retelling of the Virginia legend about Colonel Lightfoot, who dances with the devil in order to reclaim a piece of his marshy land.

Wiesmuller, Dieter. *In the Blink of an Eye.* New York: Walker & Company, 2002. Unpaged. $16.00. ISBN 0-8027-8854-8.

Author and Illustrator

Author and illustrator Dieter Wiesmuller lives in Germany.

📖 Nonfiction, Picture Book, Ages 5–8.

Summary

Each two-page spread shows the eye of a creature on the left, with two lines of descriptive text, and a habitat scene on the right, with two lines of descriptive text. The last page of the book identifies the creatures to which the eyes belong.

Curriculum Responses with Curriculum Standards

1. Read aloud and show the pictures of the eye and the habitat. Encourage children to guess what creature the eye might belong to. Turn to the last page to verify children's answers. (American Association of School Librarians Standards 1.1.2, 1.1.6, 1.1.9, 1.2.2, 1.3.4, 2.1.1, 2.1.3, 2.1.5, 3.1.3, 3.2.1, 3.2.2, 3.2.3, 3.3.2, 3.3.5, 4.1.2, 4.1.3, 4.3.1; English Language Arts Standards: 1, 2, 3, 4, 6, 11, 12; Life Science Standards: Characteristics of organisms, Organisms and environments)
2. Lead children in a group discussion about the creatures and habitats. Which of the featured creatures and habitats do you have in your

community? What other creatures and habitats do you have in your community? (American Association of School Librarians Standards 1.2.4, 2.1.3, 2.3.1, 3.1.1, 3.1.3, 3.1.5, 3.2.1, 3.2.2, 3.3.5, 4.1.2, 4.3.1; English Language Arts Standards: 3, 4, 6, 11, 12; Life Science Standards: Organisms and environments)

3. Using the book as a model, have the children create a class book by cutting animal and/or bird pictures from magazines. Paste the animal or bird on one piece of paper. Paste a habitat picture on a second piece of paper. Bind pages together into a class book. Add to the back of the book an index that identifies each of the creatures with appropriate page numbers. (American Association of School Librarians Standards 1.1.9, 1.2.2, 1.2.3, 1.3.4, 2.1.1, 2.1.2, 2.1.5, 2.1.6, 2.1.4, 2.3.1, 3.1.2, 3.1.3, 3.2.1, 3.2.2, 3.2.3, 3.3.4, 3.3.5, 4.1.2, 4.1.3, 4.1.4, 4.1.6, 4.1.7, 4.1.8, 4.3.1; English Language Arts Standards: 3, 4, 5, 6, 11, 12; Life Science Standards: Organisms and environments; Visual Arts Content Standards: 1, 3)

Wood, Audrey. *When the Root Children Wake Up*. New York: Scholastic Press. 2002. Unpaged. Illustrated by Ned Bittinger. $16.95. ISBN 0-590-42517-X.

Author and Illustrator

Audrey Wood, an American author, retells the classic German story, originally written in 1906 by Sibylle von Olfer. Illustrator Ned Bittinger is also an American.

📖   Fiction, Retelling, Picture Book. Ages 6 and Up

Summary

The Root Children wake up from the long winter to celebrate Spring. They stretch, run their fingers through their hair, tumble from their beds in husk clothing, and use scissors, needle, and thread to make blossom costumes. They rush into the world, are greeted by the animals, and dance and prance until Aunt Spring grows weary. Jolly Cousin Summer appears with laughter and music, followed by Uncle Fall with his spectacles, pencils and books. When a chilling wind blows, and brightly colored leaves fall to the ground, Mother Earth blows her horn for the Root Children to return home. Mother Earth bolts the door, tucks the children into bed, and sings them a lullaby, which is in the back of the book.

Curriculum Responses with Curriculum Standards

1. After reading, have children make puppets of the root children, Aunt Spring, Jolly Cousin Summer, Uncle Fall, and Mother Earth. (American Association of School Librarians Standards 1.1.6, 1.2.3, 2.1.6,

2.2.4, 4.1.1, 4.1.3, 4.1.8; English Language Arts Standards 1, 3, 4, 6, 12; Visual Arts Content Standards 1, 2)

2. After reading, have children draw pictures that show the changing seasons. (American Association of School Librarians Standards 1.1.6, 1.2.3, 2.1.6, 2.2.4, 4.1.1, 4.1.3, 4.1.8; English Language Arts Standards 1, 3, 4, 6, 12; Visual Arts Content Standards 1, 2)

3. Act out or create a puppet show with a narrator speaking the lines. Incorporate the song "Root Children Sleep" that is on the last page. (American Association of School Librarians Standards 1.2.3, 2.3.4, 3.1.3, 3.2.1, 3.2.2, 3.2.3, 3.3.4, 4.1.3, 4.1.8; English Language Arts Standard 3, 4, 6, 11, 12; Music Content Standard 1; Theater Content Standard 1, 2, 3, 4; Visual Arts Content Standard 1)

Related Books

Beskow, Elsa. *The Flowers' Festival*. Edinburgh: Floris Books. 1991. Unpaged. $15.95. ISBN 0-86315-120-5.

Lisa joins the plants and flowers, the birds and the bees, the crickets and frogs to celebrate Midsummer Eve.

GREENLAND, ICELAND, ARCTIC, AND ANTARCTIC

Take children on a journey to the cold northern and southern portions of the globe. Travel by kayak and dogsled with Kelly Dupre's husband as he explores the coast of Greenland. Go fishing for codfish and lumpfish with Fridrik and his grandfathers off the coast of Iceland. Fly back to the wilderness from Churchill, Manitoba, with a young polar bear named Nanuck. Look for home with little Pip the penguin. Curriculum Responses include map work, discussion, research, art, and other activities.

Dupre, Kelly. *The Raven's Gift: A True Story from Greenland*. New York: Houghton Mifflin, 2001. Unpaged. $15.00. ISBN 978-0-618-01171-1.

Author and Illustrator

The author and illustrator is an American whose husband made three trips to Greenland, traveling by kayak and dogsled to explore Greenland's west and east coasts and its far northern shores.

📖 Nonfiction, Picture Book, Ages 4–8

Summary

Using first-person narrative and linoleum block prints with watercolors, the author retells the true story of her husband's fifteen month journey along 3,200 miles of Greenland's coast by kayak, dogsled, and skis in 1997–1998. After two months of hard travel, the men are ready to quit. Tired and discouraged at the end of a long day, they find a raven whose foot is enmeshed in a tangle of fur and sticks. As the author's husband frees the raven, he speaks softly, telling the raven how sad, tired, and afraid he is—that the journey across the harsh Arctic is too hard, and that he has insufficient strength to continue the journey. Once freed, the raven picks up a rock, shows it and sets it down. The author's husband draws strength from the raven's rock when he picks it up, holds it tightly, and thinks about Greenland, his preparations for the expedition, and his family and friends.

Curriculum Responses with Curriculum Standards

1. Have the children make and illustrate a story board to retell the story of the journey. (American Association of School Librarians Standards 2.1.2, 2.1.4, 2.1.6, 2.2.4, 3.1.3, 3.1.4, 3.2.1, 3.2.2, 3.2.3, 3.3.4, 4.1.3, 4.1.6, 4.1.8, 4.3.1; English Language Arts Standard 3)
2. Have the children use a globe to locate Greenland. Have children identify places in the Northern Hemisphere and the Southern Hemisphere that are at the same latitude as Greenland. (American Association of School Librarians Standards 1.1.6, 1.1.9, 1.3.4, 2.1.4, 2.1.5, 2.3.1, 2.4.3, 3.1.2, 3.2.2, 3.2.3, 3.3.5, 4.1.3, 4.1.6, 4.1.8, 4.3.1; Social Studies Standard III)
3. Encourage children to raise questions about Greenland, research more information, and share their findings with classmates. (American Association of School Librarians Standards 1.1.1, 1.1.3, 1.1.4, 1.1.6, 1.1.8, 1.2.1, 1.2.2, 1.2.3, 1.2.5, 1.2.6, 1.3.4, 1.3.5, 1.4.1, 1.4.2, 1.4.3, 1.4.4, 2.1.1, 2.1.2, 2.1.5, 2.1.6, 2.2.4, 2.3.1, 2.4.3, 3.1.1, 3.1.2, 3.1.3, 3.2.1, 3.2.2, 3.2.3, 3.3.5, 4.1.2, 4.1.3, 4.1.7, 4.3.1; English Language Arts Standards 1, 3, 4, 6, 7, 8, 11, 12; Social Studies Standards III)

Holtei, Christa. *Nanuk Flies Home.* Grand Rapids, Michigan: Eerdmans Books for Young Readers, 2008. Unpaged. $16.00. ISBN 978-0-8-28-342-4.

Author and Illustrator

Author Christa Holtei lives in Dusseldorf, Germany, where she works as a translator and writer of books for children and young adults. Astrid Vohwinkel is a German artist. The book is set on the West Coast of Hudson Bay in Manitoba, Canada.

📖 Picture Book, Ages 6–9

Summary

Nanuck is a young polar bear. He and his mother Anaana are hungry. They wander into town and into the grocery store looking for food. The next thing he knows, Nanuck wakes up in Polar Bear Jail, with Anaana sleeping beside him! They have been tranquilized and will be transported back to the wilderness by helicopter. An Epilogue explains that in Churchill, Manitoba, a Polar Bear Alert Program tranquilizes hungry polar bears that wander into town and transports them via the Polar Bear Taxi, a helicopter with cargo nets, back to the frozen northland. A section called Facts about Polar Bears completes the book.

Curriculum Responses with Curriculum Standards

1. After reading, have children find Churchill, Manitoba, on a map. Encourage discussion by asking the following questions. Why do polar bears come to Churchill to wait for the sea to freeze over? Why do wildlife officials transport the bears back to the frozen north? (American Association of School Librarians Standards 1.1.6, 1.1.9, 1.3.4, 2.1.5, 2.3.1, 3.1.2, 3.1.3, 3.2.1, 3.2.2, 3.3.1, 3.3.2, 3.3.5, 4.1.2, 4.1.3, 4.3.1; English Language Arts Curriculum Standards 1, 3, 4, 6, 11, 12; Social Studies Standards III; Life Science Standards: Organisms and environments)

2. For more information about polar bears, have children see the Author's Note at the back of the book. In which countries can polar bears be found? Have children find those countries on a map. (American Association of School Librarians Standards 1.1.6, 1.1.9, 1.3.1, 2.1.3, 2.3.1, 3.1.3, 3.2.2, 3.2.3, 3.3.5, 4.1.2, 4.1.3, 4.1.4; English Language Arts Standards 1, 3, 4, 12; Social Studies Standard III; Life Science Standards: Organisms and environments)

3. After reading, have children make a collage featuring a polar bear, the things he does, his environment, habits, and food. (American Association of School Librarians Standards 1.1.6, 2.1.6, 2.2.4, 2.3.1, 3.3.4, 4.1.2, 4.1.3, 4.1.8; English Language Arts Standards 1, 3, 4, 12; Social Studies Standard III; Life Science Standards: Organisms and environments; Visual Arts Content Standards 1)

Related Books

1. Stafford, Liliana. *The Snow Bear.* New York: Scholastic Press, 2000. Unpaged. Illustrated by Lambert Davis. $15.95. ISBN 0-439-26977-6.

Authentic and realistic illustrations featuring the Northern Lights (Aurora Borealis) and an informative Author's Note enhance this story about the bonding and friendship between a young boy and a polar bear.

2. Miller, Debbie S. *Arctic Lights Arctic Nights.* New York: Walker & Company, 2003. 32p. Illustrated by Jon Van Zyle. $16.96. ISBN 0-8027-8856-4.

Full-color realistic illustrations and informative text take readers on a tour of Alaska, with its long summer days, long winter nights, northern lights, wildlife, and spectacular landscape.

3. Martin, Jacqueline Briggs. *The Lamp, the Ice, and the Boast Called Fish.* Boston: Houghton Mifflin Company, 2001. Unpaged. Illustrated by Beth Krommes. $15.00. ISBN 0-618-00341-X.

The true story of the survivors of the Canadian Arctic Expedition of 1913, which included Inupiaq hunters and a family with two small girls, along with crew members, scientists, explorers, sled dogs, and even a cat, is told in poetic verse with scratchboard art that reflects Inupiaq culture.

McMillan, Bruce. *Going Fishing.* Boston: Houghton Mifflin Company, 2005. 32p. $16.00. ISBN 0-618-47201-0.

Author and Illustrator

Author and illustrator Bruce McMillan is an American who lives in Maine and summers in Iceland. *Going Fishing* is his sixth book about Iceland. He has written and illustrated more children's books set in Iceland than has any other U.S. author.

📖 Nonfiction, Picture Book, Ages 6 and Up

Summary

Welcome to Iceland, a land of fish! Fish are Iceland's leading export and are depicted on Iceland's money and postage stamps. This photo essay chronicles two days in the life of young Fridrik who goes fishing, first with his Grandfather Fridrik for codfish, using lines attached to the boat, then with his Grandfather Haddi for lumpfish, using nets. The characters are real people who live in Reykjavik and Stykkisholmer and fish along coastal Iceland. The text includes a Pronunciation Guide, a Credits Page showing a map locating Iceland on the globe, illustrations of fish on the money and stamps of Iceland, and an Afterward describing Atlantic codfish and lumpfish.

Curriculum Responses with Curriculum Standards

1. Have children find Iceland on the globe and then draw a map of Iceland showing Reykjavik and Stykkisholmer. (American Association of School Librarians Standards 2.1.2, 2.1.4, 2.1.6, 2.1.4, 2.3.1, 2.4.3, 3.1.4, 3.3.4, 4.1.3, 4.1.6; English Language Arts Standards 1, 3, 4, 6, 12; Social Studies Standard III)
2. Where is Iceland in relation to Greenland? How are the two countries alike, and how are they different. Discuss and have children

make a Venn diagram. (American Association of School Librarians Standards; English Language Arts Standards 3, 4, 6, 11, 12; Social Studies Standards I, III)

3. After reading, engage children in a discussion. What more would they like to know about Fridrik if they had a chance to write text messages to him? What would they like to tell him about themselves and their lives? After discussing, have children write the text messages that they would send to Fridrik if they were able. (American Association of School Librarians Standards 1.1.3, 1.1.6, 1.1.9, 1.3.4, 2.1.6, 2.2.4, 2.3.1, 3.1.3, 3.2.2, 3.3.1, 3.3.2, 3.3.4, 3.3.5, 4.1.3, 4.1.4, 4.1.5, 4.3.1; English Language Arts Standards 1, 3, 4, 6, 11, 12; Social Studies Standards I)

Related Books

1. McMillan, Bruce. *Days of the Duckling.* Boston: Houghton Mifflin Company, 2007. 32p. $6.95. ISBN 0-618-86270-6.

This is a photo-essay of eider ducklings hatched from eggs that were recovered from neighboring islands. It features Fridrik's aunt and takes place in the same Icelandic waters as *Going Fishing*.

2. McMillan, Bruce. *How the Ladies Stopped the Wind.* Boston: Houghton Mifflin Company, 2007. 32p. Illustrated by Gunnella. $16.00 ISBN 0-618-77330-4.

Set in Iceland, which is very windy and has no trees, this is a story about the women who tried to stop the wind from blowing.

3. McMillan, Bruce. *Nights of the Pufflings.* Boston: Houghton Mifflin Company, 1997. 32p. $6.95. ISBN 0-395-85693-0.

This photo-essay of the Puffin breeding season shows Icelandic children on an island off Iceland's southern coast, ready to rescue the fledgings that don't reach the sea.

4. McMillan, Bruce. *The Problem with Chickens.* Boston: Houghton Mifflin Company, 2005. 32p. Illustrated by Gunnella. $16.00. ISBN 0-618-58581-6.

Set in Iceland, this is a humorous story of chickens who decide to act like the women in the village.

Wilson, Karma. *Where Is Home, Little Pip?* New York: Margaret K. McElderry Books, 2008. Unpaged. Illustrated by Jane Chapman. $16.99. ISBN 0-689-65083-X.

Author and Illustrator

Author Karma Wilson is American. Illustrator Jane Chapman is English.

📖 Fiction, Picture Book, Ages 4–7

Summary

Mama and Papa tell Pip, the baby penguin, not to wander far—and she doesn't. Then one day Pip sees a black feather on the white ice. The wind blows, and Pip chases the feather. Now she can't find home. The blue whale, the Kelp Gull, and the sled dogs tell Pip where their homes are. Can they help Pip find her home? Bold, colorful acrylic illustrations depict the Antarctic environment. Expository text, four-line verses describing home, and bold-print words and phrases are integrated into the page layout to enhance the visual appeal of the pages.

Curriculum Responses with Curriculum Standards

1. Read aloud and show the pictures. Reread and encourage children to chime in on the four-line verses and bold-print words and phrases. (American Association of School Librarians Standards 1.1.6, 1.3.4, 3.1.3, 3.2.2, 4.1.1, 4.1.2, 4.1.3; English Language Arts Standards 1, 3, 4, 6, 11, 12)
2. Have children retell the story using a flannel board. (American Association of School Librarians Standards 1.2.3, 1.3.4, 2.1.2, 2.1.6, 3.1.3, 3.2.1, 3.2.2, 4.1.3, 4.1.8; English Language Arts Standards 3, 4, 6, 11, 12; Theater Content Standards 1; Visual Arts Content Standards 6)
3. Engage children in a discussion about home. Have they ever been lost or moved from one home to another? How did they feel? (American Association of School Librarians Standards 1.1.2, 1.3.4, 2.3.1, 3.1.2, 3.1.3, 3.2.2, 3.3.5, 4.1.3, 4.1.5, 4.3.1; English Language Arts Standards 3, 4, 6, 11, 12)

Related Books

Wiesmuller, Dieter. *The Adventures of Marco and Polo.* New York: Walker and Company, 2000. Unpaged. Translated by Beate Peter. $16.95. ISBN 0-8027-8729-0.

Although Marco Monkey and Polo Penguin become very good friends when Marco visits Polo's home in Antarctica, and Polo visits Marco's home in the tropics, they discovers that each has to be in his own home in order to be happy.

INDIA AND PAKISTAN

Gentle picture books, a biographical story, and yoga poems depict the countries and cultures of India and Pakistan. American author Megan McDonald and English illustrator Vera Rosenberry share with young readers an Indian mother's lullaby. Indian authors write related picture books. American mountain climber,

Greg Mortenson, known for his adult book *Three Cups of Tea*, retells for young children his story of building a school in Korphi, Pakistan.

A related book adapts *Three Cups of Tea* for young adults. Other Related Books by Indian and Pakistani authors and illustrators use folk art, color photography, and rhyming verses to introduce young readers to their countries. Yoga, which originated in India and has its roots in Hindu philosophy, is reflected in a collection of sixteen illustrated poems that describe yoga moves and exercises. Music and art activities, practicing yoga moves, and writing poetry are among the suggested Curriculum Responses.

McDonald, Megan. *Baya, Baya, Lulla-by-a.* New York: Atheneum Books for Young Readers, 2003. Unpaged. Illustrated by Vera Rosenberry. $16.95. ISBN 0-689-84932-X.

Author and Illustrator

Author Megan McDonald is American. Illustrator Vera Rosenberry is English and lives with her Indian husband in England.

📖 Fiction, Picture Book, Ages 4–7

Summary

Mother weaves a blanket and sings a lullaby for her baby, while Baya Bird weaves a nest and sings. Brilliant full-page watercolors illuminate the rhythmic text. The final page lists Hindi words and meanings used in the text and provides information about the Baya bird.

Curriculum Responses with Curriculum Standards

1. Read aloud and encourage children to listen. Then reread and encourage children to chime in on the rhythmic and repetitive phrases used throughout the text. (American Association of School Librarians Standards 1.1.6, 3.1.3, 4.1.1, 4.1.3; English Language Arts Standards 3, 4, 9, 12)
2. Mother sings a lullaby to her baby. After reading, have children select or compose music for the lullaby. Encourage them to sing the lullaby. (American Association of School Librarians Standards 1.1.6, 1.2.3, 2.2.4, 3.1.2, 3.2.1, 3.2.2, 3.2.3, 3.3.4, 4.1.1, 4.1.3; English Language Arts Standards 1, 3, 11; Music Content Standards 1, 3, 4)
3. Read the last page. Focus attention to the Hindi words and their meanings. Discuss with children the baya bird nest and its many uses. (American Association of School Librarians Standards 1.1.6, 1.3.4, 2.3.1, 3.1.2, 3.1.3, 3.2.1, 3.2.2, 3.3.1, 3.3.2, 3.3.3, 3.3.5, 4.1.2, 4.1.3, 4.3.1; English Language Arts Standards 1, 3, 4, 6, 9, 11, 12)

Related Books

1. Krishnaswami. Uma. *Monsoon.* New York: Farrar, Straus, Giroux, 2003. 32p. Illustrated by Jamel Akib. $16.95. ISBN 0-374-35015-4.

Rhythmic text and brilliant illustrations depict, through the eyes of a little girl, the coming of the rains to the streets of India.

2. Rao, Sandhya. *My Mother's Sari.* New York: North-South, 2009. 24p. Illustrated by Nina Sabani. $6.95. ISBN 0-735-82233-6.

Each two-page spread has one sentence describing a sari with an illustration showing a child doing something with the sari, such as draping it as a river, a blanket, or a train.

3. Ravishankar, Anushka. *Elephants Never Forget.* New York: Houghton Mifflin Books for Children, 2008. 48p. Illustrated by Christiane Pieper. $16.00. ISBN 0-618-99784-9.

Vibrant pictures and words tell the story of the little elephant lost in a storm, who joins a herd of water buffalo.

4. Ravishankar, Anushka. *Tiger on a Tree.* New York: Farrar, Straus, Giroux, 2004. 48p. Illustrated by Pulak Biswas. $15.00 ISBN 0-374-37555-0.

Villagers capture a curious tiger, but then don't know what to do with him.

5. Ravishankar, Anushka and Rathna Ramanathan. *To Market! To Market!* Chennai, India: Tara Books, 2007. 24p. Illustrated by Emanuele Scanziou. $16.95. ISBN 8-186-21199-1.

Rhyming verses and repeated words tell the story of a little girl who goes to market with her mother.

Mortenson, Greg. *Listen to the Wind: The Story of Dr. Greg and Three Cups of Tea.* New York: Dial, 2009. 32p. Illustrated by Susan Roth. $16.99. ISBN 0-803-73058-6.

Author and Illustrator

Author Greg Mortenson is an American mountain climber, who failed to reach the summit of K2, lost his way coming down the mountain, and stumbled into a small village where he was nursed back to health. Moved by the children who had to scratch their lessons in the dirt, the author returned to Pakistan, where he built schools, many for just girls. He tells his story in *Three Cups of Tea* from which this book is drawn. Illustrator Susan Roth.

📖 Nonfiction, Picture Book, Ages 4–8

Summary

Based on his book *Three Cups of Tea*, author Greg Mortenson retells his story about building schools in Pakistan. His story is retold through the eyes of Pakistani children. Colorful illustrations using fabric and cut-paper computer-generated collages are inspired by artifacts from a place where nothing is wasted. Photos of the school and villagers are included in the back of the book.

Curriculum Responses with Curriculum Standards

1. After reading, engage children in a discussion about life in Korphi, the children's lives, and the villagers' efforts to build a school. Ask children what they might think if they lived in Korphi. (American Association of School Librarians Standards 1.1.6, 1.3.4, 2.1.5, 2.3.1, 3.1.2, 3.1.3, 3.2.1, 3.2.2, 3.3.1, 3.3.2, 3.3.3, 3.3.5, 4.1.1, 4.1.2, 4.1.3, 4.1.5, 4.3.1; English Language Arts Standards 1, 2, 3, 4, 6, 11, 12; Social Studies Standards I, 111)

2. After reading, focus attention on the illustrations, which are collages, using everyday items. Discuss with children what it might be like to use everything and waste nothing. Ask children what they use, what they waste, and how they might be able to use things that they waste. (American Association of School Librarians Standards 1.1.6, 1.3.4, 2.1.5, 2.3.1, 3.1.2, 3.1.3, 3.2.1, 3.2.2, 3.3.1, 3.3.2, 3.3.3, 3.3.5, 4.1.1, 4.1.2, 4.1.3, 4.1.5, 4.3.1; (English Language Arts Standards 1, 3, 4, 6, 11, 12; Visual Arts Content Standards 5)

3. After reading, use illustrations as a model. Have children create collages by using everyday items. (American Association of School Librarians Standards 1.1.6, 2.2.4, 2.3.1, 3.3.4, 4.1.1, 4.1.2, 4.1.3, 4.1.8; English Language Arts Standards 1, 3, 4, 13; Visual Arts Content Standards 1, 2, 3)

Related Books

1. Das, Prodeepta. *I Is for India.* London: Frances Lincoln Children's Books, 2004. 32p. $16.95. ISBN 1-845-074-83-1.

This alphabet book introduces readers to the country of India—old and new, urban and rural.

2. Jeyaveeran, Ruth. *The Road to Mumbai.* Boston, MA: Houghton Mifflin Books for Children, 2004. $16.00. ISBN 0-618-43419-4.

A map, an illustrated glossary, and colorful folk art illustrations add to the story of Shoba and her stuffed monkey, who fly to India, land in the desert, and on their way to Mumbai meet a camel, a juice seller, elephants, monks, and a snake charmer.

3. Khan, Rukhsana. *Silly Chicken.* New York: Viking Juvenile, 2005. 32p. Illustrated by Yunmee Kyong. $15.99. ISBN 0-670-05912-9.

Rani, who lives in Pakistan, is jealous of her mother's attachment to Bibi the chicken.

4. Mortenson, Greg and David Oliver (Adapted by Sarah Thomson). *Three Cups of Tea: One Man's Journey to Change the World... One Child at a Time: Young Reader's Edition.* New York: Puffin, 2009. 240p. $8.99. ISBN 0-142-41412-3.

Sarah Thomson's adaptation of Greg Mortenson's book for readers age eight and up includes an interview with Mortenson's twelve-year-old daughter Amira, maps, color photos, a time line, a glossary, and a reader's guide.

5. Razzak, Shazia. *P is for Pakistan.* London: Frances Lincoln Children's Books, 2007. 32p. Photographer Prodeepta Das. $16.95. ISBN 1-845-07483-1.

Color photography illustrates this alphabet book in which each letter begins an Urdu or English word that refers to something related to Pakistan's history, culture, or geography.

Wong, Janet S. *Twist: Yoga Poems.* New York: Margaret K. McElderry Books, 2007. 39p. Illustrated by Julie Paschkis. $17.99. ISBN 0-689-87394-8.

Author and Illustrator

Author Janet Wong is Chinese American. Illustrator Julie Paschkis is an American who studied in Norway. Yoga is a traditional physical and mental discipline that originated in India and has its roots in Hindu philosophy.

📖 Poetry, Picture Book, Ages 7–10

Summary

Sixteen illustrated poems describe yoga moves and exercises. Author's Note explains how the author acted out the moves as she wrote the poems, and that the poems were written for the illustrator.

Curriculum Responses with Curriculum Standards

1. Introduce the book by reading a poem, showing the illustration, and then acting out the yoga moves described in the poem. Encourage children to continue reading the poems and acting out the yoga

moves. (American Association of School Librarians Standards 1.1.6, 3.1.2, 4.1.1, 4.1.3, 4.1.8; Dance Content Standard 1, 3, 6; English Language Arts Standards 1, 3, 11)

2. After reading, use as a model. Encourage children to write and illustrate poems about movements they make in daily life, such as walking, running, skateboarding, and others. Allow children to share their poems with classmates, then bind them together into a class book and place where children can read independently. (American Association of School Librarians Standards 1.1.6, 1.3.4, 2.1.6, 2.2.4, 3.1.3, 4.1.1, 4.1.3, 4.1.8; English Language Arts Standards 4, 5, 12)

3. Extend the activity by doing additional yoga movements on a regular basis with your children. (Dance Content Standards 1, 3, 6)

MEXICO, LATIN AND SOUTH AMERICA, AND THE CARIBBEAN

Book selections include fractured fairy tales, realistic fiction, folktales, and biography. Several authors address the theme of social justice, in particular of children in distress. In a Related Book, author Elisa Amado features a little girl who lives between two worlds, the world of her North American grandmother and the world of her Hispanic Abuela. Isabel Campoy, Alma Flor Ada, and others entertain readers with folktales from Hispanic cultures. Readers will also meet Jose Limon, Diego Rivera, Frida Kahlo, and Roberto Clemente. Elisa Amado's book *Tricycle* was selected as an Outstanding International Book by the United States Board on Books for Young People (USBBY). Illustrator Alfonso Ruano received the Americas Award and the Jane Addams Children's Book Award. Writing a television script, writing a newspaper, oral storytelling, and creating a dance are several of the suggested Curriculum Responses.

Ada, Alma Flor. *Extra! Extra! Fairy Tale News from Hidden Forest.* New York: Atheneum Books for Young Readers, 2007. Unpaged. Illustrated by Leslie Tryon. $16.99. ISBN 973-0-680-82582-8.

Author and Illustrator

Author Alma Flor Ada grew up in Cuba, lived in Spain and Peru, and now lives in the United States. She is a prolific author who writes in Spanish and English. Illustrator Leslie Tryon is American.

📖 Fiction, Fairy Tale Retelling, Picture Book, Ages 5–8.

Summary

For the news of the day, read *Hidden Forest NEWS*. On March 3, a giant beanstalk sprouted right into the clouds near the home of Mrs. Blake and her son Jack. Mr. Geppetto closed his toy shop. Tomorrow the Tortoise and the Hare are racing against each other. In an interview on March 5, Mrs. Blake says that she is worried about her son Jack, who is missing. Pinocchio is also missing. Notice the invitation to attend a Potluck at the Red Hen's house next Thursday. Goldilocks and Little Red Riding Hood will provide childcare and entertainment. Be sure to get your paper on March 9 to find out what happened to the beanstalk and Jack and to Mr. Geppetto and Pinocchio—and to get the information you need about summer camp for the children.

Curriculum Responses with Curriculum Standards

1. After reading, use the book to write a script for a television news broadcast. Select children to broadcast the news of the day. (American Association of School Librarians Standards; English Language Arts Standards 1, 3, 4, 5, 6, 11, 12; Theater Content Standards 1, 2)
2. Using this book as a model, have the children write their own newspaper about fairy tale characters. (American Association of School Librarians Standards 1.2.3, 2.3.4, 3.1.3, 3.2.3, 3.3.4, 4.1.3; English Language Arts Standard 3, 4, 5)
3. Extend the activity by having children develop and act out conversations between fairy tale characters. (American Association of School Librarians Standards 1.1.9, 1.3.4, 2.1.5, 2.1.6, 2.2.4, 3.1.2, 3.1.3, 3.2.2, 3.2.3, 3.3.5, 4.1.3, 4.1.8; English Language Arts Standards 3, 4, 5, 6, 11, 12; Theater Content Standards 1, 2)

Related Books

1. Ada, Alma Flor. *Dear Peter Rabbit: Querido Pedrín.* New York: Aladdin Paperbacks, 2006. 32p. Illustrated by Leslie Tryon. $4.99. ISBN 1-416-91233-9.

Familiar nursery rhyme characters such as Goldilocks, The Three Pigs, Baby Bear, and Red Riding Hood write to Peter Rabbit, who is in bed with a cold after his adventure in Mr. McGregor's garden.

2. Ada, Alma Flor and F. Isabel Compoy. *Happy Birthday, Little Red Riding Hood.* Santillana United States Publishing Company, 2002. 32p. $15.95. ISBN 1-581-05961-2.

Preparations for Little Red Riding Hood's birthday party include food, decorations, gifts, cake, and music.

3. Ada, Alma Flor. *With Love, Little Red Hen.* New York: Aladdin Paperbacks. 2004. Unpaged. Illustrated by Leslie Tryon. $6.99. ISBN 0-689-87061-2.

Letters from one nursery rhyme character to another retell the familiar story of the Little Red Hen.

Amado, Elisa. *Tricycle.* Toronto: ON: Groundwood Books, 2007. Unpaged. Illustrated by Alfonso Ruano. $17.95. ISBN 978-0-88899-614-5.

Author and Illustrator

Author Elisa Amado is Guatemalan and now lives in Toronto. She is an author, illustrator, and translator. The United States Board on Books for Young People (USBBY) listed *Tricycle* as a 2008 Outstanding International Book. Illustrator Alfonso Ruano is one of Spain's best-known illustrators. He received the Americas Award and the Jane Addams Children's Book Award for his book *The Composition.*

📖 Fiction, Picture Book, Ages 6–8

Summary

Margarita's house has a library, a yard with green grass, a gardener to plant and tend the flowers, and a big tree where Margarita can climb and look over the hedge to the shacks where Rosario, Chepe, and Juanita live. One day Margarita leaves her tricycle in the hedge. As she sits in the big tree, Margarita sees Rosario and Chepe pull her tricycle out of the hedge and hide it under a big box. Margarita is afraid to tell her mother when she asks where her tricycle is, especially when she hears a luncheon guest say, "They're all thieves. They should be shot." Margarita hopes that the nearby volcano will not erupt. She realizes that she is safe in her strong house, but Rosario's house could be burned.

Curriculum Responses with Curriculum Standards

1. After reading, ask children why they think Margarita does not want to tell her mother what happened to her tricycle? Ask whether they think Margarita's mother knows what happened to her tricycle? Why do they think that she does or does not? Ask children how they think Margarita feels about Rosario and Chepe? Why do they think what they do? (American Association of School Librarians Standards 1.1.6, 1.1.9, 1.3.4, 2.1.5, 3.1.2, 3.1.3, 3.2.1, 3.2.2, 3.3.1, 3.3.2, 3.3.5, 4.1.2, 4.1.3, 4.1.5. 4.3.1; English Language Arts Standards 1, 3, 4, 5, 11, 12)
2. With children, create a Venn diagram to compare and contrast Margarita's life with the life of Rosario and Chepe. (American Association of School Librarians Standards 1.1.9, 1.3.4, 2.1.5, 2.1.6, 3.1.2,

3.1.4, 3.2.1, 3.2.2, 3.2.3, 3.3.2, 3.3.5, 4.1.3, 4.1.6, 4.3.1; English Language Arts Standards 3, 4, 5, 6, 11, 12; Social Studies Standard I)
3. Ask children what they would have done had they been Margarita. (American Association of School Librarians Standards 1.1.2, 1.1.6, 1.3.4, 2.3.1, 3.1.3, 3.2.1, 3.3.2, 3.3.5, 4.1.1, 4.1.2, 4.1.3, 4.1.5, 4.3.1; English Language Arts Standards 3, 4, 5, 11, 12)

Related Books

1. Amado, Elisa. *Cousins*. Toronto, ON: Groundwood Books, 2004. 32p. Illustrated by Luis Garay. $16.95. ISBN 0-808-9949-2.

A little girl, the narrator of the story, lives between two worlds, the comfortable world of her North American grandmother and the lively family-filled world of her Hispanic Abuela.

2. Russell, Barbara Timberlake. *The Remembering Stone*. New York: Melanie Kroupa Books, 2004. Illustrated by Claire B. Cotts. $16.00. ISBN 0-374-36242-4.

Mama dreams of her heart's desire, something that she wants, and so do Ana, Sophia, Mrs. Pettibone, and Mr. Nguyen.

3. Skarmali, Antonio. *The Composition*. Toronto, ON: Groundwood Books, 2003. 32p. Illustrated by Alfonso Ruano. $5.95. ISBN 0-888-99550-6.

This story is set somewhere in South America. After Pedro and his friends see the father of a friend taken away by the police, a policeman comes to school and tells the children to write compositions about what their families do at night.

4. Vamos, Samantha. *Before You Were Here, Mi Amor*. New York: Juvenile; Bilingual edition, 2009. 32p. Illustrated by Santiago Cohen. $15.99. ISBN 0-670-06301-0.

An expectant mother speaks to her child in English peppered with Spanish words and phrases about the family's anticipation of the baby's arrival.

5. Ziefert, Harriet. *Home for Navidad*. Boston: Houghton Mifflin Company, 2003. Illustrated by Santiago Cohen. $15.00. ISBN 0-618-34976-6.

Ten-year-old Rosa, who lives with her Abuela, her little brother John, and her Tio Pancho in Mexico, hopes that her mother, who works in the United States, will come home for Navidad.

Campoy, F. Isabel and Alma Flor Ada. *Tales Our Abuelitas Told.* New York: Atheneum Books, 2006, 118p. Illustrated by Felipe Davalos, Vivi Escriba, Susan Guevara, and Leyla Torres. $19.95. ISBN 0-689-82583-8.

Author and Illustrator

Author Isabel Campoy is an American who studied in Madrid, Spain, and chose to live there before returning to the United States. Author Alma Flor Ada was born in Cuba and now lives in the United States. The four illustrators are all leading Latino artists. Illustrator Felipe Davalos was born and educated in Mexico. Illustrator Vivi Escriva was born in Valencia, Spain. Susan Guevara is of Latino heritage, traveled in Europe, and lived in Paris and Belgium. Illustrator Leyla Torres was born and raised in Bogota, Columbia and now lives in Vermont.

📖 Folktales, Ages 5–10

Summary

This is a collection of twelve folktales, many of which originated in Spain, a country that was shaped by European, Mediterranean, Jewish, Arabic, and North African influences. Others folktales originated in Cuba and reflect Spanish and African influences. Each story ends with a brief explanation of its origins. "Welcome" explains the cultural background of Spain and the stories it produced. "To Begin a Story" and "To End a Story" suggest traditional beginnings and endings to Spanish stories. The final pages give information about the authors and illustrators.

Curriculum Responses with Curriculum Standards

1. Students may recognize some of the stories, such as the story of Juan Bebo, the boy who can't do anything right, "The Castle of Chuchurumbe," a cumulative tale similar to "The House that Jack Built," and "'Dear Deer!' Said the Turtle," a variation on Aesop's fable about the Tortoise and the Hare. Have children read and then compare and contrast familiar tales. (American Association of School Librarians Standards 1.1.2, 1.1.3, 1.1.4, 1.1.6, 1.1.9, 1.2.1, 1.3.4, 2.1.1, 2.1.3, 2.1.5, 2.4.3, 3.1.1, 3.1.2, 3.1.3, 3.2.1, 3.2.2, 3.3.5, 4.1.1, 4.1.2, 4.1.3, 4.1.4, 4.3.1; English Language Arts Standards 1, 3)

2. Stories in this book derive from the oral tradition. Have children read, block and retell the stories. (American Association of School Librarians Standards 1.1.2, 1.2.2, 1.2.3, 1.3.4, 2.1.1, 2.2.4, 3.1.2, 3.1.3, 3.2.1, 3.2.2, 3.3.5, 4.1.1, 4.1.3, 4.1.8, 4.2.2, 4.3.1, 4.4.1, English Language Arts Standards 1, 3, 4, 6, 11, 12)

3. Have children select and modify a story. Have them retell their own variation. Encourage them to use story beginnings and endings listed in the book. (American Association of School Librarians Standards 1.1.2, 1.2.2, 1.2.3, 1.3.1, 1.3.4, 2.1.1, 2.3.4, 3.1.3, 3.2.1, 3.3.5, 4.1.1, 4.1.2, 4.1.3, 4.1.8, 4.3.1; English Language Arts Standards 3, 4, 6, 11, 12)

Related Books

1. Ada, Alma Flor and F. Isabel Campoy. *Mama Goose.* New York: Hyperion Books for Children, 2004. 121p. Illustrated by Maribel Suarez. $9.99. ISBN 0-786-81953-7.

This is a collection of nursery rhymes, riddles, sayings, and songs from Spanish-speaking cultures.

2. Ada, Alma Flor. *Pio Peep.* New York: HarperCollins, 2003. 64p. Illustrated by Vivi Escriva. $16.99. ISBN 0-688-16019-0.

This is a bilingual collection of traditional rhymes from Spanish and Latin American cultures.

3. Montes, Marisa. *Juan Bobo Goes to Work: A Puerto Rican Folktale.* Unpaged. Illustrated by Joe Cepeda. $15.95. ISBN 0-688-16233-9.

Juan Bobo can't do nothing right, even when he does exactly what his mother tells him.

4. Pitcher, Caroline. *Mariana and the Merchild: A Folk Tale from Chile.* Grand Rapids, MI: Eerdmans Books for Young Readers, 2000. Unpaged. Illustrated by Jackie Morris. $17.00. ISBN 0-8028-5204-1.

Old Marianna loves and cares for the merchild until the mermaid mother returns to carry her child back to the sea.

5. Youngquist, Cathrene Valente. *The Three Billygoats Gruff and Mean Calypso Joe.* New York: Atheneum Books for Young Readers, 2002. Unpaged. Illustrated by Kristin Sorra. ISBN 0-689-82874-1.

This is a Caribbean retelling of the *Billygoats Gruff* set in the islands with a Caribbean dialect.

Freschet, Gina. *Naty's Parade.* New York: Farrar Straus Giroux, 2000. Unpaged. $16.00. ISBN 0-374-35500-2.

Author and Illustrator

Author and illustrator Gina Freschet lives in Oaxaca, Mexico, and New York City. The setting of this book is Oaxaca, Mexico, and it celebrates Guelaguetza, the festival of folkloric dances of Oaxaca.

📖 Fiction, Picture Book, Ages 5–8

Summary

It is fiesta time, Guelaguetza! Naty gets to dance in the parade. As she spins, and dances, and bumps into the other puppet people, Naty loses her whistle. She finds her whistle in the alley, but loses the parade. Night falls, and it is dark. Naty is still looking for the parade. Will she find it—and how?

Curriculum Responses with Curriculum Standards

1. Ask children to identify the musical instruments and dances that are in the parade. Have children draw pictures of instruments and dances. (American Association of School Librarians Standards 2.1.6, 4.1.3, 4.1.8; Dance Content Standards 1; Music Content Standard 6)
2. Encourage children to create a dance showing Naty dancing in the parade, getting lost, and finding the parade again. (American Association of School Librarians Standards 4.1.3, 4.1.8; Dance Content Standard 3)
3. Introduce children to the folkloric music and dance of Oaxaca. Look for two compact discs, *La Guelaguetza, la musica autentica del espectaculo folklorico mas importante de America* (1998, 1996*)*, and two videocassettes, *Folklorico,* vol. 1 (59 min. 1999) and vol. 2 (53 min. 1999) at your public or university libraries. Use the CDs and videos to demonstrate and teach Mexican folk dances. (American Association of School Librarians Standards 1.1.6; Dance Content Standard 5; Music Content Standards 6, 9)

Related Books

1. Freschet, Gina. *Beto and the Bone Dance.* New York: Farrar, Straus, Giroux, 2001. Unpaged. $16.00 ISBN 0-374-31720-8.

Beto and his family celebrate Halloween, which is *el dia de los muertos,* the Day of the Dead, in Mexico.

2. Freschet, Gina. *La procesión de Naty.* New York: Farrar Straus Giroux, 2000. Unpaged. $16.00. ISBN 0-374-36136-3.

This is a Spanish version of *Naty's Parade.*

3. Toledo, Natalia. *Light Foot: Pies Ligeros.* Illustrated by Francisco Toledo. Translated by Elisa Amado.

The animals jump rope with Death in this bilingual story that the author wrote to accompany a series of engravings of Death created by her father, Francisco Toledo, an indigenous Mexican contemporary artist.

Reich, Susanna. *Jose! Born to Dance.* New York: Simon & Schuster Books for Young Readers, 2005. Unpaged. Illustrated by Raul Colon. $16.95 ISBN 0-689-86576-7.

Author and Illustrator

Author Susanna Reich is American. Illustrator Raul Colon lived in Puerto Rico when he was young; he now lives in New York.

   📖 Biography, Picture Book, Ages 5–8

Summary

This is a picture biography of the Mexican-born dancer and choreographer, José Limón. Before he became a dancer, José wanted to become an artist. He traveled from his home in California to New York City in order to pursue his dream. In New York, he missed his family and the warmth and sunshine of California, and he lost his heart for painting. When he attended a dance concert with a friend, his spirits rebounded, and he knew that he wanted to make dance his way of life. A brief Historical Note completes the book.

Curriculum Responses with Curriculum Standards

1. After reading, engage children in a discussion about José Limón. Have them generate and write questions, then visit the Web site www.limon.org to learn more about him. Provide opportunities for children to share their findings with their classmates. (American Association of School Librarians Standards 1.1.1, 1.1.3, 1.1.4, 1.1.4, 1.1.6, 1.1.8, 1.1.9, 1.2.1, 1.3.1, 1.3.4, 2.1.1, 2.1.4, 2.1.5, 2.1.6, 2.2.4, 3.1.1, 3.1.2, 3.1.3, 3.1.4, 3.1.6, 3.2.1, 3.2.2, 3.3.3, .3.3.5, 4.1.1, 4.1.3, 4.1.4, 4.1.7, 4.3.1; English Language Arts Standards 1, 2, 4, 5, 6, 7, 8, 11, 12)

2. Look for and show films or videos that feature José Limón. Two are listed in the back of the book: "Three Modern Dance Classics—The Moor's Pavane, The Traitor, The Emperor Jones" and "Limon: A Life Beyond Words." (American Association of School Librarians Standards 1.1.6, 4.1.1; English Language Arts Standards 7, 8).

3. Engage children in a discussion. José Limón experienced hardships in his early life. What were those hardships, and how did he respond to them? Ask children where their parents, caregivers, or family members experienced hardships in their early lives. How did they respond to their hardships? Ask children whether they are experiencing hardships in their lives and how they can respond to their hardships? (American Association of School Librarians Standards 1.1.1, 1.1.2, 1.1.3, 1.1.6, 1.1.9, 1.3.4, 2.1.5, 2.2.1, 2.3.1, 3.1.1, 3.1.2, 3.1.3, 3.1.5, 3.2.1, 3.2.2, 3.2.3, 3.3.1, 3.3.2, 3.3.3, 3.3.5, 4.1.2, 4.1.3, 4.1.4, 4.1.5, 4.1.7, 4.2.2, 4.3.1; English Language Arts Standards 1, 3, 4, 6, 11, 12; Social Studies Standards IV)

Related Books

1. Winter, Jonah. *Diego.* New York: Knopf Books for Young Readers, 2007. 40p. Illustrated by Jeanette Winter. $16.95. ISBN 0-679-81997-8.

A bilingual focus on the early life of painter Diego Rivera features Mexican folk art designs that reflect his painting style.

2. Winter, Jonah. *Frida.* New York: Arthur A. Levine Books, 2002. Unpaged. Illustrated by Ana Juan. $16.95 ISBN 0-590-20320-7.

Bold, colorful illustrations and simple text tell the story of Frida Kahlo, the Mexican artist who was married to another Mexican artist, Diego Rivera.

3. Winter, Jonah. *Roberto Clemente: Pride of the Pittsburgh Pirates.* New York: An Anne Schwartz Book, 2005. Illustrated by Raul Colon. $16.95. ISBN 0-689- 85643-1.

Roberto Clemente grows up playing baseball in Puerto Rico until he is invited to play for the Pittsburgh Pirates, a losing team that he helps to win the World Series.

MIDDLE EAST

Introduce readers to the land of Israel, Jewish holidays, and poems by a Palestinian-American writer. Using lyrical text and dream-like illustrations, American author Sue Alexander, who was inspired by a visit to Israel, and Russian-born illustrator Leonid Gore trace the history of the land from a time of abundant trees, through denuding by development, wars, and neglect, to restoration by the intentional planting of trees. Israeli-born Ora Eitan illustrates Leslie Kimmelman's book about eleven Jewish holidays, and a related book about Georgia O'Keeffe. Finally, Palestinian-American Naomi Shihab Nye writes sixteen poems about journeys. Illustrator Ora Eitan was nominated for the Hans Christian Anderson Award. Curriculum Responses include creating and illustrating a timeline, celebration of earth Day, selecting or composing background music, and others.

Alexander, Sue. *Behold the Trees.* New York: Arthur A. Levine Books, 2001. Unpaged. Illustrated by Leonid Gore. $16.96. ISBN 0-590-76211-7.

Author and Illustrator

Author Sue Alexander is American and was inspired to write this book following a trip to Israel. Illustrator Leonid Gore is a Russian who now lives in the United States. The setting of the book is Israel.

📖 Nonfiction, Picture Book, All Ages

Summary

Israel, from the time when it is called Canaan until the present, is a land of abundant trees gradually denuded by development, wars, and neglect, until it is restored by the intentional planting of trees. Dream-like, Impressionist acrylic paints and colored pencil illustrations enhance the lyrical text. Page headings indicate dates and events. A time line at the back of the book traces the history of the land from 5000 BCE to 1948 CE. The Author's Note speaks to the importance of trees to human life across countries and cultures.

Curriculum Responses with Curriculum Standards

1. Read this book either to or with your children. Be sure to show and call attention to the illustrations. Use the timeline in the back of the book as a guide. Have children use a roll of wide shelf paper to create and illustrate a timeline showing historic eras and events. (American Association of School Librarians Standards 1.1.6, 1.2.3, 1.4.3, 2.1.2, 2.1.5, 2.1.6, 2.3.4, 3.1.2, 3.1.3, 3.1.4, 3.2.1, 3.2.2, 3.2.3, 3.3.4, 3.3.5, 3.4.1, 3.4.2, 4.1.1, 4.1.2, 4.1.3, 4.1.6, 4.1.8; English Language Arts Standards 1, 2, 3, 4, 5, 11, 12; Social Studies Standards II, III)

2. Discuss with your children the history of the land and its peoples, how the trees were used, and what happened to the land when the trees were gone. (American Association of School Librarians Standards 1.3.4, 2.1.3, 2.2.3, 3.1.2, 3.1.3, 3.2.1, 3.2.2, 3.3.5, 4.1.3, 4.3.1; English Language Arts Standards 3, 6, 11, 12; Life Science Standards: Life cycles of organisms, Organisms and environments, Populations and ecosystems; Social Studies Standards II, III)

3. Consider using this book prior to Earth Day, which is observed on April 22. Plan to participate in your community's celebration of Earth Day. Encourage children to plant a tree. (American Association of School Librarians Standards 2.3.1, 3.1.5, 3.2.3, 4.1.3; Life Science Standards: Life cycles of organisms, Organisms and environments, Populations and ecosystems)

Kimmelman, Leslie. *Dance, Sing, Remember: A Celebration of Jewish Holidays.* New York: HarperCollins Publishers, 2000. 34p. Illustrated by Ora Eitan. $18.95. ISBN 0-06-027725-4.

Author and Illustrator

Author Leslie Kimmelman is an American. Illustrator Ora Eitan was born in Tel Aviv and lives in Jerusalem. She was nominated for the Hans Christian Andersen Prize.

     Nonfiction, Picture Book, Ages 4–8

Summary

Illustrated two-page spreads describe eleven holidays, such as Yom Kippur, Purim, Sukkot, and others. Prepare a Seder Plate, play the dreidel game, or dance the Hora. Directions are given for games, foods, music, and dance.

Curriculum Responses with Learning Extensions

1. This book lends itself to reading aloud and discussing with your children. The book can be read in short sittings, two to four pages at a time. If you prefer, you can also read about a holiday when that holiday occurs. Some children may be familiar with the holidays and may celebrate them with their families, but others may not. As you read about each holiday, engage children in discussion by asking what they already know about the holiday and whether and how they celebrate it. Encourage students who are not familiar with the holiday to ask questions of those who are. (American Association of School Librarians Standards 1.1.1, 1.1.2, 1.1.3, 1.1.6, 1.3.4, 2.1.5, 2.3.1, 3.1.2, 3.1.3, 3.2.1, 3.2,2, 3.3.1, 3.3.2, 3.3.3, 3.3.5, 4.1.1, 4.1.2, 4.1.3, 4.3.1; English Language Arts Standards 1, 2, 3, 4, 6, 11, 12; Social Studies Standards I)

2. Teach your children to dance the Hora using the directions on page 29. (American Association of School Librarians Standards 4.1.3; Dance Content Standards 1, 4; Social Studies Standards I)

3. Have children read about Purim, and then make groggers using the directions on page 21. (American Association of School Librarians Standards 1.1.6, 1.1.9, 2.2.4, 2.3.1, 3.1.2, 3.2.2, 3.2.3, 3.3.4, 4.1.1, 4.1.2, 4.1.3, 4.1.8; English Language Arts Standards 1, 3, 11; Visual Arts Content Standards 1, 2, 3, 4; Social Studies Standards I)

4. Have children use the directions on page 19 to plant parsley for Tu B'Shevat and take it home for Passover. (American Association of School Librarians Standards 1.1.6, 1.1.9, 2.1.5, 2.2.4, 2.3.1, 3.1.2, 3.2.2, 3.2.3, 3.3.4, 4.1.2, 4.1.3; English Language Arts Standards 1, 3, 11; Science Standards: Life cycles of organisms; Social Studies Standards I)

5. Have your children bake Harvest Muffins using the recipe on page 10, after reading about Sukkot. (American Association of School Librarians Standards 1.1.6, 2.1.5, 2.2.4, 3.1.2, 3.2.2, 3.2.3, 3.3.4, 4.1.2, 4.1.3; English Language Arts Standards 1, 2, 3, 11, 12; Social Studies Standards I)

Related Books

Lasky, Kathryn. *Georgia Rises: A Day in the Life of Georgia O'Keeffe.* Unpaged. Illustrated by Ora Eitan. $16.96. ISBN 0-374-32529-4.

Georgia rises before sunup, fixes tea for herself and water for her dogs, packs her bag with paints and canvas, walks into the desert for a day of painting; she returns to her home in the evening to fix her dinner and watch the night sky from her rooftop, then slips into bed for a good night's sleep.

Nye, Naomi Shihab. *Come With Me: Poems for a Journey.* New York: Green Willow Books, 2000. Unpaged. Illustrated by Dan Yaccarino. $15.95. ISBN 0-688-1596-X.

Author and Illustrator

Author and poet Naomi Shihab Nye is Palestinian American; she lived in Jordan and Jerusalem, traveled in the Middle East and Asia for the United States Information Agency, and now lives in the United States. Illustrator Dan Yaccarino is an American author and illustrator.

📖 Poetry, Picture Book, Ages 5 and Up

Summary

Sixteen poems illustrated with mixed media collages take young readers on journeys around the town, through the field, on an airplane, in a covered wagon, and more.

Curriculum Responses with Curriculum Standards

1. Introduce the book by selecting a poem to read aloud. Have children select poems to read aloud to their classmates. Encourage them to listen for repetitive phrases, rhythms, and similes. (American Association of School Librarians Standards 1.1.6, 4.1.1, 4.1.2; English Language Arts Standards 1)
2. With your children, write and illustrate whole-class poems about journeys—journeys in dreams and fantasies, journeys to places, journeys by car, bus, or airplane. Help children use repetitive phrases, rhythms, and similes. Use the poems to compile a class book. (American Association of School Librarians Standards 2.1.2, 2.1.5, 2.1.6, 3.2.3, 3.3.5, 4.1.5, 4.3.1, 4.4.1; English Language Arts Standards 4, 5, 6, 11, 12; Visual Arts Content Standards 1)
3. Extend the activity by having children collect and read aloud other poems about journeys. Select or compose background music to accompany the poetry readings. (American Association of School

Librarians Standards 1.1.6, 1.2.2, 1.2.3, 1.3.4, 3.3.5, 4.1.1, 4.1.2, 4.1.3, 4.1.4, 4.1.8, 4.2.4, 4.3.1; English Language Arts Standards 1; Music Content Standards 3, 6)

UNITED KINGDOM AND IRELAND

Readers will discover classical titles and contemporary titles; fiction, poetry, fables, and fairy tales; stories about people and animals, some humorous, others tender. Anthony Browne introduces readers to Mom, Dad, Beauty the kitten, and Willy the chimp. Caroline Church introduces readers to Digby the sheep dog, who learns to say please and thank you. Readers will meet Principessa and others who learn that it really is okay to have a new sibling. Creative book making, nonsense language, and a trip to the art museum appeal to the imagination.

There are even lessons to be learned from Aesop's fables and Wanda the witch. Authors include those who are well-known, such as Edward Lear, C. S. Lewis, Charles Dickens, and Clement Moore. Three authors are award winners. Anthony Browne received the Hans Christian Andersen Prize. He and Emily Gravett have had books selected by the United States Board on Books for Young People (USBBY) as Outstanding International Books. The children's laureate of Britain, Michael Morpurgo, is also included. Discussion, writing, book making, puppetry, choral reading, and a visit to the art museum are only a few of the suggested Curriculum Responses.

Browne, Anthony. *My Mom.* New York: Farrar Straus Giroux, 2005. Unpaged. $16.00. ISBN 0-374-35098-1.

Author

Author Anthony Browne is a British recipient of the Hans Christian Andersen Prize and other awards. His books, *My Mom, Silly Billy,* and *Little Beauty* were selected by the United States Board on Books for Young People (USBBY) as Outstanding International Books in 2006, 2007, and 2009 respectively.

📖 Fiction, Picture Book, Ages 4–8

Summary

My mom is nice, strong, beautiful, and many other good things. She could be a dancer, an astronaut, or something else, but she is my mom who makes me laugh and who loves me. This companion book to *My Dad* is similar with simple text and simple illustrations.

Curriculum Responses with Curriculum Standards

1. Introduce this book by reading aloud. Then engage children in conversation about their moms. Ask the children how they would describe their moms? (American Association of School Librarians Standards 1.1.6, 1.3.4, 2.3.1, 3.1.2, 3.1.3, 3.2.1, 3.2.2, 3.3.5, 4.1.1, 4.1.3, 4.3.1; English Language Arts Standards 1, 3, 4, 6, 11, 12)

2. Extend the activity by having children write about their moms. (American Association of School Librarians Standards 2.1.6, 2.2.4, 3.1.3, 4.1.3, 4.1.8; English Language Arts Standards 3, 4, 5, 6, 12)

3. Follow up by encouraging children to make illustrated books to take home to their moms. (American Association of School Librarians Standards 2.1.6, 2.2.4, 3.1.3, 4.1.3, 4.1.8; English Language Arts Standards 3, 4, 5, 6, 12)

Related Books

1. Browne, Anthony. *Little Beauty.* New York: Candlewick Press, 2008. Unpaged. $16.99. ISBN 978-0-7636-3959-4.

When the ape in the zoo, who knows sign language, signs to his keepers that he is lonely, they bring him a kitten named Beauty.

2. Browne, Anthony. *My Dad.* New York: Farrar Straus Giroux, 2000. Unpaged. $16.00. ISBN 9-780374-351014.

My dad is a hero, a sportsman, and many other good things, who makes me laugh and loves me.

3. Browne, Anthony. *The Shape Game.* New York: Farrar Straus Giroux, 2003. Unpaged. $16.00. ISBN 0-374-36764-7.

Directions for a shape game are given on the last two pages of this book, which is about a boy and his family who visit the art museum and bring the pictures to life.

4. Browne, Anthony. *Silly Billy.* New York: Candlewick Press, 2006. Unpaged. $15.99. ISBN 0-7636-3124-8.

Billy is a worrier who even worries that his worry dolls have too many worries.

5. Browne, Anthony. *Willy's Pictures.* Cambridge, MA: Candlewick Press, 2000. Unpaged. $16.99. ISBN 0-7637-0962-5.

In *Willy's Pictures,* one of six books about Willy the chimp, readers can view Willy's sketchbook and even see the paintings that inspired Willy.

Church, Caroline Jayne. *Digby Takes Charge.* New York: Margaret K. McElderry Books, 2007. Unpaged. $14.99. ISBN 978-1-4169-3441-7.

Author and Illustrator

Author and illustrator Caroline Jayne Church is British and lives in England.

📖 Fiction, Picture Book, Ages 4–7

Summary

Digby is a sheepdog who cannot herd his six sheep. No matter what he does, his sheep just ignore Digby. They ignore him when he comes at them with a roaring engine, with a roaring tank, and with a helicopter. Finally the cows and the pigs teach Digby the magic word that they use to get what they want. What do you think that magic word is? What do you think happens when Digby uses the magic word?

Curriculum Responses with Curriculum Standards

1. Have children role-play the use of please and thank you. (American Association of School Librarians Standards 1.1.9, 1.3.4, 2.1.5, 2.3.1, 3.1.3, 3.2.2, 4.1.3, 4.1.8, 4.3.1; English Language Arts Standards 3, 4, 11, 12; Social Studies Standards IV; Theater Content Standards 2)
2. Ask children whether they know any other "magic" words, such as: I'm sorry, and excuse me. Have children role-play the use of other "magic" words. (American Association of School Librarians Standard 1.1.2, 1.1.9, 1.3.4, 2.1.5, 2.3.1, 3.1.3, 3.2.2, 3.3.5, 4.1.3, 4.1.8, 4.3.1; English Language Arts Standards 3, 4, 11, 12; Social Studies Standards IV; Theater Content Standards 2)
3. Engage children in a discussion about using good manners. What difference does the use of manners make? (American Association of School Librarians Standards 1.1.2, 1.3.4, 2.1.5, 2.3.1, 3.1.3, 3.2.1, 3.2.2, 3.3.5, 4.1.3, 4.1.8, 4.3.1; English Language Arts Standards; Social Studies Standards IV; Theater Content Standards 2)

Related Books

1. Ives, Penny. *Celestine: Drama Queen.* New York: Arthur A. Levine Books, 2008. Unpaged. $16.99. ISBN 0-545-08149-1.

Celestine was born to be a star, and dresses and talks like a star, but when her moment for stardom comes, she can't move and can't speak.

2. Hayes, Sarah. *Dog Day.* New York: Farrar Straus Giroux, 2008. Unpaged. Illustrated by Hannah Broadway. $16.95. ISBN 0-374-31810-7.

When Ben's new teacher turns out to be a dog, Ben and his classmates learn to wag their bottoms, scratch their ears and chins, stick out their tongues and pant, and do other things that dogs do.

3. David Lucas. *The Robot and the Bluebird.* New York: Farrar Straus and Giroux, 2007. Unpaged. New York: Farrar Straus Giroux, 2007. Unpaged. $16.95. ISBN 0-374-36330-7.

This is a gentle and touching story of a rusty, broken-hearted old robot whose life is changed by a cold and weary bluebird who makes a nest where the robot's heart used to be.

4. Shields, Gillian. *Dogfish.* New York: Atheneum Books for Young Readers, 2008. Unpaged. $16.99. ISBN 1-4189-7127-0.

When a little boy decides that he will treat his goldfish like a dog by taking him for walks and teaching him to catch a stick, everyone is happy—the boy, his mom, and the goldfish.

5. Stewart, Joel. *Addis Berner Bear Forgets.* New York: Farrar, Straus and Giroux, 2008. Unpaged. $16.95. ISBN 0-374-30036-4.

When Addis Bear arrives in the big city, it is all so confusing that he forgets why he came—and then he is robbed!

Enderle, Judith Ross Enderle & Stephanie Jacob Gordon. *Smile, Principessa!* New York: Margaret K. McElderry Books. 2007. Unpaged. Illustrated by Serena Curmi. $16.99. ISBN 978-1-4169-1004-6.

Author and Illustrator

Authors Judith Ross Enderle and Stephanie Jacob Gordon are an American writing team. Illustrator Serena Curmi is English.

📖 Fiction, Picture Book, Ages 3–6

Summary

Until the birth of her little brother, Principessa is the focus of her parents' attention. Papa takes pictures of her smiling, crying, eating, and sleeping. Now Papa takes pictures of her brother smiling, crying, eating, and sleeping. Principessa doesn't like it! What do you think she does?

Curriculum Responses with Curriculum Standards

1. Engage children in a discussion. How did Principessa feel about her baby brother? Ask children whether they have younger brothers or

sisters. Ask them how they felt when a new brother or sister joined the family. (American Association of School Librarian Standards 1.1.6, 2.3.1, 3.1.3, 4.1.2, 4.1.5, 4.3.1; English Language Arts Standards 1, 3, 4, 12; Social Studies Standards IV)

2. What did Principessa do when Papa took pictures of her baby brother? What did you do when you had a new baby brother or sister in the family? (American Association of School Librarian Standards 1.1.6, 2.3.1, 3.1.3, 4.1.2, 4.1.5, 4.3.1; English Language Arts Standards 1, 3, 4, 12; Social Studies Standard IV)

3. What made Principessa change her mind about her baby brother? Did you change your mind about your baby brother or sister? Why? (American Association of School Librarian Standards 1.1.6, 2.3.1, 3.1.3, 4.1.2, 4.1.5, 4.3.1; English Language Arts Standards 1.3, 4, 14; Social Studies Standard IV)

Related Books

1. Bunting, Eve. *Jin Woo*. New York: Clarion Books, 2001. 30p. Illustrated by Chris Soentpiet. $16.00 ISBN 0-395-93872-4.

Davey hopes that the new baby his parents are adopting from Korea won't come.

2. Hojer, Dan and Lotta. *Heart of Mine: A Story of Adoption*. Stockholm: R&S Books, 2001. Unpaged. $14.00. ISBN 91-29-65301-0.

While baby Tu Thi grows in her mommy's tummy, she also grows in the minds and hearts of the mommy and daddy who adopt her.

3. Lloyd, Sam. *Mr. Pusskins and Little Whiskers*. New York: Atheneum Books for Young Readers, 2007. Unpaged. $15.99. ISBN 1-4169-5796-0.

Mr. Pusskins is not happy with his fabulous surprise from Emily, a kitten named Little Whiskers.

4. Mendes, Valerie. *Look at Me, Grandma!* New York: The Chicken House, 2001. Unpaged. Illustrated by Claire Fletcher. $15.95. ISBN 0-439-29654-4.

Jamie doesn't want to be a big brother, until Grandma tells him about her big brother, who died when he was ten.

5. Young, Ed. *My Mei Mei*. New York: Philomel, 2006. 40p. $16.99. ISBN 0-399-24339-9.

The author tells his eldest daughter's story of being adopted from China, of her desire to be a big sister, and of her disappointment in the adopted little sister who also comes from China.

Gravett, Emily. *The Odd Egg.* New York: Simon & Schuster Books for Young Readers, 2008. Unpaged. $15.99. ISBN 1-4169-6872.

Author

Author Emily Gravett is British. Two of her books, *Wolves* and *Meerkat Mail* were selected by the United States Board on Books for Young People (USBBY) as Outstanding International Books in 2007 and 2008 respectively.

📖 Fiction, Picture Book, 4–8

Summary

The hen, the parrot, the flamingo, and the owl have eggs to hatch. Duck has no egg until he finds a very big white egg with green spots on it. Duck sits and sits and sits upon his egg while all of the others hatch. The other birds tell Duck that his egg won't hatch, but one day it does. What do you suppose is in Duck's very large white egg with green spots?

Curriculum Responses with Curriculum Standards

1. The humor of this book is in the illustrations. Introduce the book by reading aloud. Focus children's attention on the illustrations and have them discuss what is happening in the pictures. After reading place the book where children can select it for independent reading. (American Association of School Librarians Standards 1.1.6, 1.1.9, 1.3.4, 2.1.5, 3.1.2, 3.1.3, 3.2.1, 3.2.2, 3.3.5, 4.1.1, 4.1.3, 4.2.4, 4.3.3; English Language Arts Standards 1, 3, 4, 6, 11, 12; Visual Arts Content Standards 3, 5)

2. Use this book as a model for picture layout and design. Call attention to the balance and flow of each two-page spread. Have children make pictures using a similar balance and flow. (American Association of School Librarians Standards 1.1.6, 2.1.6, 2.2.4, 4.1.3; English Language Arts Standards 1, 3, 4, 6, 12; Visual Arts Content Standards 1, 2, 3, 5)

3. Use this book as a model for book making. Note, in particular, the short pages with their illustrations. Encourage children to make their own books using a similar technique. (American Association of School Librarians Standards 2.1.6, 2.2.4, 4.1.3; English Language Arts Standards 1, 3, 4, 6, 12; Visual Arts Content Standards 1, 2, 3, 5)

Related Books

1. Gravett, Emily. *Little Mouse's Big Book of Fears.* New York: Simon and Schuster Books for Young People. Unpaged. $17.99. ISBN 1-4169-5930-0.

Torn pages, fold-outs, words with definitions at the tops of pages, and the invitation to record your fears on each page invite the reader to participate in this gentle story of the little mouse who is afraid of creepy crawlies, what's under the bed, sharp knives, bathing, accidents, loud noises, the dark, getting lost, birds, and dogs, but who can scare a human.

2. Gravett, Emily. *Meerkat Mail*. New York: Simon and Schuster Books for Young People, 2007. Unpaged. $17.99. ISBN 978-1-4169-3473-8.

Sunny Meerkat writes postcards to his family in the Kalahari Desert as he travels to visit relatives.

3. Gravett, Emily. *Monkey and Me*. New York: Simon and Schuster Children's Publishing, 2008. 32p. $15.99. ISBN 1-146-95457-0.

Repetitive text invites children to guess what the next animal will be and to chime in on the verse, while art work invites children to imitate the animals that the little girl imagines as she plays with her stuffed monkey.

4. Gravett, Emily. *Orange Pear Apple Bear*. New York: Simon and Schuster Books for Young Readers, 2007. Unpaged. $12.99. ISBN 1-4169-3999-7.

Intended for very young children, this simple picture book of five words and four pictures can be used with primary grade children as an art lesson involving the use of color and shading, and also as a lesson involving word play.

5. Gavett, Emily. *Wolves*. New York: Simon and Schuster Books for Young People. Unpaged. $15.95. ISBN 1-4169-1491-9.

Rabbit is reading a book about wolves as he walks home from the library and doesn't notice the real wolf following behind, getting closer and closer, bigger and bigger.

Lear, Edward. *The Owl and the Pussy Cat*. New York: Simon and Schuster Books for Young Readers, 2001. Unpaged. Illustrated by Hilary Knight. $17.00. ISBN 0-689-83927-8.

Author, Illustrator, Music Composer

Author Edward Lear is a British author who traveled extensively throughout southern Europe, Egypt, and India and wrote about his travels, but who is best known for his limericks and nonsense verses. He was also a landscape painter and Queen Victoria's drawing instructor. Illustrator Hilary Knight is an American, as is music composer Douglas Colby.

📖 Poetry, Picture Book, Ages 4–8

Lively cartoon-like illustrations featuring Bernadette Peters as the Pussy Cat enliven this Victorian era version of the poem about the Owl and the Pussy-cat, who were married and went to sea in a pea green boat. Concept drawings from Hilary Knight's sketchbook are on the inside front and back covers. The poem set to sheet music by Douglas Colby is included in the front of the book.

Curriculum Responses with Curriculum Standards

1. Introduce the book by reading aloud. Encourage children to chime in on repetitive language, and especially on the center page that begins with "All together now!" After reading aloud, place the book where children can select it for independent reading. (American Association of School Librarians Standards 1.1.6, 3.1.2, 3.1.3, 3.2.2, 3.2.3, 4.1.1, 4.1.3, 4.2.4, 4.3.1; English Language Arts Standards 1, 3, 4, 6, 11, 12)

2. Have the children reread and develop reader's theater or choral reading scripts. Have them rehearse and present their reader's theater or choral reading to other classmates or another group of children. (American Association of School Librarians Standards 1.1.6, 1.1.9, 1.2.2, 1.3.4, 2.1.5, 2.1.6, 2.2.4, 3.1.2, 3.1.3, 3.2.1, 3.2.2, 3.2.3, 3.3.5, 4.1.1, 4.1.3, 4.1.8, 4.3.1; English Language Arts Standards 1, 3, 4, 5, 6, 11, 12)

3. Have children use the illustrations as a guide and create a board game with written questions and activities. (American Association of School Librarians Standards 1.1.6, 1.3.4, 2.1.5, 2.1.6, 2.2.4, 3.1.2, 3.1.3, 3.2.1, 3.2.2, 3.2.3, 3.3.5, 4.1.3, 4.1.8, 4.3.1; English Language Arts Standards 3, 4, 5, 6, 11, 12; Visual Arts Content Standards 1, 2, 3, 5)

Related Books

1. Lear, Edward. *"A" Was Once An Apple Pie.* New York: Orchard Books, 2005. 32p. Illustrated by Suse Macdonald. $12.99. ISBN 439-66-56-4.

Boldly colored collage illustrations, silly rhyming verses, and word play take the reader through the alphabet.

2. Lear, Edward. *Nonsense!* New York: Atheneum, 2004. 40p. Illustrated by Valorie Fisher. $9.95. ISBN 0-689-863-802.

Fifteen illustrated limericks are featured, with one on each two-page spread, and an Afterword and Map adding biographical information at the end of the book.

3. Lear, Edward. *The Owl and the Pussycat.* New York: HarperCollins, 2006. 32p. 16.95. ISBN 0-060-27228-7.

The owl and the pussycat go to sea with each verse on a separate page illustrated by realistic sea-creatures, lush tropical flowers, and stylized borders.

Lewis, C. S. *The Lion, the Witch, and the Wardrobe.* HarperCollins Publishers, 2000. Unpaged. Illustrated by Christian Birmingham. $15.95. ISBN 0-06-029011-0.

Author and Illustrator

Author C. S. Lewis was Irish. Illustrator Christian Birmingham is British. This story is set in England during World War II, and is the second in a series of seven books entitled *The Chronicles of Narnia.*

📖 Fiction, Picture Book, Ages 6–10

Summary

Lucy, Susan, Edmund, and Peter enter the magical land of Narnia through the back of the wardrobe. In Narnia, it is always winter and Christmas never comes because the White Witch has cast a spell. The White Witch has cast a spell on Edmund too, and she is holding him a prisoner. Now Aslan is on the move. How will he save Edmund, defeat the White Witch, and free Narnia from her spell? This 50th Anniversary Issue of the C. S. Lewis's classic is an abridged version using a nontraditional picture book format.

Curriculum Responses with Curriculum Standards

1. Have children create scenes of Narnia. (American Association of School Librarians Standards 1.2.3, 2.1.2, 2.2.4, 4.1.3, 4.1.8; Visual Arts Content Standard 1)
2. Have children retell the story by creating puppets and putting on a puppet show, or by writing a reader's theater script and putting on a reader's theater presentation. (American Association of School Librarians Standards 1.2.3, 1.3.4, 2.1.2, 2.1.6, 2.2.4, 3.1.3, 3.2.1, 3.2.2, 3.2.3, 4.1.3, 4.1.8. 4.3.1; Theater Content Standards 1, 2; English Language Arts Standards 5)
3. See Related Books for additional reissued classics illustrated by Christian Birmingham. Feature these books and encourage children to read them as part of an Illustrator of the Month theme. The additional classics also lend themselves to the creation of shoe box dioramas or retellings using puppet shows or reader's theater presentations. (American Association of School Librarians Standards 4.1.1., 4.1.2, 4.2.4; English Language Arts Standard 1; Visual Arts Content Standard 5)

Related Books

1. Andersen, Hans Christian. *The Classic Treasury of Hans Christian Andersen*. Philadelphia, PA: Courage Books, 2002. 55p. Illustrated by Christian Birmingham. $16.95. ISBN 0-762-41393-X.

Full color illustrations enhance this collection of stories by Hans Christian Andersen.

2. Dickens, Charles. Retold by Jane Parker Resnick. *A Christmas Carol: The Heirloom Edition*. Philadelphia, PA: Running Press Book Publishers, 2002. 55p. Illustrated by Christian Birmingham. $16.95. ISBN 0-762-41299-2.

The story of Ebenezer Scrooge and the ghosts of Christmas Past, Present, and Future, and of the Cratchit family and Tiny Tim is retold in an abridged version with full-color illustrations.

3. Geras, Adele. *Sleeping Beauty*. New York: Orchard Books, 2003. Unpaged. Illustrated by Christian Birmingham. $18.95. ISBN 0-439-58180-X.

Soft dream-like illustrations embellish this retelling of Princess Aurora, the jealous witch, and the handsome prince.

4. Lewis, C. S. *The Chronicles of Narnia*. New York: Harper Collins, 1994. $8.95. ISBN 46594-00895.

A series of seven books begins with the origin of the land of Narnia and its king, Aslan, then continues with the saga that ends with the great battle between the forces of good and evil. Titles in the series are *The Magician's Nephew, The Lion, the Witch and the Wardrobe, The Horse and His Boy, Prince Caspian, The Silver Chair,* and *The Last Battle*.

5. Moore, Clement C. *The Night Before Christmas: The Heirloom Edition*. Philadelphia, PA: Running Press Book Publishers, 2001. 48p. Illustrated by Christian Birmingham. $16.95. ISBN 0-762-41069-8.

This well loved classic poem of St. Nick's Christmas Eve visit is reissued with full color illustrations.

Mayhew, James. *Katie's Sunday Afternoon*. New York: Orchard Books, 2004. Unpaged. $16.95. ISBN 0-439-60678-0.

Author and Illustrator

Author and illustrator James Mayhew is British and lives in England. This book is set in England and is one of several books about Katie's visits to British art museums.

📖 Fiction, Picture Book, Ages 4–7

Summary

Katie's adventures begin when she steps into the pointillist paintings at the art museum. Katie starts by swimming with *The Bathers* at Asnieres in Georges Seurat's painting until the river overflows into the art gallery. Then she invites the elegant people in Seurat's *Sunday Afternoon on the Island of La Grande Jatte* to come wading. As the water gets deeper and deeper, Katie and her new friend Jacques drag a rowboat from Seurat's *Port of Honfleur* into the art gallery. An elegant lady steps into the rowboat, slips, and falls into the water. Fortunately the washerwoman in Camille Pissarro's *Woman Hanging up the Washing* has dry clothes for the lady to wear and hangs up her wet dress to dry. Just then, Jacques calls a warning that the museum guard is coming. Now Katie must get rid of the water in the art museum and get all of the people back into their paintings? How will she ever do that?

Curriculum Responses with Curriculum Standards

1. Ask children which picture they would like to step into. What will they do in the picture? Where will they go? With whom will they talk or play? Where will they sit? (American Association of School Librarians Standards 1.3.4, 3.2.2, 4.3.1; English Language Arts Standard 3)
2. Have the children recreate their own scenes from the story by making pointillist paintings. (American Association of School Librarians Standards 2.2.4, 4.1.3; Visual Arts Content Standard 1)
3. Consider taking children on a visit to a nearby art museum to see pointillist paintings. (American Association of School Librarians Standard 2.3.1; Visual Arts Content Standard: 5)
4. Borrow pointillist paintings from your local library or pointillist slides from your local art museum to use in your library or classroom. (American Association of School Librarians Standard 2.3.1; Visual Arts Content Standard 5)
5. Introduce the children to other well-known painters and their works by using the additional titles about Katie's visits to the art museum that are listed in Related Books. Follow up with questions and discussion about the paintings, by recreating scenes, visiting an art museum, or borrowing paintings or slides to use with your children. (American Association of School Librarians Standards 4.1.2, 4.1.3; English Language Arts Standard 2; Visual Arts Content Standard 3)

Related Books

1. Mayhew, James. *Katie and the Mona Lisa.* New York: Orchard Books, 1999. 32p. $10.80 ISBN 1-860-30706-9.

Katie invites Mona Lisa out of her frame. Together they visit other Italian Renaissance masterpieces.

2. Mayhew, James. *Katie and the Sunflowers.* New York: Orchard Picture Books, 2001. 32p. $10.80. ISBN 1-841-21634-8.

In this museum adventure, Katie meets Van Gogh and other Post-impressionists.

3. Mayhew, James. *Katie in London.* New York: Orchard Books. 2003. 32p. $10.80. ISBN 1-843-62285-8.

Katie explores London with the lion from Trafalgar Square.

4. Mayhew, James. *Katie Meets the Impressionists.* New York: Orchard Books, 2007. 32p. $16.95. ISBN 0-439-93508-1.

In this museum adventure, Katie meets the Impressionists.

5. Mayhew, James. *Katie's Picture Show.* New York: Orchard Books, 2004. 32p. $10.80. ISBN 1-843-62397-8.

Katie and her grandmother visit a London art gallery, where Katie stumbles into one painting after another.

Morpurgo, Michael. *The McElderry Book of Aesop's Fables.* New York: Margaret K. McElderry Books, 2004. 96p. Illustrated by Emma Chichester Clark. $19.95. ISBN 1-4169-0290-2.

Author and Illustrator

Author Michael Morpurgo is the Children's Laureate of Britain. Illustrator Emma Chichester Clark is an award-winning British illustrator.

📖 Fables, Picture Book, Ages 6–10

Curriculum Responses with Curriculum Standards

1. After reading, encourage children to retell the stories using a flannel board, puppetry, reader's theater, or by making masks and acting out. (American Association of School Librarians Standards 1.1.6, 1.1.9, 1.2.2, 1.2.3, 2.1.6, 2.1.5, 2.2.4, 3.1.2, 3.1.3, 3.2.2, 3.2.3, 3.3.1, 3.3.2, 3.3.4, 3.3.5, 4.1.1, 4.1.3, 4.1.8, 4.2.4, 4.3.1; English Language Arts Standards 1, 3, 4, 5, 6, 11, 12, Theater Content Standards 1, 2; Visual Arts Content Standards 1, 2)

2. Select and display other versions of the stories, encourage children to read, compare the variations, and share their responses with classmates. (American Association of School Librarians Standards 1.1.2, 1.1.3, 1.1.4, 1.1.6, 1.1.9, 1.2.2, 1.2.3, 1.3.4, 2.1.5, 2.2.4, 3.1.1, 3.1.2, 3.1.3, 3.2.1, 3.2.2, 3.2.3, 3.3.1, 3.3.2, 3.3.5, 4.1.1, 4.1.2, 4.1.3, 4.2.4, 4.3.1; English Language Arts Standards 1, 3, 11, 12)

3. Feature the author or illustrator as Author or Illustrator of the Week/ Month. Select and display books. Encourage children to read and share responses with classmates. (American Association of School Librarians 1.1.6, 1.2.2, 1.3.4, 2.1.5, 3.1.2, 3.1.3, 3.2.1, 3.2.2, 3.3.5, 4.1.1, 4.1.2, 4.1.3, 4.2.4, 4.3.1; English Language Arts Standards 1, 3, 11, 12)

Related Books

1. French, Vivian. *Stories from Favorite Nursery Rhymes: The Daddy Goose Treasury.* New York: The Chicken House, 2006. 92p. Illustrated by AnnaLaura Cantone, Ross Collins, Joelle Dreidemy, Andrea Huseinovic. $18.99. ISBN 0-439-79608-3.

Daddy Goose tells you what happens when Old King Cole calls for his pipe, his bowl, and his fiddlers three; what happens when the mouse runs up and down the clock; and what happens in ten other nursery rhymes.

2. Green, Alison. *Mother Goose's Storytime Nursery Rhymes.* New York: Arthur A. Levine Books, 2006. 127p. Illustrated by Axel Scheffler. $19.99. ISBN 0-439-9306-8.

Mother Goose has three little goslings who are full of questions. She answers each question with a short story that introduces a set of three or four nursery rhymes. Twenty-five sets of illustrated nursery rhymes will entertain young children as read-alouds or for independent browsing and reading.

3. Pirotta, Saviour. *The McElderry Book of Grimms' Fairy Tales.* New York: Margaret K. McElderry Books. 127p. Illustrated by Emma Chichester Clark. $19.95. ISBN 1-4169-11798-5.

Ten fairy tales from the Brothers Grimm, some familiar, like the story of Snow White, and others not so familiar, such as the story of the cat and mouse, are retold.

Sperring, Mark. *Wanda's First Day.* London: The Chicken House, 2004. Unpaged. Illustrated by Kate & Liz Pope. $15.95. ISBN 0-439-62773-7.

Author and Illustrator

Author Mark Sparring is English. Illustrators Kate and Liz Pope are Americans.

📖 Fiction, Picture Book, Ages 4–6

Summary

It is the first of day school, and Wanda the witch discovers that she is in a school for fairies, not for witches. Even so, she likes her teacher, has a good time on the first day of school, and makes new friends. She learns that it is okay to be different.

Curriculum Responses with Curriculum Standards

1. After reading, engage children in a discussion. How did Wanda feel about being different? What did she learn? (American Association of School Librarians Standards 1.1.2, 1.1.6, 1.3.4, 3.2.2, 4.3.1; English Language Arts Standards 1, 3, 4, 6, 11, 12; Social Studies Standard IV)

2. Personalize the discussion by asking the children whether they have ever felt different from everyone else. Did it feel okay to be different? (American Association of School Librarians Standards 1.1.2, 1.1.6, 1.3.4, 3.2.2, 4.3.1; English Language Arts Standards 3, 4, 6, 11, 12; Social Studies Standard IV)

3. Extend the conversation by asking whether the children know someone who is different from them. How do they treat the person who is different? How do they think that person feels? (American Association of School Librarians Standards 1.1.2, 1.3.4, 3.2.2, 4.3.1; English Language Arts Standards 3, 4, 6, 11, 12; Social Studies Standard IV)

Related Books

Rickards, Lynne. *Pink!* New York: Scholastic Inc., 2009. Unpaged. Illustrated by Margaret Chamberlain. 16.95. ISBN 0-545-08608-6.

Patrick the pink penguin swam for seven days and seven nights to Africa, and another seven days and seven nights home again, only to learn that it's okay to be different.

Ages 8–12

AFRICA

Invite students to explore and experience Africa through the eyes of authors from South Africa, and from the North African countries of Algeria, Tunisia, Morocco, and Libya, through the eyes of American and British authors with ties to Africa, and a European author who lived in Sumatra and set his book in Kenya. Introduce readers to the wildlife of Tanzania, Botswana, the African savannah, and the Democratic Republic of Congo, and to the culture and history of the people of Ghana, North Africa, and Kenya. Students can step into traditional Muslim society of the late nineteenth century in Southern Libya, and experience life among the Masai and Kekuyu tribes of Kenya.

Fiction and nonfiction titles include photodocumentaries, nontraditional picture books, mystery, adventure, humor, and a historical coming-of-age story. The United States Board on Books for Young People (USBBY) selected three books for younger readers by South African author/illustrator Niki Daly as Outstanding International Books. Niki Daly was also nominated for the Hans Christian Andersen Prize. Two books, *The Shadows of Ghadames* by Joelle Stolz and *The Baboon King* by Anton Quintana received the Batchelder Award. Curriculum Responses include research, discussion, retelling, art, and other activities.

Daly, Niki. *Bettina Valentino and the Picasso Club.* New York: Farrar, Straus and Giroux, 2009. 104p. $15.95. ISBN 0-374-30753-9.

Author

Niki Daly is an author and illustrator who lives in Cape Town, South Africa, which is the setting for many of his books. Three of his books for younger readers were listed by the United States Board on Books for Young People (USBBY) as Outstanding International Books. He was also nominated for the Hans Christian Andersen Prize.

📖 Fiction, Ages 9–12

Summary

Bettina doesn't like pink, or pastels. She likes black and white, and wild art that hits you in the eye. And that is just what the new art teacher, Mr. Popart, encourages. Bettina not only adores art, she adores her teacher too. But not everyone thinks Mr. Popart is wonderful in his bare feet, red vest, and too-short, flared trousers. Maxine Rattle and her parents don't like him. Because of them, Mr. Popart might lose his job. The school might lose a lot of money too, even though students are producing exciting art projects. Lively illustrations, lively text, and lively characters introduce readers to artists and styles, and even encourage the creation of lively art projects.

Curriculum Connections with Curriculum Standards

1. As students read, encourage them to search for, collect, and display examples of art work by the artists that they read about, for example: Klee, Picasso, and others. (American Association of School Librarians Standards 1.1.1, 1.1.3, 1.1.4, 1.1.6, 1.1.8, 1.2.1, 1.2.2, 1.2.3, 1.3.4, 2.1.2, 2.2.4, 3.1.1, 3.1.2, 3.2.1, 3.2.2, 3.2.3, 3.3.3, 3.3.5, 4.1.1, 4.1.3, 4.1.7, 4.2.1, 4.3.1, 4.4.1; English Language Arts Standards 1, 2, 3, 4, 6, 7, 8, 11, 12; Visual Arts Content Standards 3, 4, 5)

2. After reading, encourage students to create and display their own art projects. (American Association of School Librarians Standards 1.1.6, 1.2.3, 2.1.6, 2.2.4, 4.1.1, 4.1.3, 4.1.8, 1.4.1; English Language Arts Standards 1, 2, 4, 6, 11, 12; Visual Arts Content Standards 1, 2, 3)

3. In addition to a focus on art and artists, this book uses fun, lively language and expressions. While you are reading, encourage students to record in their journals language and expressions that appeal to them. After reading, have them create their own expressions. Provide opportunities for students to share with classmates language and expressions that they recorded and those that they created. (American Association of School Librarians Standards 1.1.6, 1.3.4, 2.1.6, 2.2.4, 3.1.3, 3.2.1, 4.1.1, 4.1.3, 4.1.5, 4.3.1; English Language Arts Standards 1, 3, 4, 5, 6, 11, 12)

Hatkoff, Juliana, Isabella Hatkoff, Craig Hatkoff, and Dr. Paula Kahumbu. *Looking for Miza: The True Story of the Mountain Gorilla Family Who Rescued One of Their Own.* New York: Scholastic Press, 2008. Unpaged. Photography by Peter Greste. $16.99. ISBN 0-545-08540-3.

Authors and Photographer

Authors Isabella, Juliana, and Craig Hatkoff are Americans. Dr. Paula Kahumbu is the Conservation Director of Wildlife Direct and lives in Kenya. Photographer Peter Greste is a broadcaster and photojournalist who spent twenty years in Australia, Africa, Latin America, the Middle East, and who now lives in Kenya. The book is set in the Democratic Republic of Congo, Africa.

📖 Nonfiction, Photodocumentary, Ages 9–12

Summary

Baby mountain gorilla, Miza, and her mother, Lessinjina, are missing from their mountain gorilla family. Miza's father, Kabirizi, a silverback gorilla, leads his gorilla family to the safety of the high mountains before he goes in search of Miza and Lessinjina. Rangers Innocent and Diddy also search for the missing gorillas. It is Kabirizi, not the rangers, who find Miza and bring her back to her family. She is frightened, sick, hungry, and struggling to feed herself, now that she cannot nurse from her mother. Although Lessinjina is never found, Miza, with the help of her family, does recover from her ordeal. The purpose of this book is to highlight the plight of the mountain gorilla in the Virunga National Park in the Democratic Republic of the Congo in Africa. The last pages identify threats to the mountain gorillas and their habitat with suggestions for solutions and a listing of four organizations that help mountain gorillas.

Curriculum Responses and Curriculum Standards

1. Call attention to and have children discuss similarities between a gorilla family and a human family, for example, young children's need for nurturing and protection, the father's protection of the family, and family members' support and assistance to the young one in need. (American Association of School Librarians Standards 1.1.2, 1.1.3, 1.1.9, 1.3.4, 2.1.5, 2.3.1, 2.4.3, 3.1.2, 3.1.3, 3.2.1, 3.2.2, 3.3.5, 4.1.5, 4.3.1; English Language Arts Standards 4, 11, 12; Life Science Standards; Social Studies Standards I)
2. Encourage children to learn more about mountain gorillas and report their findings by visiting the Web sites of the organizations listed in

the back of the book. (American Association of School Librarians Standards 1.1.1, 1.1.2, 1.1.3, 1.1.4, 1.1.5, 1.1.6, 1.1.8, 1.1.8, 1.2.1, 1.2.2, 1.2.3, 1.2.4, 1.2.5, 1.2.6, 1.2.7, 1.3.1, 1.3.3, 1.3.4, 1.3.5, 1.4.1, 2.1.1, 2.1.2, 2.1.3, 2.1.4, 2.2.1, 2.2.3, 2.4.1, 3.1.1, 3.1.3, 3.2.1, 3.3.5, 4.1.2, 4.1.7, 4.3.1; English Language Arts Standards 1, 7, 8, 11; Life Science Standards)

3. Extend the activity by encouraging interested children to use Related Books and other print and nonprint sources to learn about other animals in Africa. Invite them to share their findings with their classmates. (American Association of School Librarians Standards 1.1.1, 1.1.2, 1.1.3, 1.1.4, 1.1.5, 1.1.6, 1.1.8, 1.2.2, 1.2.3, 1.2.4, 1.2.5, 1.2.6, 1.2.7, 1.3.1, 1.3.3, 1.3.4, 1.3.5, 1.4.1, 1.4.2, 1.4.3, 1.4.4, 2.1.1, 2.1.2, 2.1.3, 2.1.4, 2.3.4, 2.3.1, 2.4.1, 2.4.3, 3.1.1, 3.1.3, 3.1.6, 3.2.1, 3.2.2, 3.3.5, 4.1.2, 4.1.4, 4.1.5, 4.1.7, 4.2.1, 4.2.2, 4.3.1, 4.3.2, 4.3.4, 4.4.1, 4.4.3; English Language Arts Standards 1, 4, 7, 8, 11, 12; Life Science Standards)

Related Books

1. Goodall, Jane. *The Chimpanzees I Love: Saving Their World and Ours.* New York: Scholastic Press, 2001. 80p. $17.95. ISBN 0-439-21320-X.

Scientist Dr. Jane Goodall tells the story of her life among and study of the chimpanzees of Gombe National Park in Tanzania, and her dedication to preserving wildlife habitats and environments in Tanzania and elsewhere.

2. Lewin, Ted and Betsy. *Elephant Quest.* New York: Harper Collins Publishers, 2000. 47p. $15.95. ISBN 0-688-14111-0.

Realistic paintings and field sketches of hippos, Cape buffalo, lions, leopards, wildebeests, lechwe, giraffes, and elephants illustrate the descriptive text that tells about the authors' trip to the Moremi Reserve in the Okavango Delta of Botswana, Africa.

3. London, Jonathan and Paul Morin. *What the Animals Were Waiting For.* New York: Scholastic, 2001. Unpaged. $16.95. ISBN 0-439-33630-9.

Free verse and mixed media illustrations depict, through the eyes of the Masai grandmother and her grandson, the drama of the changing seasons on the African savannah.

Mussi, Sarah. *The Door of No Return.* New York: Margaret K. McElderry Books, 2007. 394p. $17.95. ISBN 1-4169-1550-8.

Author

Author Sarah Mussi is English, lived in Ghana for many years, is married to a Ghanaian, and currently lives in England. The book is set in England and in Ghana, Africa.

📖 Fiction, Mystery, Ages 12 & up

Summary

Pops was murdered, his apartment ransacked, and his diaries were stolen, all but the one in Zac's pocket. Now someone is after Zac. Pops always said that he was the descendant of an African king sold into slavery, that there was a fortune in gold, and that he had the map to find the gold. Might there be some truth to Pops' story? Is that why Pops was murdered? Zac is determined to find out. Why do the police seem to be against Zac? Are they tied in with the murderers? Is there anyone whom Zac can trust? This is a gripping, fast-moving, suspenseful, and thought-provoking mystery.

Curriculum Responses with Curriculum Standards

1. Encourage students to read a chapter, predict what will happen next, then read to confirm their predictions. Encourage discussion among students and ask them to support their predictions with clues from their reading. (American Association of School Librarians Standards 1.1.6, 1.3.4, 1.4.1, 1.4.2, 1.4.3, 2.1.1, 2.1.5, 2.2.3, 2.4.1, 3.1.2, 3.2.1, 3.2.2, 3.2.3, 3.4.1, 4.2.3, 4.3.1; English Language Arts Standard 3, 11, 12)

2. Zac's ancestor was sold into slavery in 1701. Why did the British government not want the old African bond and treasure found? (American Association of School Librarians Standards 1.1.4, 1.1.6, 1.2.4, 1.2.5, 1.2.6, 1.2.7, 1.3.4, 1.4.1, 1.4.2, 1.4.3, 1.4.4, 2.1.1, 2.1.3, 2.2.2, 2.2.3, 2.4.1, 2.4.2, 3.1.1, 3.1.2, 3.1.3, 3.2.1, 3.2.2, 3.3.1, 3.3.5, 3.4.1, 4.1.3, 4.3.1, 4.4.3; English Language Arts Standards 11, 12; Social Studies Standards I, II, V, IX)

3. Find Ghana on a map. Discuss the relationship between Ghana's location and its role in the slave trade. (American Association of School Librarians Standards 1.1.6, 1.3.2, 1.3.4, 1.4.1, 1.4.2, 1.4.3, 1.4.4, 2.1.1, 2.1.3, 2.2.2, 2.2.3, 2.3.1, 2.3.2, 2.4.1, 2.4.3, 3.1.1, 3.1.2, 3.1.3, 3.2.1, 3.2.2, 3.3.5, 3.4.1, 4.1.3, 4.3.1; English Language Arts Standards 1, 11, 12; Social Studies Standards III)

Related Books

Mussi, Sarah. *The Last of the Warrior Kings*. London: Hodder Children's Books, 2008. 464p. $8.67. ISBN 0-340-90322-8.

Just a few hours after witnessing the death of Mogul King, Max's brother is dead, and Max's life is threatened as he runs through the streets of London.

Nikly, Michelle. *The Perfume of Memory.* New York: Arthur A. Levine Books, 1998. Unpaged. Illustrated by Jean Claverie. $16.95. ISBN 0-439-08206-4.

Author and Illustrator

Author Michelle Nikly was born in Algeria and grew up in Algeria, Tunisia, and Morocco. Illustrator Jean Claverie is French and lives near Lyons.

📖 Fiction, Nontraditional Picture Book, Ages 8–10

Summary

Yasmin's only wish is to become a perfume maker like her father. But the laws of her country do not allow girls to become perfume makers. The people have forgotten that once upon a time women were perfume makers. The people have also forgotten perfume formulas, birthdays, songs, how to think, and even their own history. And then one day the Queen forgets who she is. Yasmin believes that she can help! She has the scent of lilies that grew on the walls of the Queen's house and the scent of the oil that was used when the Queen became Queen. She also has the scent of the rules that the Queen signed into laws. Can Yasmin help the Queen to remember? If she does, will the Queen remember that girls must not become perfume makers?

Curriculum Responses with Curriculum Standards

1. Have children retell the story by writing a script and putting on a puppet show. (American Association of School Librarians Standards 1.1.9, 1.3.4, 2.1.6, 2.2.4, 3.1.2, 3.1.3, 3.2.1, 3.2.2, 3.2.3, 3.3.4, 3.3.5, 4.1.3, 4.1.8, 4.3.1; English Language Arts Standards 3, 4, 5, 6, 11, 12; Theater Content Standards 1, 2)

2. Call students' attention to the motif on the top of each printed page. Have them identify, compare, and analyze the geometric shapes used in the motif. Then have students design geometric motifs for their script and puppet show. (American Association of School Librarians Standards 2.1.6, 2.2.4, 3.1.2, 3.2.3, 3.3.4, 3.3.5, 4.1.3, 4.1.8; English Language Arts Standards 4, 11, 12; Visual Arts Content Standards 1, 2, 3, 4)

3. Some children might be interested in aromatherapy, the mixing of essential oils with carrier oils to produce a pleasing scent and beneficial effect. Encourage them to research and mix simple blends

such as lavender with almond oil. (American Association of School Librarians Standards 1.1.1, 1.1.6, 1.1.8, 1.1.9, 1.2.1, 1.2.2, 1.2.3, 1.4.1, 2.1.1, 2.1.4, 2.1.5, 2.1.6, 2.2.1, 2.2.4, 2.3.1, 3.3.4, 4.1.1, 4.1.2, 4.1.3, 4.1.4, 4.1.5, 4.1.8, 4.2.1, 4.2.2, 4.3.3; English Language Arts Standards 7, 8, 11)

Related Books

1. Fowles, Shelley. *The Bachelor and the Bean: A Jewish Moroccan Folk Tale*. London: Frances Lincoln Children's Books, 2007. 32p. $7.95 ISBN 0-7112-2001-8.

Younger children might enjoy the story of the grumpy old bachelor who ends up with a grumpy old wife, just because he drops a bean down a well.

2. Freedman, Russell. *The Adventures of Marco Polo*. New York: Arthur A. Levine Books, 2006. 63p. Illustrated by Bagram Ibatoulline. $17.99. ISBN 0-439-52394-X.

Illustrations reflecting the cultures that Marco Polo visited enrich this account of his travels from Venice to China by way of Constantinople, the Persian Gulf, India, Sumatra, and Vietnam.

3. Jungman, Ann. *The Most Magnificent Mosque*. London: Frances Lincoln Children's Books, 2004. Unpaged. Illustrated by Shelley Fowles. $15.95. ISBN 1-84507-012-7.

The Christian, Muslim, and Jewish people of Cordoba, Spain, save their beloved Great Mosque, built by the Moors in the eighth century, from being torn down by the new Christian King Ferdinand in the twelfth century.

4. Rumford, James. *The Traveling Man: The Journey of Ibn Battuta, 1325-1354*. Boston: Houghton Mifflin Company, 2001. Unpaged. $16.00 ISBN 0-618-08366-9.

Over one hundred years before Columbus sailed to the New World, Ibn Battuta left his home in Morocco to travel 75,000 miles to China and Russia.

5. Shulevitz. Uri. *The Travels of Benjamin of Tudela: Through Three Continents in the Twelfth Century*. New York: Farrar Straus Giroux, 2005. Unpaged. $17.00 ISBN 0-374-37754-5.

This is a fictionalized account of the true story about Benjamin of Tudela, who traveled to Rome, Constantinople, Jerusalem, Baghdad, Persia, and Egypt from his home in Spain one hundred years before Marco Polo visited China.

Quintana, Anton. *The Baboon King*. New York: Walker and Company, 1996. 183p. Translated by John Nieuwenhuizen. $16.95. ISBN 0-8027-8711-8.

Author

Author Anton Quintana grew up in Amsterdam, traveled the world as a young man, and spent a period of time in the jungles of Sumatra. This book is set in Africa. It received the Batchelder Award in 2000.

📖 Fiction, Adventure, Ages 10–14

Summary

Morengaru is part Masai and part Kikuyu. Morengaru's grandfather, Mauro, sold his daughter, Morengaru's mother, to the Masai in exchange for great wealth—all of two cows. Morengaru grew up with his father's Masai people, fearless nomadic hunters, who looked down on the boy of mixed blood. When Morengaru's life with the Masai became unbearable, he returned to his mother's people, the Kikuyu, who tilled the soil. Unfortunately, the Kikuyu did not welcome the young man of mixed blood, with the heart of a hunter, nor did Mauro welcome his grandson, who was a reminder of the evil deed by which he acquired his first wealth. When Morengaru was banished by the Kikuyu for killing a young man, he found himself utterly alone in the world, not accepted by his own people, the Masai, or the Kikuyu, and not accepted by neighboring tribes.

Curriculum Responses with Curriculum Standards

1. After reading, have students compare and contrast the life and customs of the Masai, the Kikuyu, and the baboons. (American Association of School Librarians Standards 1.1.3, 1.1.6, 1.3.4, 2.1.5, 3.1.1, 3.1.2, 3.1.3, 3.2.1, 3.2.2, 3.2.3, 3.3.1, 3.3.2, 3.3.3, 3.3.5, 4.1.1, 4.2.3, 4.3.1; English Language Arts Standards 1, 3, 4, 6, 11, 12; Social Studies Standards I, III, V, VI)
2. After reading, engage students in a discussion. How did Morengaru discover his humanity while living with the baboons? (American Association of School Librarians Standards 1.1.3, 1.1.6, 1.3.4, 2.1.5, 3.1.1, 3.1.2, 3.1.3, 3.2.1, 3.2.2, 3.2.3, 3.3.1, 3.3.2, 3.3.3, 3.3.5, 4.1.1, 4.2.3, 4.3.1; English Language Arts Standards 1, 4, 6, 11, 12; Social Studies Standards IV)
3. After reading, have students use the map in the front of the book to find Africa, Kenya, and the lands of the Masai and Kikuyo on a large map. Extend the activity by having students mark and label this area of Africa on the world map that they are creating to show the places about which they are reading. Encourage students to compare and contrast Kenya and the lands of the Masai and Kikuyo geographically, socially, and culturally, with additional areas of Africa about which they are reading, such as South Africa, Ghana, Libya, and others. (American Association of School Librarians Standards 1.1.3,

1.1.4, 1.1.5, 1.1.6, 1.3.4, 2.1.5, 3.1.1, 3.1.2, 3.1.3, 3.2.1, 3.2.2, 3.2.3, 3.3.1, 3.3.2, 3.3.3, 3.3.4, 3.3.5, 4.1.1, 4.1.2, 4.1.5, 4.1.7, 4.2.3, 4.3.1; English Language Arts Standards 1, 3, 4, 6, 11, 12; Social Studies Standards I, III, V, VI)

Stolz, Joelle. *The Shadows of Ghadames.* New York: Delacorte Press, 2004. 119p. Translated by Catherine Temerson. $15.95. ISBN 0-385-73104-3.

Author

Joelle Stolz is a French journalist who reports for *Le Monde* and Radio France Internationale in Vienna. *The Shadows of Ghadames,* which is her first children's novel, received the Batchelder Award in 2005. The setting of this book is in Southern Libya.

📖 Historical Fiction, Ages 10–13

Summary

Something awakens eleven-year-old Malika from her sleep. Bilkisu hears it too. As they look out the window, they can see that someone is being chased and is possibly injured. Although Malika protests, Bilkisu goes into the street and returns with an injured young man. In the morning, Malika's mother Meriem is horrified to learn about the injured stranger in her house. Having given him shelter, the women cannot turn him out and must keep his presence secret until he is strong enough to leave. It is the late nineteenth century in Southern Libya in the city of Ghadames. Malika will soon be of marriageable age. When she marries, she will leave her parents' home and be restricted to the women's quarters. Yet she wants to learn, and her traditional Muslim mother says no. As the stranger recovers his strength, he tutors Malika, and her world begins to change.

Curriculum Responses with Curriculum Standards

1. After reading, engage students in a discussion of how the learning that Malika acquired from Abdelkarim's tutoring changed her world. (American Association of School Librarians Standards 1.1.6, 1.1.9, 1.3.4, 2.1.1, 2.1.5, 3.1.2, 3.1.3, 3.2.1, 3.2.2, 3.2.3, 3.3.2, 3.3.5, 4.1.1, 4.1.3, 4.3.1; English Language Arts Standards 1, 3, 4, 6, 11, 12; Social Studies Standards IV)
2. Ghadames is a city on the trade route in Southern Libya near Algeria and Tunisia. The city of Tripoli was a twelve-day caravan trek to the north. After reading, encourage students to locate Ghadames and Tripoli on a map. Suggest that students Google Ghadames and

Tripoli to learn more about the city. (American Association of School Librarians Standards 1.1.6, 1.1.8, 1.1.9, 2.1.4, 2.1.6, 2.3.1, 3.1.2, 3.1.4, 3.2.3, 4.1.1, 4.1.3, 4.3.1; English Language Arts Standards 1, 2, 8, 11; Social Studies Standards III)

3. After reading, have students use descriptions in the book to create models of Malika's house and the city. (American Association of School Librarians Standards 1.1.6, 1.1.9, 1.2.3, 1.3.4, 2.1.2, 2.1.5, 2.1.6, 2.2.4, 3.1.2, 3.2.1, 3.2.3, 3.3.4, 3.3.5, 4.1.1, 4.1.3, 4.1.8; English Language Arts Standards 1, 2, 3, 6, 11, 12; Visual Arts Content Standards 1, 2)

ASIA

American, Chinese American, Chinese-Korean-American, and Chinese authors provide readers with four very different Asian perspectives. Andrea Warren is an American who adopted her Amerasian daughter via Operation Babylift, just prior to the North Vietnamese Army's entrance into Saigon. She writes a biographical account of a young Vietnamese American boy's adoption via Operation Babylift by an American family. Laurence Yep is a well-known, award-winning Chinese American Author, who carefully researched his Chinese heritage to provide readers with historical fiction accounts of Chinese culture and tradition.

Chinese-Korean-American author Janet Wong writes in verse about the contemporary experience of being American and about being Asian American. Chinese author Chen Yu, writes an autobiographical account of her experiences growing up in China during the Cultural Revolution. A Related Book, *The Diary of Ma Yan: The Struggles and Hopes of a Chinese Schoolgirl,* was selected by the United States Board on Books for Young People (USBBY) as on Outstanding International Book in 2005. Curriculum Responses include discussion of political, social, and economic conditions, as well as reader's theater, listening, art, writing, and other activities.

Warren, Andrea. *Escape from Saigon.* New York: Farrar, Straus, and Giroux, 2004. 110p. $9.95. ISBN 0-3374-40023-7.

Author

Author Andrea Warren is an American who adopted her Amerasian daughter via Operation Babylift, the U.S. government's airlift rescue of children in advance of the North Vietnamese Army's entrance into Saigon. This book is set in Vietnam and the United States.

📖 Nonfiction, Biography, Ages 11 and Up

Summary

Matt Steiner's biography begins with his birth and early childhood as Hoang-V-Long, an Amerasian child in Vietnam. Poverty and the frailties of age prompt his grandmother to leave him at the Holt Center, an orphanage for children waiting to be adopted by American families. Eight-year-old Long is one of 2,300 orphans rescued by Operation Babylift as Saigon falls to North Vietnam. The Steiners, his new family, await his arrival. Long becomes Matt and grows up as an American boy in Ohio. As an adult, Matt returns to Vietnam to rediscover his Vietnamese heritage and identity.

Photos enrich the text. In the Introduction, the author tells the story of adopting her Vietnamese daughter, who was also rescued via Operation Babylift. A Prologue gives a brief description and history of Vietnam. The Afterword includes a postscript about the people in the book, a summary of Operation Babylift, overviews of international adoption and Amerasian children, and statistics about the war in Vietnam. The book concludes with multimedia recommendations.

Curriculum Responses with Curriculum Standards

1. Long is a Vietnamese-American (Amerasian) boy. Have students discuss the development of his personal identity as Vietnamese, as American, and, finally, as Vietnamese American. (American Association of School Librarians Standards 1.1.9, 1.2.1, 1.2.5, 1.3.2, 1.3.4, 2.1.1, 2.1.3, 2.1.5, 2.2.2, 2.2.3, 2.3.2, 2.4.3, 3.1.2, 3.1.3, 3.2.1, 3.2.2, 3.3.1, 3.3.2, 3.3.5, 4.2.3, 4.3.1, 4.4.2, 4.4.3; English Language Arts Standards 11, 12; Social Studies Standards I, IV, V)

2. Have students discuss the social and economic conditions that cause Long's grandmother to place him at the Holt Center. (American Association of School Librarians Standards 1.1.9, 1.2.1, 1.2.4, 1.3.2, 1.3.4, 2.1.1, 2.1.3, 2.1.5, 2.2.2, 2.2.3, 2.3.2, 2.4.3, 3.1.2, 3.1.3, 3.2.1, 3.2.2, 3.3.1, 3.3.2, 3.3.5, 4.2.3, 4.3.1, 4.4.2, 4.4.3; English Language Arts Standards 11, 12; Social Studies Standards I, IV)

3. Have students discuss the political conditions that lead to Operation Babylift. (American Association of School Librarians Standards 1.1.9, 1.2.1, 1.2.4, 1.3.2, 1.3.4, 2.1.1, 2.1.3, 2.1.5, 2.2.2., 2.2.3, 2.3.2, 2.4.3, 3.1.2, 3.1.3, 3.2.1, 3.2.2, 3.3.1, 3.3.2, 3.3.5, 4.2.3, 4.2.1, 4.4.2, 4.4.3; English Language Arts Standards 11, 12; Social Studies Standards VI, IX)

4. Have students find Vietnam on a world map, locate the city of Saigon, trace the route of the Operation Babylift flight from Vietnam to Guam, to Hawaii, Seattle, Chicago and New York. Why was the flight route across the Pacific Ocean to New York instead of across Europe

and the Atlantic Ocean to New York and on to Chicago and Seattle? (American Association of School Librarians Standards 1.1.1, 1.1.3, 1.1.9, 1.2.5, 1.3.4, 2.1.3, 2.1.5, 2.2.1, 2.2.2, 2.2.3, 2.3.1, 3.1.2, 3.1.3, 3.2.1, 3.2.2, 3.2.3, 3.3.1, 3.3.5, 4.1.7, 4.2.3, 4.3.1, 4.4.2; English Language Arts Standards 1, 11, 12; Social Studies Standards III)

5. Use the multimedia recommendations in the back of the book to learn more about Vietnam. (American Association of School Librarians Standards 1.1.6, 1.1.8, 1.2.3, 1.3.5, 3.1.6, 3.3.1, 4.1.4, 4.1.7, 4.2.2, 4.3.2, 4.3.4; English Language Arts Standards 1, 7, 8, 11, 12; Social Studies Standards I, II, III, V, VI, IX)

Wong, Janet S. *Minn and Jake's Almost Terrible Summer.* New York: Frances Foster Books, 2008. 99p. Illustrated by Genevieve Cote. $15.00 ISBN 0-375-34977-0.

Author and Illustrator

Author Janet Wong is Chinese-Korean-American, and studied art history in France. Illustrator Genevieve Cote is French Canadian.

📖 Fiction, Poetry, Ages 8–12

Summary

Written in verse, this is the story of Jake's summer in Los Angeles. He says he wants to do nothing—no camps, no lessons, no activities. Unfortunately, his old friends have new activities that don't include him. At home, his five-year-old brother is jumping on his bed early every morning. His grandma is trying to feed him. His mom is trying to learn to play his video games. The summer drags on until Minn comes to visit. Instead of getting better, the summer gets worse, and their friendship almost comes to an end.

Curriculum Responses and Curriculum Standards

1. After reading, have students reread and discuss the two stanzas on page 24 about friendship. Do they agree? Ask them what their experiences are in talking with friends and talking with strangers? (American Association of School Librarians Standards 1.1.2, 1.1.3, 1.1.6, 1.1.9, 1.3.4, 2.1.5, 2.3.1, 3.1.2, 3.1.3, 3.2.1, 3.2.2, 3.3.1, 3.3.2, 3.3.3, 3.3.5, 4.1.1, 4.1.2, 4.1.3, 4.3.1; English Language Arts Standards 1, 3, 4, 6, 11, 12)

2. After reading, encourage students to write using the verse format in the book. (American Association of School Librarians Standards 1.1.6, 2.1.6, 2.2.4, 3.1.3, 4.1.1, 4.1.3; English Language Arts Standards 1, 3, 4, 6, 12)

3. Consider choosing Janet Wong as author of the Week/Month. Collect and display her books. Encourage students to read and respond. (American Association of School Librarians Standards 1.1.6, 4.1.1, 4.1.2, 4.2.4; English Language Arts Standards 1, 3, 4, 6, 11, 12)

Related Books

1. Janet Wong, *Before It Wriggles Away.* Katonah, NY: Richard C. Owen Publishers, 2006. 32p. $14.95. ISBN 1-572-74861-3.

Color photos and rough drafts illustrate what Janet Wong has to say about her books and poetry writing.

2. Wong, Janet S. *Minn and Jake.* New York: A Sunburst Book, 2003. 145p. Illustrated by Genevieve Cote. $6.95. ISBN 0-374-4002-0.

This is the story of Minn, the tallest girl in the class, and Jake, the shortest boy in the class, who become friends when Jake needs help, and Minn needs an after-school friend.

3. Wong, Janet S. *Night Garden: Poems from* the *World of Dreams.* 32p. New York: Aladdin Books, 2007. 32p. Illustrated by Julie Paschkis. $10.99. ISBN 1-416-96816-4.

Fourteen poems about dreams and nightmares encourage readers to write about and illustrate their own dreams.

4. Wong, Janet S. *The Rainbow Hand: Poems about Mothers and Children.* Amazon. com: Book Surge Publishing, 2008. Illustrated by Jennifer Hewitson. $12.00. ISBN 1-439-20700-3.

Children and their mothers will find their feelings and experiences voiced in this collection of poems that celebrate the connections between mothers and children.

5. Wong, Janet S. *You Have to Write.* New York: Margaret K. McElderry Books, 2002. Illustrated by Teresa Flavin. $17.00. ISBN 0-689-83409-8.

This is a motivating, inspirational source of practical ideas for young and not-so- young writers to spark up their writing topics, approaches, and points of view.

Yep, Lawrence. *Lady of Ch'iao Kuo: Warrior of the South.* New York: Scholastic Inc., 2001. 224p. $10.95. ISBN 0-439-21598-6.

Author

Author Lawrence Yep is Chinese American, has researched his Chinese identity, and is an award-winning author. This book is set in Southern China, A.D. 531.

Historic Fiction, Ages 8–14

Summary

One of the Royal Diaries series, this is the fictional diary of the young Princess Redbird, officially known as Lady of Ch'iao Kuo, who lived in Southern China from A.D. 516 to 601. Her father, who rules the Hsien people, sends her to the Chinese Colony to study with a Chinese teacher so she can learn from the Chinese and be among them as his "ears and eyes." Princess Redbird's father fears attacks on his people by the Dog Heads and by the Chinese. Although he is a brave warrior, he wants to establish peace for his people and their neighbors. When the feared attack by the Dog Heads comes, first on the Chinese Colony, and then on the Hsien, Princess Redbird proves her bravery in battle and her wisdom as a peacemaker. An Epilogue, Historical Note, Glossary of Characters, and About the Author section complete the book.

Curriculum Responses with Curriculum Standards

1. After reading, have students compare and contrast Chinese ways and culture with Hsien ways and culture. (American Association of School Librarians Standards 1.1.3, 1.1.6, 1.1.9, 1.3.4, 2.1.1, 2.1.3, 2.1.4, 2.3.1, 3.1.2, 3.1.3, 3.2.1, 3.2.2, 3.3.1, 3.3.2, 3.3.3, 3.3.5, 4.1.1, 4.1.2, 4.1.3, 4.3.1; English Language Arts Standards 1, 3, 4, 6, 11, 12; Social Studies Standards I, V)
2. Princess Redbird became known for her wisdom as a peacemaker. After reading, encourage student discussion. How did she develop that wisdom? What values and beliefs guided her thinking? (American Association of School Librarians Standards 1.1.3, 1.1.6, 1.1.9, 1.2.1, 1.3.4, 2.1.3, 2.1.5, 2.3.1, 3.1.2, 3.1.3, 3.2.1, 3.2.2, 3.3.1, 3.3.2, 3.3.5, 4.1.1, 4.1.3, 4.3.1; English Language Arts Standards 1, 2, 3, 4, 5, 11, 12; Social Studies Standards I, IV)
3. Encourage students to read the Historical Note in the back of the book to learn more about the history and origin of the Southern Chinese, about the Chinese calendar, and about Chinese measurements. Call attention to the map of China on page 291, and have students locate China on a world map. (American Association of School Librarians Standards 1.1.6, 2.3.1, 4.1.1, 4.1.2; English Language Arts Standards 1, 2, 3, 11, 12; Social Studies Standards II, III)

Related Books

1. Yep, Lawrence. *Spring Pearl: The Last Flower.* 2002. New York: American Girl, 2002. 224p. Illustrated by Kazuhiko Sano. $10.00. ISBN 1-584-85519-3.

Twelve-year-old Spring Pearl and the Sung family, who took Spring Pearl in when her parents died, get caught up in the Opium Wars in Canton, China, in 1857, when Mr. Sung, the head of the family, is arrested for being a traitor.

2. Yep, Lawrence, and Dr. Katherine Yep. *The Dragon's Child: A Story of Angel Island.* New York: HarperCollins, 2008. 144p. $15.99. ISBN 0-060-27692-8.

The story of ten-year-old Gem Lew, his travels to America with his father, and the experience of his arrival on Angel Island are based on the Author's conversations with his father and on his niece's research about their family immigration history.

3. Yep, Lawrence. *The Tiger's Apprentice: Book One.* New York: HarperCollins. 2004. 208p. $6.99. ISBN 0-060-01015-0.

In this modern-day fantasy set in San Francisco against a backdrop of Chinese folklore, culture, and mythology, Tom learns magic as an apprentice to his grandmother, and, after her death he becomes an apprentice to Mr. Hu, a shape-shifting tiger, who is the guardian of the Phoenix egg.

4. Yep, Lawrence. *Tiger's Blood: The Tiger's Apprentice Book Two.* New York: HarperCollins, 2006. 240p. $16.99. ISBN 0-060-01018-8.

As Mr. Hu's health fails, Tom assumes increasing responsibility as guardian of the Phoenix egg until the egg is stolen, and Tom must risk his life to find it.

5. Yep, Lawrence. *Tiger Magic: The Tiger's Apprentice Book Three.* New York: HarperCollins, 2006. 288p. $16.99. ISBN 0-060-01019-3.

In the conclusion of the *Tiger's Apprentice* series, Tom tries to be teacher and parent to the baby Phoenix, who believes that Tom is his mother, while Tom, Mr. Hu, and the Alliance battle the evil Lord Vattner and his forces.

Yu, Chun. *Little Green.* NY: Simon and Schuster, 2005. 112p. $15.95. ISBN 0-689-86943-6.

Author

Author Chun Yu was born in China, grew up there, and graduated from Peking University, then moved to the United States, where she now lives. This book is set in China during the Cultural Revolution.

📖 Biography, Verse Format, Ages 12 and Up

Summary

Using a poetic verse format with black and white photographs, the author writes her memoirs, an account of growing up during China's Cultural Revolution. The Cultural Revolution began shortly after she was born and ended when she was ten years old. She introduces readers to her family (father, mother, brother, little sister, and grandparents) and to her childhood during a time of turmoil, upheaval, and change. She tells of her father being sent away to be reeducated, of her mother going to work, of being left alone at night while her mother attends political meetings, of her experiences in school, and finally of Chairman Mao's death. Epilogue and Glossary complete the book.

Curriculum Responses with Curriculum Standards

1. Encourage students to read the book and prepare reader's theater presentations by selecting and reading entries of their choice. Form small groups and have each group select and read its entries. (American Association of School Librarians Standards 4.1.2, 4.1.3, 4.1.8; English Language Arts Standards 1, 3; Social Studies Standards I, III, V, VI)

2. Descriptive language lends itself to a listening and art activity. Select a passage such as "Breakfast with Taiye and Taitai" on pages 22–23. Read aloud a portion, such as the fourth verse. Tell students to listen for the images the author is creating and to create in their mind's eye an image or images that they want to recreate, using colored pencils (or crayons, paint, or colored chalk) on paper. (American Association of School Librarians Standards 2.1.6, 2.2.4, 4.1.1, 4.1.3, 4.1.8; English Language Arts Standards 1, 2, 3, 4, 12; Visual Arts Content Standards 1, 6)

3. Use as a writing model. Have students write an episode or episodes from their lives, using headings such as the headings that Chun Yu uses, e.g.: "The House," "Spring," or "My Birthday." Encourage students to write using the free verse format that Chun Yu uses. For some, it may be easier to write first in prose, and then reformat their writing from prose to free verse. (American Association of School Librarians Standards 2.1.6, 3.1.3, 4.1.3, 4.1.5; English Language Arts Standards 4, 5, 6; Social Studies Standard IV)

4. Have students discuss China's Cultural Revolution. What was it? How did it affect Little Green's life, her family, and her family's lives? (American Association of School Librarians Standards 1.3.4, 3.1.3, 3.2.1, 3.2.2, 3.3.3, 3.3.5, 4.1.3, 4.3.1; Social Studies Standards I, V, VI)

5. Encourage students to research and report on China's' Cultural Revolution by posing questions and using print and nonprint sources to gather information. (American Association of School Librarians

Standards 1.1.1, 1.1.3, 1.1.4, 1.1.5, 1.1.6, 1.1.8, 1.2.1, 1.2.2, 1.2.3, 1.2.4, 1.2.5, 1.2.6, 2.3.7, 1.3.1, 1.3.3, 1.3.4, 1.3.5, 1.4.1, 1.4.3, 1.4.4, 2.1.1, 2.1.2, 2.1.4, 2.1.5, 2.1.6, 2.2.1, 2.2.4, 2.3.1, 2.4.1, 2.4.3, 2.4.4, 3.1.1, 3.1.2, 3.1.3, 3.1.4, 3.3.3, 3.3.4, 3.3.5, 3.4.1, 4.1.4, 4.1.6, 4.1.7, 4.2.1, 4.2.2, 4.3.1, 4.3.1, 4.4.1, 4.4.3, English Language Arts Standards 1, 7, 8; Social Studies Standards I, V, VI)

Related Books

1. Compestine, Ying Chang. *Revolution Is Not A Dinner Party.* New York: Henry Holt and Company, Inc., 2007. 256p. $16.95. ISBN 0-805-08207-7.

The author writes her memoirs of growing up during China's Cultural Revolution.

2. Yan, Ma. *The Diary of Ma Yan: The Struggles and Hopes of a Chinese Schoolgirl.* New York: HarperCollins, 2005. 176p. Translated by Lisa Appignanesi. $15.99. ISBN 0-06-076496-1.

Proceeds from Ma Yan's journals, in which she recorded her determination to stay in school in remote northwest China, when she was twelve and thirteen years old, have funded scholarships for 250 other children, mostly girls, from her area of China to continue their studies.

AUSTRALIA AND NEW ZEALAND

Australian and New Zealand authors engage readers with fantasy and realistic fiction. Readers travel to exotic worlds with Australian authors Kate Constable and Garth Nix in their two fantasy series, the *Chantras of Tremaris* trilogy and *The Keys of the Kingdom* series. In *Dreamhunter,* a fantasy that appeals to older girls, written by New Zealand author Elizabeth Knox, readers make some chilling discoveries, as the mystery of The Place unfolds. *Being Bee,* by Australian author Catherine Bateson, is a coming-of-age story that appeals to girls, and *Chicken Feathers,* by New Zealand author Joy Cowley, is a gentle read that appeals to both boys and girls. The United States Board on Books for Young People (USBBY) selected Catherine Bateson's *Being Bee* as an Outstanding International Book in 2008. Retellings, board games, conversations between book characters, and map-making are only a few of the possible Curriculum Responses.

Bateson, Catherine. *Being Bee.* New York: Holiday House, 2007. 126p. $16.95. ISBN 0-8234-21104-X.

Author

Author Catherine Bateson is Australian. Her book *Being Bee* was selected by the United States Board on Books for Young People (USBBY) as an Outstanding International Book in 2008.

📖 Realistic Fiction, Ages 8–12

Summary

Bee is happy with her life until her dad's girlfriend starts changing things. First it's the cleaning. Then there is no time alone with Dad. Bee even feels left out. Worst of all, Jazzi throws out Bee's box of treasures, the few things she has left from her mom. Then Bee meets Jazzi's brother, the brother that no one knew about. Bee likes Harley, and Harley likes Bee. Even though Jazzi asks Bee not to tell anyone about her brother, Bee spills the beans by insisting that Harley be invited to the dinner party. Life begins to change again.

Curriculum Responses with Curriculum Standards

1. After reading, ask students how they would have felt if they had been Bee. What might they have done in Bee's place? Encourage discussion. (American Association of School Librarians Standards 1.1.6, 1.1.9, 1.3.4, 2.1.5, 2.3.1, 3.1.2, 3.1.3, 3.2.1, 3.2.2, 3.3.1, 3.3.2, 3.3.5, 4.1.1, 4.1.2, 4.1.3, 4.3.1; English Language Arts Standards 1, 3, 4, 6, 11, 12)

2. After reading, engage students in a discussion of Jazzi's brother Harley. Why do they think Jazzi did not tell her friends or Bee's dad that she had a brother? (American Association of School Librarians Standards 1.1.6, 1.1.9, 1.3.4, 2.1.5, 2.3.1, 3.1.2, 3.1.3, 3.2.1, 3.2.2, 3.3.1, 3.3.2, 3.3.5, 4.1.1, 4.1.2, 4.1.3 ; English Language Arts Standards 1, 3, 4, 6, 11, 12)

3. Bee wrote letters to her guinea pigs. Ask students what kind of letters they would write to their real or imaginary pets. Set aside classtime each day for writing, for several days, or for a week. Have students keep a writing journal in which they write letters to their pets. Then, for another few days, have students select letters that they are willing to share anonymously. Randomly select and distribute those letters so classmates can respond. Finally, collect and bind letters and responses together in a class book for students to read. (American Association of School Librarians Standards 1.1.6, 1.1.9, 1.3.4, 2.1.5, 2.1.6, 2.2.4, 2.3.1, 3.1.2, 3.1.3, 3.2.1, 3.2.2, 3.3.1, 3.3.2, 3.3.4, 3.3.5, 4.1.1, 4.1.2, 4.1.3, 4.1.5, 4.3.1; English Language Arts Standards 1, 3, 4, 5, 6, 11, 12)

Related Books

1. Bateson, Catherine. *Stranded in Boringsville.* New York: Holiday House, 2007. 138p. $6.95. ISBN 0-823-42113-9.

Friendship grows between twelve-year-old Rain, who moved from Melbourne to the country when her parents separated, and Daniel, who must have corrective heart surgery.

2. Bateson, Catherine. *The Boyfriend Rules of Good Behavior.* New York: Holiday House, 2006. 181p. $16.95. ISBN 0-823-42026-4.

In this coming-of-age story, not only must Millie make new friends when she and her single mother move, she must also come to terms with her mother's boyfriends.

Constable, Kate. *The Waterless Sea.* New York: Arthur A. Levine Books, 2005. 314p. $16.95. ISBN 0-439-55480-2.

Author

Author Kate Constable is Australian. She grew up in Papua, New Guinea, and now lives in Australia.

Fiction, Fantasy, Ages 10–14

Summary

In this second book of the *Chantras of Tremaris* trilogy, Calwyn and her friends sail to Merithuros, then trek across the desert, first to the Palace of Cobwebs, then on to the Black Palace in their quest to rescue the captive children who have the gift of enchantment. Darrow follows them. After the Palace of Cobwebs is destroyed, and the Black Palace is freed from the sorcerers, and Calwyn heals the land with her magical powers, Darrow, aided by the power of the evil sorcerer Samis's ruby ring, becomes the new leader. Much to his dismay, Darrow learns that Samis may still be alive. Although he wants to establish peace in Merithuros, Darrow realizes that he must go in search of Samis and destroy him.

Curriculum Responses with Curriculum Standards

1. After reading, encourage students to retell the story by creating a storyboard based on settings, characters, and events that occur in each setting. (American Association of School Librarians Standards 1.1.6, 1.1.9, 1.2.3, 1.3.4, 2.1.2, 2.1.5, 2.1.6, 2.2.4, 3.1.2, 3.1.3, 3.2.1, 3.2.2, 3.2.3, 3.3.1, 3.3.2, 3.3.5, 4.1.1, 4.1.3, 4.1.8, 4.3.1; English Language Arts Standards 1, 3, 4, 5, Visual Arts Content Standards 1, 2, 3)

2. Much travel occurs in the book. After reading, have students create a board game that traces the journey and events experienced by Calwyn and her friends. Write questions and answers about places, characters, and events. Provide an opportunity for students to play the board game. Extend the activity by developing a collection of book-related board games created by students. Place board games with the Related Books where students can access, read, and play. (American Association of School Librarians Standards 1.1.6, 1.1.9, 1.2.3, 1.3.4, 2.1.1, 2.1.2, 2.1.5, 2.1.6, 2.2.4, 3.1.2, 3.1.3, 3.2.1, 3.2.2, 3.2.3, 3.3.1, 3.3.2, 3.3.5, 4.1.1, 4.1.3, 4.1.8, 4.3.1; English Language Arts Standards 1, 3, 4, 5, 6, 11, 12; Visual Arts Content Standards 1, 2, 3)

3. After reading, encourage students to develop conversations between the characters of this book and characters in other fantasy books that students are reading. Provide opportunities for students to engage in conversations between book characters. (American Association of School Librarians 1.1.6, 1.1.9, 1.2.2, 1.2.3, 1.3.4, 2.1.5, 2.3.4, 3.1.2, 3.1.3, 3.2.1, 3.2.2, 3.2.3, 3.3.1, 3.3.2, 3.3.5, 4.1.1, 4.1.3, 4.1.8, 4.3.1; English Language Arts Standards 1, 3, 4, 11, 12)

Related Books

1. Constable, Kate. *The Singer of All Songs.* New York: Scholastic Paperbacks, 2005. 320p. $6.99. ISBN 0-439-55479-4.

In the first book of the *Chanters of Tremaris* trilogy Calwyn joins her new friend Darrow and his small band of followers in an attempt to save Tremais from the evil Sorcerer Samis, who threatens to take over the land.

2. Constable, Kate. *The Tenth Power.* New York: Scholastic Paperbacks, 2007. 320p. $5.00. ISBN 0-439-55483-7.

In the third book of the *Chanters of Tremaris* trilogy, Tremaris is trapped in never-ending winter, many of the chanters are deathly sick, and Calwyn no longer has the power to work magic, when she discovers new gifts that lead her to become the Singer of All Songs.

Cowley, Joy. *Chicken Feathers.* New York: Philomel Books, 2008. 149p. Illustrated by David Elliott. $15.99. ISBN 978-0-399-24791-0.

Author and Illustrator

Author Joy Cowley and illustrator David Elliot are both from New Zealand.

📖 Realistic Fiction, Ages 8–12

Summary

When Josh's dad shows him the chicken feathers, the blood, and the silver ring, they know what happened to Semolina. The fox got her, just as she had feared. Semolina is Josh's pet, a talking chicken, who talks only to Josh, and who likes Grandma's brew. It was she who told Josh that the fox was stealing eggs from the henhouse, and who showed him the loose board. Now Semolina's gone because Grandma wouldn't let her in the house and because Josh was careless about locking the shed door. But is she really gone? Did the fox get Semolina, or did Semolina get the fox? This book is a gentle read about a loving family, a boy, and his pet.

Curriculum Responses with Curriculum Standards

1. This book is a gentle read with thought-provoking statements interspersed throughout. Encourage children to select a statement such as, "Sad always comes with happy (page 97)" or Grandma talks about her worries, and Josh vows that "he'd never let his worries make him say mean things to people (page 107)." Ask children what they think, and engage them in a discussion. (American Association of School Librarians Standards 1.1.2, 1.1.6, 1.1.9, 1.2.1, 1.3.4, 2.1.5, 2.3.1, 3.1.2, 3.1.3, 3.2.1, 3.2.2, 3.2.3, 3.3.1, 3.3.2, 3.3.3, 3.3.5, 4.1.1, 4.1.2, 4.1.3, 4.1.5, 4.3.1; English Language Arts Standards 1, 3, 4, 6, 11, 12)

2. Josh looks for Semolina for two days after she disappears. When his father finds Semolina's feathers, ring, and blood, everyone believes that she is dead. Josh is worried, heavy-hearted, and sad. After reading, encourage children to discuss how Josh felt. Ask whether they have lost a pet, and encourage them to discuss how they felt. (American Association of School Librarians Standards 1.1.2, 1.1.6, 1.1.9, 1.3.4, 2.1.5, 2.3.1, 3.1.2, 3.1.3, 3.3.1, 3.3.2, 3.3.5, 4.1.1, 4.1.2, 4.1.3, 4.1.3, 4.3.1; English Language Arts Standards 3, 4, 6, 11, 12)

3. Dialogue, action, and descriptive text lend themselves to acting out. Have children form small groups and select scenes to act out. Sequence the acting out so that children retell the story. (American Association of School Librarians Standards 1.1.3, 1.1.6, 1.1.9, 1.2.1, 1.2.2, 1.3.4, 2.1.5, 2.1.6, 2.2.4, 3.1.2, 3.1.3, 3.2.1, 3.2.2, 3.2.3, 3.3.1, 3.3.2, 3.3.3, 3.3.4, 3.3.5, 3.4.3, 4.1.1, 4.1.3, 4.1.8, 4.3.1; English Language Arts Standards 1, 3, 4, 6, 11, 2; Theater Content Standards 1, 2)

Related Books

Cowley, Joy. *Hunter.* New York: Philomel, 2004. 154p. ISBN 0-3999-24227-9.

Jordan, a mixed-race fourteen-year-old girl in 2005, hears in her head the voice of Hunter, a runaway Maori slave in 1805, guiding her to safety after the plane that she and her brothers are riding in crashes in a remote area of New Zealand.

Knox, Elizabeth. *Dreamhunter.* New York: Francis Foster Books, 2005. 365p. $19.00. ISBN 0-374-31853-0.

Author

Author Elizabeth Knox lives in Wellington, New Zealand.

📖 Fiction, Fantasy, Ages 12 and Up

Summary

Laura's father is a dreamhunter. So is Rose's mother. Laura and her cousin Rose expect to become dreamhunters too, soon, even, in just two weeks. Both girls try, but only Laura passes. For the first time, the girls are separated. Laura is very much alone when she discovers that it is she who must unravel the mystery and overcome the evil surrounding her father's disappearance.

Curriculum Responses with Curriculum Standards

1. Engage students in a group activity. Have students create a map of The Place, the locations that Laura visited, and the events that occurred there. (American Association of School Librarians Standards 1.1.8, 1.3.4, 2.1.2, 2.1.5, 3.1.2, 3.1.4., 3.2.2, 3.2.3, 3.3.5, 4.1.3, 4.1.8; English Language Arts Standards 3, 4, 11, 12)
2. The bonds of friendship and family loyalty are strong between Laura and Rose. Have students discuss friendships and family loyalties. What are their experiences and the experiences of people in their lives? What have they read about? What do they see portrayed in the media or in the news? (American Association of School Librarians Standards 2.3.1, 3.3.5, 4.1.1, 4.1.2, 4.1.4, 4.1.5, 4.3.1; English Language Arts Standards 1, 3, 4, 6, 11, 12; Social Studies Standards IV)
3. Encourage students to identify clues as they read, predict, and then confirm the outcomes that the clues point to. (American Association of School Librarians Standards 1.1.2, 1.1.6, 1.3.4, 1.4.1, 1.4.2, 1.4.3, 2.1.1, 2.2.2, 2.2.3, 2.4.1, 3.1.2, 3.1.3, 3.2.1, 3.2.2, 3.2.3, 3.3.1, 3.3.5, 3.4.1, 4.1.1, 4.1.3, 4.2.3, 4.3.1, 4.4.3; English Language Arts Standards 1, 3, 4, 6, 11, 12)

Related Books

Knox, Elizabeth. *Dreamquake.* New York: Farrar, Straus, and Giroux, 2007. 464p. $19.00. ISBN 0-374-31854-9.

In Book Two of *The Dreamhunter Duet,* the mystery, evil, and terror that unfolded in *Dreamhunter* continues to unravel, as Laura reveals the truth through her dreams. Note: Laura's sexual desires develop in her relationship with the "sandman."

Nix, Garth. *Lady Friday.* New York: Scholastic, Inc., 2007. 304p. $6.99. ISBN 0-439-43658-3.

Author

Author Garth Nix was born and raised in Melbourne, Australia, traveled the United Kingdom, and now lives in Sydney, Australia.

📖 Fiction, Fantasy, Ages 9 and Up

Summary

In the fifth book of *The Keys to the Kingdom* series, parallel stories of Arthur and Leaf in the Middle House unfold. Leaf awakens to find herself among the sleepers, while Arthur, now Lord Arthur Rightful Heir of the Architect, is in possession of the Fourth Key. Lady Friday, Mistress of the Middle House, sends a letter of abdication to Arthur, Superior Saturday, and the Piper. Is Lady Friday sincere, or is her letter a trap? Arthur wants to return to Earth to see his family, but he must stay in the Kingdom and search for the Will. What about Leaf? Will her memories and feelings be stolen by Lady Friday? Will she be able to rescue Aunt Mango from the sleepers? The complexity of this fantasy series is such that readers who begin by reading the first book will find it much easier to follow the action and characters.

Curriculum Connections with Curriculum Standards

1. When Arthur rescues the sleepers from Lady Friday, he uses the Key to restore their memories and their happiness. As an afterthought, he also restores their sorrows. After reading, discuss with students why sorrows are important as well as happiness. (American Association of School Librarians Standards 1.1.2, 1.1.3, 1.1.6, 1.1.9, 1.2.1, 1.3.2, 2.1.5, 2.3.1, 3.1.2, 3.1.3, 3.2.1, 3.2.2, 3.2.3, 3.3.1, 3.3.2, 3.3.3, 3.3.5, 4.1.2, 4.1.3, 4.1.5, 4.3.1; English Language Arts Standards 1, 2, 3, 4, 6, 11, 12; Social Studies Standards IV)

2. While students are reading, encourage them to predict what will happen next and write down their predictions. Then have them read to confirm their predictions. (American Association of School Librarians Standards 1.1.2, 1.1.3, 1.1.6, 1.1.9, 1.2.4, 1.2.5, 1.3.2,

1.3.4, 1.4.1, 1.4.2, 1.4.3, 2.1.1, 2.1.3, 2.1.5, 2.2.2, 2.2.3, 2.4.1, 2.4.3, 3.1.1, 3.1.2, 3.1.3, 3.2.1, 3.2.2, 3.2.3, 3.3.1, 3.3.5, 3.4.1, 4.1.1, 4.1.3, 4.3.1, 4.4.3; English Language Arts Standards 1, 3, 4, 5, 6, 11, 12)

3. After reading, have students create masks for the many different characters, for example: Lady Friday, the Denizens, the Piper, the various looks of the Will, and others. (American Association of School Librarians Standards 1.1.6, 1.2.3, 2.1.6, 2.2.4, 4.1.1, 4.1.3, 4.1.8, 4.4.1; English Language Arts Standards 1, 3, 4, 11, 12; Visual Arts Content Standards 1, 2, 3)

Related Books

1. Nix, Garth. *Drowned Wednesday.* New York: Scholastic, Inc., 2005. $16.99. ISBN 0-439-70086-8.

In the third book in the *Keys of the Kingdom* series, Arthur, who has a broken leg and suffers from asthma, is adrift on the Border Sea, where he must rescue Leaf and the denizens from Feverfew.

2. Nix, Garth. *Grim Tuesday.* New York: Scholastic, Inc., 2005. $16.99. ISBN 0-439- 70370-0.

In the second book in the *Keys of the Kingdom* series, Arthur must fight to gain possession of the second key in order to save his home on Earth.

3. Nix, Garth. *Mister Monday.* New York: Scholastic, Inc., 2005. $16.99. ISBN 0-439-70369-7.

In the first book in the *Keys of the Kingdom* series, mysterious events begin, and mysterious characters appear when Arthur wakes from a dream with a mysterious key in his hand.

4. Nix, Garth. *Sir Thursday.* New York: Scholastic, Inc., 2006. $16.99. ISBN 0-4389-70087-6.

In the fourth book in the *Keys of the Kingdom* series, Arthur wants to return home to Earth, but must join Sir Thursday's army to fight against the Nithlings, while a Nithling disguised as Arthur infects Earth with a mind-control disease.

5. Nix, Garth. *Superior Saturday.* New York: Scholastic, Inc., 2008. 336p. $17.99. ISBN 0-439-700089-2.

In the sixth book of the *Keys of the Kingdom* series, Arthur defeats five of the evil Trustees of the Will, takes their keys, and now faces Superior Saturday and her powerful sorcerers.

CANADA

Four Canadian authors write realistic fiction and fantasy, and another writes a biographical graphic novel. Sarah Ellis tells the story of twelve-year-old Kip, who learns more about his deceased father and comes to terms with his mother's remarriage and his new step-father. L. M. Montgomery tells the story of Anne, the young orphan girl, who finds a new home and a new life with Marilla Cuthbert and her brother Matthew. Tim Wynne-Jones writes about Rex Norton-Norton, called Rex Zero by his new friends, who has to make a new life in Ottawa after moving across Canada from Vancouver. Jamieson Findlay offers a change of pace with his fantasy about Syeira and the wild horses from Arva. Finally, Nicolas Debon writes a graphic novel about the strongman and circus owner Louis Cyr. Three books, two by Tim Wynne-Jones and one by Nicolas Debon, were selected by the United States Board on Books for Young People (USBBY) as Outstanding International Books for Young People in 2007 and 2008. Curriculum Responses include writing and illustrating a class book, creating a game show, retelling by creating a storyboard, and other activities.

Debon, Nicolas. *The Strongest Man in the World: Louis Cyr.* Toronto: Groundwood Books, 2007. 27p. $17.95. ISBN 0-88899-731-0.

Author

Author Nicolas Debon was born and educated in France, spent ten years in Canada, where he worked for the French consulate in Toronto, became a Canadian citizen, and then returned to France, where he now lives. His book, *The Strongest Man in the World: Louis Cyr,* was selected by the United States Board on Books for Young People (USBBY) as an Outstanding International Book in 2008.

📖   Biography, Graphic Novel, Ages 8–12

Summary

This illustrated biography of Louis Cyr, written as a graphic novel, is told from the perspective of Louis Cyr, who is talking to his daughter Emiliana. The book opens with a picture of the circus wagons surrounding the circus tent and a voice warning Louis St. Cyr that he must take care of himself. As he looks back on his life, he remembers his childhood and his family: his mother, a tall, strong woman; his grandfather, the strongest man in the area, who urged him to eat and be strong. Louis became a weight-lifting champion at the age of seventeen by lifting a horse off the ground. From then on Louis continued to win competitions until he became the strongest man in the world. He traveled with the circus until he founded his own, the Louis St. Cyr Circus. The Afterward adds information and photos to the text. Endpapers show advertising posters of other strong men of the time.

Curriculum Responses with Curriculum Standards

1. After reading, students might enjoy engaging in weight-lifting contests among themselves. Have them plan the contests and identify the weights or objects that they will lift. (American Association of School Librarians Standards 1.1.6, 1.1.9, 1.2.2, 1.3.4, 2.1.5, 2.3.1, 3.1.2, 3.2.1, 3.2.2, 3.2.3, 3.3.1, 3.3.2, 3.3.5, 4.1.1, 4.1.3, 4.1.8, 4.3.1; English Language Arts Standards 1, 11)

2. After reading, encourage students to research information about the weight-lifters and circus performers featured in the endpapers and report their findings to their classmates. (American Association of School Librarians Standards 1.1.1, 1.1.2, 1.1.3, 1.1.4, 1.1.5, 1.1.6, 1.1.7, 1.1.9, 1.2.2, 1.2.3, 1.2.7, 1.3.4, 2.1.1, 2.1.3, 2.1.5, 2.3.4, 2.3.1, 3.1.1, 3.1.2, 3.1.3, 3.2.1, 3.2.2, 3.3.1, 3.3.2, 3.3.3, 3.3.5, 4.1.1, 4.1.2, 4.1.3, 4.3.1; English Language Arts Standards 1, 3, 4, 6, 11, 12)

3. Engage students in a discussion about the circus. Ask how many have gone to a circus. What do they know about the circus? How has the circus changed since Louis St. Cyr was a performer? Encourage students to research further information and share their findings with their classmates. (American Association of School Librarians Standards 1.1.1, 1.1.2, 1.1.3, 1.1.4, 1.1.5, 1.1.6, 1.1.9, 1.2.2, 1.3.4, 2.1.1, 2.1.5, 2.2.4, 2.3.1, 3.1.1, 3.1.2, 3.1.3, 3.2.1, 3.2.2, 3.2.3, 3.3.1, 3.3.2, 3.3.3, 3.3.5, 4.1.1, 4.1.2, 4.1.3, 4.1.4, 4.1.5, 4.3.1; English Language Arts Standards 1, 3, 4, 6, 11, 12)

Related Books

1. Debon, Nicolas. *A Brave Soldier.* Toronto: Groundwood Books, 2002. 32p. $4.87. ISBN 0-888-99481-8.

When two young Canadian boys, Frank and his friend Michael, go off to France to fight in the first World War, they discover that war is not easy, and that they'll not be home by Christmas.

2. Debon, Nicolas. *Four Pictures by Emily Carr.* Toronto: Groundwood Books, 2007. 40p. $6.95. ISBN 0-888-99814-7.

This biography of Canadian artist Emily Carr (1871–1945) based on her journals, shows her development as a painter over four periods of her life.

3. Zemlieka, Shannon, Florence Zemlieka, and Shannon Knudsen. *Florence Nightingale.* Lerner Publishing Group, 2003. Minneapolis, MN: 48p. Illustrated by Nicolas Debon. $6.95. ISBN0-876-14102-5.

This illustrated biography of Florence Nightingale, who was a pioneer in women's nursing, tells about her early life, her hospital work in the Crimea, and her school for nurses.

Ellis, Sarah. *Odd Man Out.* Toronto: Groundwood Books, 2006. 162p. $6.95. ISBN 0-88899-703-6.

Author

Author Sarah Ellis is Canadian. This book is set in Canada.

📖　Realistic Fiction, Ages 10–14

Summary

Twelve-year-old Kip is an imaginative writer. He creates spy mysteries and mysterious worlds. This summer with Gran and his cousins, Kip discovers and unravels a mystery. While his mother and new stepfather honeymoon in Hawaii, Kip spends a month with his grandmother and five girl cousins. Because Gran's house is about to be torn down, Kip and the girls are allowed to write on and even demolish the walls. Cousin Emily thinks she is a dog. Jane and Daffodil think they are ballerinas. They also think they are twins. Alice is the girl sitting on the ladder. Hilary is the tall girl. To escape the "girlatorium," Kip claims the attic room for himself. There he creates his own world and uncovers secrets of his father.

Curriculum Responses with Curriculum Standards

1. After reading, see page 128 and engage students in a discussion of the following line. "The gracious relinquishing of power can be a great source of personal strength." What do you suppose Gran means? Ask students whether they know of anyone who has graciously relinquished power. Ask students whether this line has any meaning in their lives. (American Association of School Librarians Standards; English Language Arts Standards 1, 2, 3, 4, 6, 11, 12; Social Studies Standards IV, VI)
2. As students read, encourage them to record meaningful lines as Philosophical Gems. Provide opportunities for students to share with their classmates the lines they selected and what the lines mean to them. (American Association of School Librarians Standards 1.1.6, 1.3.4, 2.1.2, 2.1.6, 2.2.4, 2.3.1, 3.1.1, 3.1.2, 3.1.3, 3.2.1, 3.2.2, 3.3.1, 3.3.2, 3.3.5, 4.1.1, 4.1.2, 4.1.3, 4.1.4, 4.1.5,

4.1.6, 4.1.7, 4.3.1; English Language Arts Standards 1, 2, 3, 4, 5, 6, 11, 12)

3. After reading, encourage students to discuss Kip's feelings about his father's death, his feelings about his new stepfather, and his relationship with his mother. (American Association of School Librarians Standards 1.1.2, 1.1.6, 1.1.9, 1.2.1, 1.3.2, 1.3.4, 2.1.5, 2.3.1, 3.1.2, 3.1.3, 3.2.1, 3.2.2, 3.3.1, 3.3.2, 3.3.3, 3.3.5, 4.1.1, 4.1.2, 4.1.3, 4.1.4, 4.1.5, 4.2.3, 4.3.1; English Language Arts Standards 1, 2, 3, 4, 6, 11, 12; Social Studies Standards IV)

Related Books

1. Ellis, Sarah. *Out of the Blue.* Toronto: Groundwood Books, 2001. 120p. $5.95. ISBN 0-888-99236-X.

Twelve-year-old Megan discovers that she has a new sister, when her mother rediscovers the child she gave up for adoption when the mother was seventeen.

2. Ellis, Sarah. *Pick-Up Sticks.* Toronto: Groundwood Books, 2001. 124p. $7.95. ISBN 0-888-99162-2.

Thirteen-year-old Polly discovers what is important to her life when she goes to live with her affluent uncle.

3. Ellis, Sarah. *The Several Lives of Orphan Jack.* Toronto: Groundwood Books, 2005. 88p. Illustrated by Bruno St. Alban. $7.95. ISBN 0-888-99618-7.

Twelve-year-old Jack leaves the Opportunities School for Orphans and Foundlings with his treasured dictionary to find his calling, not as a book-keeper but as an "ideas peddler."

Findlay, Jamieson. *The Blue Roan Child.* NY: Chicken House, 2004. 252p. $16.95. ISBN 0-439-62752-4.

Author

Author Findlay Jamieson is Canadian. This book was first published in the United Kingdom.

📖 Fiction, Fantasy, Ages 9–12

Summary

The horses are her family. Syeira was born in the king's stables, lives there, and works there, even though her mother has died. She has her favorites, especially the three wild horses from Arva, the blue roan and her two colts. Syeria's journey with Arwin, the blue roan, begins when Lord Ran buys the two colts from the king and takes them from their mother. Syeira rides Arwin from Haysele, across the dark cold river to Braywick and Withers, through the Forest of Deire and Storm Sythe to the ancient city of Thurck-port, where Lord Ran stables his horses before boarding them on his ship and sailing across the Grey Sea. Syeira must now devise a plan to rescue Arwin's colts and escape to safety.

Curriculum Responses with Curriculum Standards

1. This book is filled with vivid and colorful descriptions. After read-ing, have students select scenes of their choice, create pictures using the media of their choice, and then share with classmates and orally describe the scenes that they have recreated. Extend the activity by having students add in their own words written descriptions of the scenes, identify a page or pages, and then combine them sequen-tially into a class book. (American Association of School Librarians Standards 1.1.6, 1.1.9, 1.2.2, 1.2.3, 1.3.4, 2.1.5, 2.1.6, 2.2.4, 3.1.2, 3.1.3, 3.2.1, 3.2.2, 3.2.3, 3.3.5, 4.1.1, 4.1.3, 4.1.8, 4.3.1; English Language Arts Standards 1, 3, 4, 5, 6, 11, 12; Visual Arts Content Standards 1, 3)

2. Syeira forms a strong, unspoken bond with Arwin. Engage students in a discussion of bonds that they have formed with a pet, a family member, a friend, or a teacher. (American Association of School Librarians Standards 1.1.9, 1.3.4, 2.1.5, 2.3.1, 3.1.2, 3.1.3, 3.2.1, 3.2.2, 3.3.2, 3.3.3, 3.3.5, 4.1.3, 4.1.5, 4.3.1; English Language Arts Standards 3, 4, 6, 11, 12)

3. After reading, have students retell the story by creating a storyboard of settings, characters, and events. (American Association of School Librarians Standards 1.1.6, 1.1.9, 1.2.2, 1.2.3, 1.3.4, 2.1.2, 2.1.5, 2.1.6, 2.3.4, 3.1.2, 3.1.3, 3.2.1, 3.2.2, 3.2.3, 3.3,4, 3.3.5, 4.1.1, 4.1.3, 4.1.8, 4.3.1; English Language Arts Standards 1, 3, 4, 5, 6, 11, 12)

4. Much of the vocabulary is likely to be new to students: such terms include batterjack, fletcher, scrabbled, and others. Encourage students to make a list of new words as they read. Be sure that they record the new words as used in context. Have them find and record mean-ings, and then create a game-show using the new words. (American Association of School Librarians Standards 1.1.1, 1.1.6, 1.1.9, 1.2.2, 1.2.3, 1.3.4, 2.1.2, 2.1.5, 2.1.6, 2.3.4, 2.3.1, 3.1.2, 3.1.3, 3.2.1, 3.2.2, 3.2.3, 2.3.4, 2.3.5, 4.1.1, 4.1.3, 4.1.4, 4.1.5, 4.1.7, 4.1.8, 4.3.1; Eng-lish Language Arts Standards 1, 3, 4, 5, 6, 11, 12)

5. Smells figure prominently in the book. Engage students in a dis-cussion. How are smells important to the horses and Syeira? How are smells important in students' lives? (American Association of

School Librarians Standards 1.1.2, 1.1.3, 1.1.9, 1.3.4, 2.3.1, 3.1.2, 3.1.3, 3.2.1, 3.2.2, 3.3.5, 4.1.3, 4.1.5, 4.3.1; English Language Arts Standards 3, 4, 6, 11, 12)

Montgomery, L. M. *Anne of Green Gables.* New York: Putnam Adult, 2008. 320p. $19.95. ISBN 0-486-42239-9.

Author

Author Lucy Maud Montgomery is Canadian. She was born and raised in the maritime province of Prince Edward Island, which is the setting of her books about Anne Shirley.

📖 Realistic Fiction, Ages 8–12

Summary

Matthew Cuthbert and his sister Marilla request a boy from the orphanage to help them as they are getting older. They are surprised and disappointed to receive a girl, and they even consider sending her back to the orphanage. So begins Anne Shirley's life on Prince Edward Island. Anne is an eleven-year-old orphan, an imaginative, spirited red-head, when she comes to live with Matthew and Marilla. A series of eight books tells the story of how she grew into young womanhood, became a teacher, went off to college, married her school friend Gilbert, who had taunted and teased her as a child, and raised six children.

Curriculum Responses with Curriculum Standards

1. Call students' attention to Anne's use of words, phrases, and statements such as "scope for the imagination," or "But the worst of imagining things is that the time comes when you have to stop, and that hurts." Encourage students to keep a journal of Philosophical Gems in which they record significant phrases or statements of their choice with a personally meaningful paraphrase. Provide opportunities for students to share their significant phrases or statements and paraphrases with their classmates. (American Association of School Librarians Standards 1.3.1, 2.1.1, 2.1.6, 2.2.4, 2.3.1, 2.4.3, 3.1.1, 3.1.2, 3.1.3, 3.2.1, 3.2.2, 3.3.5, 4.1.1, 4.1.2, 4.1.3, 4.1.4, 4.1.5, 4.1.7, 4.2.2, 4.3.3, 4.4.4; English Language Arts Standards 3, 4, 5, 6, 9, 11, 12)

2. Encourage students to add to their journals significant phrases or statements used by people around them, or from song lyrics, favorite television programs, and other books. (American Association of School Librarians Standards 1.1.6, 1.2.2, 1.3.4, 2.1.6, 2.2.4, 2.3.1,

3.1.3, 3.2.1, 3.2.2, 3.3.1, 3.3.2, 3.3.4, 3.3.5, 4.1.1, 4.1.4, 4.1.5, 4.1.7, 4.2.1, 4.2.2, 4.2.4, 4.3.3, 4.4.4; English Language Arts Standards 4, 5, 6, 9, 11, 12)

3. Prepare a class book, a bulletin board, or a display for the school library by having students select and write their favorite phrases and statements using calligraphy. (American Association of School Librarians Standards 1.1.9, 1.2.2, 1.2.3, 1.3.4, 2.1.2, 2.1.6, 2.2.4, 3.1.2, 3.1.3, 3.2.1, 3.2.3, 3.3.1, 3.3.2, 3.3.4, 3.3.5, 4.1.3, 4.1.8; English Language Arts Standards 4, 5, 6, 11, 12)

4. Encourage interested students to read additional books in the series about Anne, to read related resources, or to view the DVDs. (American Association of School Librarians Standards 1.1.6, 1.2.2, 4.1.1, 4.1.2, 4.2.4; English Language Arts Standards 1, 2)

5. Extend the activity by having students read about and discuss the experience of orphans in the early 1900s, as described in the beginning of the book and in *We Rode the Orphan Train.* (American Association of School Librarians Standards 1.1.6, 1.1.4, 2.1.5, 3.1.3, 3.3.5, 4.1.1, 4.1.2, 4.2.4, 4.3.1, 4.4.4; English Language Arts Standards 1, 2, 4, 6, 11, 12; Social Studies Standards II, V)

Related Books

1. Collins, Carolyn Strom and Christina Wyss Erickson. *The Anne of Green Gables Treasure—Special Edition Commemorating the 100th Anniversary of Anne of Green Gables, 1908–2008.* St. Paul, MN: Ingleside Impressions: Special Commemorative Edition, 2008. 168p. $19.95. ISBN 0-981-67340-6.

Step into Anne's world by learning how to prepare a tea party with recipes, create Anne's garden and handicrafts, and view maps, photographs, and floor plans of Green Gables, and more.

2. McDonald, Kate, and L. M. Montgomery. *The Anne of Green Gables Cookbook.* Mississauga, ON. CA: Seal Books 1988. 48p. Illustrated by Barbara Di Lella. $3.16. ISBN 0-770-42258-6.

The author, who is L. M. Montgomery's granddaughter, has compiled twenty-five simple recipes and directions including Marilla's Plum Pudding and a nonalcoholic version of Diana Barry's Favorite Raspberry Cordial.

3. Warren, Andrea. *We Rode the Orphan Trains.* Sandpiper, 2004. 144p. $9.95. ISBN 0-618-43235-3.

The author interviews eight adults, who as children rode the orphan trains as part of the "outplacing" program of the Children's Aid Society of New York City (1854–1929), in which young children with no families or families who could not care for them were placed on the trains, and traveled west to families who would take them in as workers.

Wynne-Jones, Tim. *Rex Zero and The End of the World.* New York: Farrar, Straus and Giroux, 2007. 186p. $16.00. ISBN 0-274-33467-6.

Author

Tim Wynne-Jones is a Canadian award-winning author who was born in London and grew up in British Columbia and Ontario. *Rex Zero and the End of the World,* and its sequel *Rex Zero, King of Nothing,* were selected by United States Board on Books for Young People (USBBY) as Outstanding International Books for Young People in 2007 and 2008 respectively. Ottawa, Ontario, is the setting for the books about Rex.

📖 Realistic Fiction, Ages 9–12

Summary

Ten-year-old Rex's friends call him "Rex Zero," because they say his hyphenated last name, Norton-Norton, means Norton minus Norton equals Zero. Is the end of the world really coming at noon on October 23, as Dump Orbit says? Maybe! It is summer 1962, when Rex and his family (Mom, Dad, four sisters: Cassiopeia, Letitia, Annie Oakley, Flora Bella, and one brother, Rupert the Sausage) move across Canada from Vancouver to Ottawa. Rex needs to learn French, the Russians have recently launched Sputnik, people are building bomb shelters, the Cuban missile crisis threatens, and Kathy Brown says there is a panther loose in Adams Park. British terminology, French dialogue, similes, metaphors, and puns enrich the language of this book.

Curriculum Responses with Curriculum Standards

1. After reading, build on the language of the book by encouraging students to identify British word usage and by helping them to translate the French dialogue. Discuss with students why British and French language would be appropriate to this story, set in Ottawa, Ontario, Canada. (American Association of School Librarians Standards 1.1.6, 1.3.4, 2.1.3, 2.1.5, 2.3.1, 3.1.2, 3.1.3, 3.2.1, 3.2.2, 3.3.5, 4.1.1, 4.1.2, 4.3.1; English Language Arts Standards 1, 3, 4, 6, 9, 11, 12)
2. After reading, using similes, metaphors, and puns from the book as models, encourage students to use them in their own writing. (American Association of School Librarians Standards 1.1.6, 2.1.6, 2.2.4, 3.1.3, 4.1.1, 4.1.3; English Language Arts Standards 1. 3, 4, 5,

6, 9, 11, 12)3. Rex says that his life is like a board game. After reading, encourage students to develop a board game with game board, directions, written questions and answers based on this book. (American Association of School Librarians Standards 1.1.6, 1.1.9, 1.2.3, 1.3.4, 2.1.5, 2.1.6, 2.2.4, 3.1.2, 3.1.3, 3.2.1, 3.2.2, 3.2.3, 3.3.4, 3.3.5, 4.1.1, 4.1.3, 4.1.6, 4.1.8, 4.3.1; English Language Arts Standards 1, 3, 4, 5, 6, 11, 12)

Related Books

1. Wynne-Jones, Tim. *The Book of Changes.* New York: Puffin, 1997. 160p. $6.95. ISBN 0-140-38072-8.

Seven unrelated short stories set in Ontario, about ordinary events such as a class project and a class bully, take unusual twists.

2. Wynne-Jones, Tim. *The Boy in the Burning House.* New York: Farrar, Straus, and Giroux, 2003. 224p. $6.95. ISBN 0-374-40887-4.

Humor, suspense, and heavy topics of possible murder and suicide entwine with the struggles fourteen-year-old Jim and his mother face following the disappearance of Jim's father.

3. Wynne-Jones, Tim. *Rex Zero, King of Nothing.* New York: Farrar, Straus, and Giroux, 2008. 224p. $16.95. ISBN 0-374-36259-9.

In this sequel to *Rex Zero and the End of the World,* Rex's coming of age adventures continue as he moves into sixth grade with a new set of mysteries to solve.

CROSS COUNTRIES AND CULTURES

Many books are international in that the author, illustrator, and setting of the book represent different countries and cultures; for example, Louise Borden's *The Greatest Skating Race,* Ralph Helfer's *Mosey: The Remarkable Friendship of a Boy and His Elephant,* and Philip Pullman's *Aladdin and the Enchanted Lamp.* In other cases stories, myths, and legends from a number of different countries and cultures are collected into one book, such as in Geraldine McCaughrean's *Starry Tales.* Then there is the nonfiction series *Insiders.* Books are about topics such as space, oceans, dinosaurs, and other matters. Authors of the books are experts in their fields and are from different countries. Geraldine McCaughrean and Philip Pullman are both international award–winning authors who had books selected as Outstanding International Books by the United States Board on Books for Young People (USBBY) in 2006. Curriculum Responses include mathematics, science, theater, and drama, as well as research, retelling, and other activities.

Borden, Louise. *The Greatest Skating Race.* New York: Margaret K. McElderry Books, 2004. 44p. Illustrated by Niki Daly. $18.95. ISBN 0-689-84502-2.

Author and Illustrator

Author Louise Borden is American. Illustrator Niki Daly is South African. The story is set in the Netherlands and Belgium during World War II.

📖 Realistic Fiction, Verse Format, Picture Book, Ages 9–12

Summary

It is 1942, the second winter of World War II. Ten-year-old Piet loves to skate and dreams of skating the Elfstedentocht (Eleven Town Race), like Pim Hubies. Piet's opportunity to skate and to be brave comes after the father of his nine-year-old friend Johanna is arrested by Germans for having a hidden radio. Johanna's mother decides that for safety she will send Johanna and her seven-year-old brother Joop to an aunt who lives in Bruegge (Belgium). Piet's grandfather tells Piet that he must skate to Bruegge with Johanna and Joop. The text is tightly written, using a lean, spare, lyrical verse format. The author includes brief histories of the Elfstedentocht and skating, with a pronunciation guide and definitions at the bottoms of the pages. The frontispiece shows a map of Europe in 1942.

Curriculum Responses with Curriculum Standards

1. Mother told Piet, "This is what it means to be Dutch, . . . Not only to love skating on our canals, but also to be brave in our hearts." (p12) After reading, ask students why a love of skating on the canals is part of being Dutch. Have students find the Netherlands on a map. Where is it located? Why are the canals important? (American Association of School Librarians Standards 1.1.1, 1.1.2, 1.1.4, 1.1.6, 2.1.5, 2.3.1, 2.4.3, 3.3.5, 4.1.2, 4.1.3, 4.3.1; English Language Arts Standards 1, 3, 4, 6, 11, 12; Social Studies Standards I, III, IV)

2. After reading, lead a class discussion on bravery. What does it mean to be "brave in our hearts?" How did Piet become brave in his heart? Have you ever had to be brave in your heart? What is it to be brave? Ask children to recall their own or others' experiences, including experiences they have read about or know about from the media. List characteristics and examples of bravery; then have children write a Prescription for Bravery. Using the book as a model, have the children write using free verse. (American Association of School Librarians Standards 1.1.2, 1.1.3, 1.1.6, 1.1.9, 1.3.4, 2.1.5, 2.1.6, 2.3.1, 2.4.3, 3.1.3, 3.3.5, 4.1.3, 4.3.1; English

Language Arts Standards 1, 3, 4, 6, 11, 12; Social Studies Standards IV)

3. Use the 1942 map of Europe in the frontispiece as a guide. Have children find Friesland and Brussels on a map of Europe. Then have children draw their own maps, showing the route along which the children skated. (American Association of School Librarians Standards 1.1.1, 1.1.6, 2.1.2, 2.1.6, 2.2.4, 2.3.1, 3.3.4, 4.1.3; English Language Arts Standards 1, 3, 4, 6, 11, 12; Social Studies Standards III)

Related Books

1. Dodge, Mary Mapes. *Hans Brinker or The Silver Skates.* New York: Cosimo Classics, 2005. 244p. Illustrated by Alice Casey. $16.95. ISBN 1-596-05415-8.

In this replica of the 1917 edition of a well loved story first published in 1865, two Dutch children, Hans and his sister, Gretel, wear their wooden skates to compete in a race on the frozen canal against skaters wearing fine steel blades.

2. Lunge-Larsen, Lise. *The Race of the Birkebeiners.* Boston, Houghton Mifflin Company, 2001. Unpaged. Illustrated by Mary Azarian. $16.00. ISBN 0-618-10313-9.

The Birkebeiner, a crosscountry ski race, has its origins on Christmas Eve, A.D. 1206, in the town of Lillehammer, Norway, where the infant prince Hakon and his mother meet eight Birkebeiners, who ski them across the stormy, snowcapped mountains to the safety and protection of the Birkebeiner chieftains.

3. Miller, Debbie S. *The Great Serum Race: Blazing the Iditarod Trail.* New York: Walker Books for Young Readers, 2006. 40p. Illustrated by Jon Van Zyle. $8.95. ISBN 0-802-77723-2.

The 1000-mile dogsled relay of serum through severe winter conditions from Anchorage to Nome, Alaska, to save the children in the 1925 diphtheria epidemic serves as the inspiration for the Iditarod Dogsled race run each year in March from Anchorage to Nome, Alaska.

4. Borden, Louise. *The Little Ships: The Heroic Rescue at Dunkirk in World War II.* New York: Aladdin, 2003. Unpaged. Illustrated by Michael Foreman. $6.99. ISBN 0-689-85396-3.

A little girl wearing her father's cap and her brother's trousers sails with the men who man the large ships and small boats to rescue the French and British soldiers waiting on the beaches at Dunkirk.

5. Borden, Louise. *Sea Clocks: The Story of Longitude.* New York: Margaret K. McElderry Books, 2004. Unpaged. Illustrated by Erik Blegvad. $18.95. ISBN 0-689-84216-3.

John Harrison develops the sea clock, a large watch that enables sailors to determine the exact longitude of their ships while they are at sea.

Dyer, Alan. *INSIDERS: Space.* New York: Simon and Schuster Books for Young Readers, 2007. 64p. $16.99. ISBN 1-4169-3860-5.

Author

Author Alan Dyer is a Canadian astronomer and philosopher. *Space* is one of several titles in the *INSIDERS* Series written by recognized experts in their fields from countries such as Canada, England, Australia, and the United States.

📖 Nonfiction, Ages 9–12

Summary

Simple, informative, fact-filled text and colorful, realistic graphics introduce readers to origins of the universe, objects in space, space exploration, the solar system, stars, and galaxies. Each two-page spread focuses on a specific topic, such as the Big Bang, a Spacesuit, Saturn, and others. A Glossary at the end of the book alphabetically lists and defines technical terms.

Curriculum Responses with Curriculum Standards

1. Use this book as a reference in conjunction with a unit on astronomy or space exploration. Clear, specific illustrations will aid students in visualizing and understanding information and concepts. The Glossary will enhance comprehension. (American Association of School Librarians Standards 1.1.6, 4.1.1, 4.1.2, 4.1.4, 4.2.4; English Language Arts Standards 1, 3, 7; Life Science Standards)

2. Encourage students to develop questions about space and space exploration, then go to the Web site of the National Aeronautics and Space Agency (NASA) (www.//nasa.gov) to research more information. Provide opportunities for students to share their findings with their classmates. If you live near a NASA Visitor Center, plan to take students on a field trip or encourage them to visit such a center with their families and friends. Ask students to report back to classmates about their visit. (American Association of School Librarians Standards 1.1.1, 1.1.2, 1.1.3, 1.1.4, 1.1.5, 1.1.6, 1.1.7, 1.1.8, 1.1.9, 1.2.2, 1.2.3, 1.2.4, 1.2.7, 1.3.4, 1.3.5, 2.1.1, 2.1.2, 2.1.3, 2.1.4, 3.1.1, 3.1.2, 3.1.3, 3.1.6, 3.2.1, 3.2.2, 3.3.3, 3.3.5, 4.1.2, 4.1.7, 4.3.1;

English Language Arts Standards 1, 4, 6, 7, 8, 11, 12; Life Science Standards)

3. Have students begin their studies by creating a KWL Chart. (What do we Know? What do we Want to know? What did we Learn?) Have them record their knowledge, questions, and learning by completing the chart as they go along. (American Association of School Librarians Standards 1.1.2, 1.1.3, 1.3.4, 2.1.2, 2.1.4, 2.1.5, 2.1.6, 2.2.4, 2.3.1, 2.4.3, 3.1.1, 3.1.2, 3.1.3, 3.1.4, 3.2.1, 3.2.2, 3.2.3, 3.3.4, 3.3.5, 4.1.5, 4.1.6, 4.1.7, 4.2.1, 4.3.1; English Language Arts Standards 4, 5, 6, 11, 12)

Related Books

1. Long, John. *INSIDERS: Dinosaurs.* New York: Simon and Schuster Books for Young Readers, 2007. 64p. ISBN 1-4169-3857-5.

Find in these pages everything you want to know about dinosaurs: the different kinds, how they lived, when they lived, and how we learn what we know about them.

2. McMillan, Beverly. *INSIDERS: Oceans.* New York: Simon and Schuster Books for Young Readers, 2007. 64p. $16.99. ISBN 1-4169-3859-1.

Informative text and graphics depict ocean life and explorations, plants, and animals along the shorelines and in the depths, and more.

3. Rubin, Ken. *INSIDERS: Volcanoes & Earthquakes.* New York: Simon and Schuster Books for Young Readers, 2007. ISBN 1-1469-3860-5.

Detailed information, 3-D illustrations, and glossary provide an easily understandable reference about volcanoes and earthquakes.

4. Seidensticker, John, and Susan Lumpkin. *INSIDERS: Predators.* New York: Simon and Schuster Books for Young Readers, 2008. ISBN 1-1469-3863-X.

Informative text and vivid 3-D illustrations provide readers with an abundance of data about different kinds of predators.

5. Tyldesley, Joyce. *INSIDERS: Egypt.* New York: Simon and Schuster Books for Young Readers, 2007. 64p. $16.99. ISBN 1-4169-3858-3.

Explore every aspect of ancient Egyptian civilization, including pyramid building and the chambers of King Tut's tomb.

Helfer, Ralph. *Mosey: The Remarkable Friendship of a Boy and His Elephant.* New York: Scholastic Press, 2002. 144p. $16.95. ISBN 0-439-29313-8.

Author

Author Ralph Helfer is an American animal trainer, who uses affection and kindness to train wild animals. He lives in Los Angeles and in Kenya, where he leads wildlife safaris. The author purchased Mosey in the 1970s, and owned the elephant during its last 20 years of life. The story of Mosey begins in Germany and ends in The United States.

📖 Nonfiction, Ages 12 and up

Summary

This is a true story of the bonds of love and friendship between the elephant Modoc, affectionately known as Mosey, and her young trainer, Bram Gunterstein. Mosey and Bram were born on the same day in 1896 into a circus family in Germany. Bram's father trains Mosey and teaches Bram to be his assistant. As Bram's father is dying, he tells Bram to take care of Mosey. However, the circus is being sold, and the new owner has his own animal trainers. When Mosey and the circus animals are taken aboard ship for the voyage to America, Bram steals aboard as a stowaway. A hurricane destroys the ship in the Indian Ocean as it heads toward India to deliver its cargo to Calcutta. The crew is rescued, but Bram chooses to stay adrift with Mosey until a larger boat can come for them. They are rescued as they begin to drown. The Epilogue describes how Mosey and Bram stay in India until the circus owner finds them. From India, Mosey and Bram travel on and eventually arrive in the United States.

Curriculum Responses with Curriculum Standards

1. After reading, engage students in a discussion of their experiences with pets and animals. What have they learned about using affection and kindness with animals and with people? (American Association of School Librarians Standards 1.1.2, 2.3.1, 2.4.3, 3.1.2, 3.1.3, 3.2.1, 3.2.2, 3.3.5, 4.1.5, 4.1.7, 4.3.1; English Language Arts Standards 1, 2, 3, 4, 6, 11, 12; Social Studies Standards IV)

2. Have students use information in the book to create a map by which Bram and Mosey traveled from Germany to Calcutta, India and finally to the United States. (American Association of School Librarians Standards 1.1.1, 1.1.6, 1.1.9, 1.2.3, 1.3.4, 1.4.1, 1.4.3, 2.1.1, 2.1.2, 2.1.3, 2.1.5, 2.1.6, 2.2.4, 2.3.1, 3.1.1, 3.1.2, 3.1.3, 3.2.1, 3.2.2, 3.2.3, 3.3.4, 3.3.5, 4.1.1, 4.1.2, 4.1.3, 4.1.8, 4.3.1; English Language Arts Standards 1, 3, 4, 5, 6, 11, 12; Social Studies Standards II)

3. The epilogue says Bram and Mosey lived in India in the palace and elephantarium of a maharajah. Encourage students to research information about elephants in India. With the information they

gather, have them write a fictional story or nonfiction essay about the life that Bram and Mosey might have led in the maharajah's palace and elephantarium. (American Association of School Librarians Standards 1.1.1, 1.1.2, 1.1.3, 1.1.4, 1.1.5, 1.1.6, 1.1.7, 1.1.8, 1.1.9, 1.2.2, 1.2.3, 1.2.5, 1.2.6, 1.2.7, 1.3.1, 1.3.2, 1.3.3, 1.3.4, 1.3.5, 1.4.1, 1.4.2, 1.4.3, 1.4.4, 2.1.1, 2.1.2, 2.1.3, 2.1.4, 2.1.5, 2.1.6, 2.2.1, 2.2.3, 2.2.4, 2.4.1, 2.4.3, 3.1.1, 3.1.2, 3.1.3, 3.1.4, 3.1.6, 3.2.1, 3.2.2, 3.2.3, 3.3.5, 4.1.1, 4.1.2, 4.1.3, 4.1.4, 4.1.7, 4.2.1, 4.2.2, 4.3.1; English Language Arts Standards 1, 4, 5, 6, 7, 8, 11, 12; Social Studies Standards I)

McCaughrean, Geraldine. *Starry Tales.* New York: Margaret K. McElderry Books, 2001. 109p. Illustrated by Sophy Williams. $21.00. ISBN 0-689-83-15-7.

Author and Illustrator

Author Geraldine McCaughrean and illustrator Sophy Williams are both British. Geraldine McCaughrean received England's Carnegie Medal. Her young adult book, *Not the End of the World,* was selected by the United States Board on Books for Young People (USBBY) as an Outstanding International Book in 2006. *Starry Tales,* which was first published in Great Britain, is a collection of stories from thirteen different cultures.

📖 Fiction, Short Stories, Myths, Legends, Ages 8–12

Summary

Fifteen stories of the stars are collected from the cultures of Afghanistan, Ancient Greece, Arabia, Australia, China, the Cook Islands, France, Guatemala, North American Indian, Peru, Rome, Spain, and West Africa. Some may be familiar, such as the story from Ancient Greece about Orion the Hunter. Other stories, such as "The White Cockatoo" and "The White Gum Tree," both of which are about the sky in the Southern Hemisphere, may be new to readers.

Curriculum Responses with Curriculum Standards

1. Show students pictures of the constellations. Have them use a map of the sky to identify the constellations. Ask students which constellations they can identify when they look up at the sky at night. (American Association of School Librarians Standards 1.1.6, 1.1.9, 1.3.4, 2.3.1, 3.1.2, 3.1.3, 3.2.1, 3.2.2, 3.2.3, 3.3.1, 3.3.2, 3.3.5, 4.1.2, 4.1.3, 4.3.1; English Language Arts Standards 1, 3, 4, 6, 11, 12; Life Science Standards)

2. Invite students to research and retell stories about the constellations. (American Association of School Librarians Standards 1.1.1, 1.1.4, 1.3.4, 1.4.1, 2.4.3, 3.1.2, 3.1.3, 4.1.2; English Language Arts Standards 1, 2, 3, 4, 11, 12; Life Science Standards)

3. Geraldine McCaughrean is a prolific author who collects stories, myths, and legends across cultures. Feature her as Author of the Week or Month. Display her books and encourage students to read and retell stories from her collections. In their retellings, have students identify the cultures from which the stories are selected and ways in which cultures are reflected in the stories. (American Association of School Librarians Standards 1.1.2, 1.1.6, 1.2.2, 1.3.4, 3.1.1, 3.1.2, 3.1.3, 3.2.1, 3.2.2, 3.2.3, 3.3.5, 4.1.1, 4.1.2, 4.1.3, 4.2.4, 4.3.1, 4.4.1, 4.4.4; English Language Arts Standards 1, 2, 3, 4, 6, 11, 12; Social Studies Standards I)

Related Books

1. McCaughrean, Geraldine. *The Bronze Cauldron: Myths and Legends of the World.* New York: Margaret K. McElderry Books, 1998. 144p. Illustrated by Bee Willey. $17.85. ISBN 0-689-81758-8.

Twenty-seven myths and legends from around the world include familiar tales, such as stories of The Golem, Cupid and Psyche, and less well-known stories, such as the "Sun's Son," from Tonga.

2. McCaughrean, Geraldine. *Gilgamesh the Hero.* Grand Rapids, MI: Eerdmans Books for Young Readers, 2003. 95p. Illustrated by David Parkins. $18.00. ISBN 0-8028-5262-9.

The story of Gilgamesh, believed to have been a ruler in Mesopotamia (now Iraq) between 3200 and 2700 BC, is the oldest recorded story in the world.

3. McCaughrean, Geraldine. *Greek Gods and Goddesses.* New York: Margaret K. McElderry Books, 1998. 112p. Illustrated by Emma Chichester Clark. $19.95. ISBN 0-689-82084-4.

Fifteen stories of Greek gods and goddesses include stories about Persephone, Cassandra, Paris, and others.

4. McCaughrean, Geraldine. *The Jesse Tree.* Grand Rapids, MI: Eerdmans Books for Young Readers, 2005. 96p. Illustrated by Bee Willey. $20.00. ISBN 0-8028-5288-2.

As the old carpenter carves a Jesse tree, the family tree of Jesus, he tells the little boy the Old Testament Bible stories represented in the tree.

5. McCaughrean, Geraldine. *Roman Myths.* New York: Margaret K. McElderry Books, 2001. 96p. Illustrated by Emma Chichester Clark. $8.46. ISBN 0-689-83822-0.

Fifteen myths about Aeneas, Jupiter, Venus, Diana, and others are retold.

Pullman, Philip. *Aladdin and the Enchanted Lamp.* New York: Arthur A. Levine Books, 2005. 72p. Illustrated by Sophy Williams. $16.95. ISBN 0-439-69255-5.

Author and Illustrator

Author Philip Pullman is English, lived in Australia, graduated from Oxford University, and is the recipient of England's Carnegie Medal and the Guardian Fiction Award. His book, *The Scarecrow and His Servant,* was selected as an Outstanding International Books in 2006 by the United States Board on Books for Young People (USBBY). Illustrator Sophy Williams is also English. The original story of Aladdin was written in Arabic, comes from the Middle East, and is set in China. Pullman's retelling is also set in China.

📖 Fiction, Retelling, Nontraditional Picture Book, Ages 7–11

Summary

Aladdin is a poor tailor's son. His mother is a poor widow. How did this poor boy meet the beautiful princess Badr-al-Budur and become a wealthy, powerful prince? How did he lose his princess and then reclaim her? Aladdin's adventures begin when he meets the Moor and discovers the magic lamp and jinnee. The Introduction explains that Pullman's retelling of Aladdin is set in China, like the original story, even though it was written in Arabic and comes from the Middle East. The story of Aladdin is well established in the British theatrical tradition of pantomime and is played in toy theaters.

Curriculum Responses with Curriculum Standards

1. Encourage children to read and compare other retellings of the story of Aladdin. (American Association of School Librarians Standards 1.1.6, 4.1.1, 4.1.2, 4.1.4, 4.2.4; English Language Arts Standards 1, 3, 4, 6, 11, 12)
2. Encourage older children to use print and nonprint sources to research and report on the British theatrical tradition of pantomime and toy theaters. (American Association of School Librarians Standards 1.1.1, 1.1.3, 1.1.4, 1.1.5, 1.1.8, 1.2.2, 1.2.4, 1.2.5, 1.2.6, 1.2.7, 1.3.3, 1.3.4, 1.3.5, 1.4.1, 1.4.2, 1.4.3, 1.4.4, 2.1.1, 2.1.2, 2.1.3, 2.1.4, 2.1.6, 2.2.1, 2.4.3, 3.1.1, 3.1.2, 3.1.3, 3.1.4, 3.2.1, 3.3.5, 4.1.4, 4.1.7, 4.2.1; English Language Arts Standards 1, 3, 4, 6, 7, 8, 11, 12; Theater Content Standards 5, 6)

3. Encourage those who are interested to develop pantomime and/or toy theater productions of the story of Aladdin, or of episodes from the story. (American Association of School Librarians Standards 1.1.9, 2.1.5, 2.2.4, 3.1.3, 3.2.2, 3.2.3, 4.1.3, 4.1.8; English Language Arts Standards 3, 4, 6, 11, 12; Theater Content Standards 1, 2, 3, 4)

Related Books

1. McCaughrean. Geraldine. *One Thousand and One Arabian Nights.* New York: Oxford University Press, USA, 2000. 288p. Illustrated by Rosamund Fowler. $14.95. ISBN 0-192-75013-5.

Ali Baba, Sinbad the Sailor, the Chinese Princess, and others come to life, as each night Shaherezade, in an attempt to save her life, tells her husband one more story.

2. Pullman, Philip. *Clockmaker.* UK: Corgi Yearling Books, 2004. 96p. Illustrated by Paul Bailey. $6.93. ISBN 0-440-86638-3.

What is Karl to do? He is the first clockmaker's apprentice in hundreds of years to fail to produce a new clock figure, and the townspeople of Glockenheim are awaiting the unveiling of the clock.

3. Pullman, Philip. *The Fire-Maker's Daughter.* New York: Arthur A. Levine Books, 1999. 97p. $15.95. ISBN 0-590-18719-8.

Even though her father wants her to marry when she grows up, Lila, who lives in India, is determined to become a fire-maker just like her father.

4. Pullman, Philip. *The Scarecrow and His Servant.* New York: Knopf Books for Young Readers, 2005. 96p. Illustrated by Peter Bailey. $15.95. ISBN 0-375-81531-7.

When lightening brings the scarecrow to life, Jack, an orphan boy, becomes his servant, adventures begin, and friendship grows.

5. Sunami, Kitoba. *How the Fisherman Tricked the Genie: A Tale Within a Tale Within a Tale.* New York: Atheneum Books for Young Readers, 2002. Unpaged. Illustrated by Amiko Hirao. $16.00. ISBN 0-689-83399-7.

Younger readers may enjoy the story of the fisherman who told the wicked genie a story, within a story, within a story in order to trick him back into the bottle.

EUROPE

German authors Cornelia Funk, Karin Gundisch, Kai Meyer, Dietlof Reiche, and Bohemian Josef Holub dominate the selection of European books. In addition, books by Kate Banks, an American living in the South of France, Tove Jannssen from Finland, author and illustrator Peter Sis from Czechoslovakia, and French writer Jules Verne complete the selection. Genres include fantasy series by Cornelia Funk, Tove Jannssen, and Kai Meyer, realistic fiction by Kate banks, historical fiction by Karin Gundisch and Josef Holub, mystery by Dietrich Rieche, autobiography by Peter Sis, and science fiction by Jules Verne. Five authors are international award winners. Peter Sis received the BolognaRagazzi award for nonfiction for his book *The Tree of Life*. Cornelia Funk's *Igraine the Brave* and Josef Holub's *The Innocent Soldier* were selected by the United States Board on Books for Young People (USBBY) as Outstanding International Books. *The Innocent* Soldier and *The Robber and Me*, by Josef Holub, and *How I Became An American,* by Karin Gundisch, received the Batchelder Award. Finally, author Tove Janssen is a recipient of the Hans Christian Andersen Prize. A wide array of Curriculum Responses includes the creation of storyboards, board games, and character webs, as well as research, writing, discussion, and other activities.

Banks, Kate. *Friends of the Heart: amici del cuore.* New York: Frances Foster Books, 2005. 138p. $16.00. ISBN: 0-374-32455-7.

Author

Author Kate Banks is American and lives in the South of France. She writes in English, speaks French and Italian, and publishes in France and the United States. This book is set in Italy. Characters are both French and Italian.

📖 Realistic Fiction, Ages 11 and Up

Summary

Ollie and Lukey (her real name is Lucrezia) have been friends since they were born, since even before they were born. After Ollie's family moves to Milan, he spends every summer with Lukey and her family at their house by the sea south of Rome. This summer, Ollie and Lukey are thirteen. They pass the summer days swimming and boating and playing cards, badminton, and chess with their neighborhood friends, Martin and Anna Marie. This first person narrative, gently told from Lukey's point of view, is peppered with a sense of foreboding, a sense of ominous change. Suddenly, the peace and joy of Lukey's world is shattered by Ollie's tragic death, when a terrorist's bomb explodes in the waiting room of Rome's airport where Ollie is awaiting his flight to Milan. Lukey, family, and friends feel the impact of Ollie's death. Three years later, Lukey still struggles with her acceptance of Ollie's death and addresses him as "Amicomio. Amico del cuore."—My friend. Friend of my heart.

Curriculum Responses with Curriculum Standards

1. Engage students in a discussion of loss, grief, and mourning. How did Lukey, her family, and friends react to Ollie's death? Why does Lukey refer to Ollie as "friend of my heart?" Have students experienced the loss of someone they knew well: a friend, relative, pet, or perhaps a famous person? Encourage students to relate their experiences to the experiences of Lukey, her family, and friends. (American Association of School Librarians Standards 1.1.2, 1.1.3, 1.3.4, 2.3.1, 2.4.3, 3.1.3, 3.2.2, 3.3.2, 3.3.5, 4.1.5, 4.3.1; English Language Arts Standards 1, 2, 3, 4, 6, 11, 12; Social Studies Standards IV)

2. Extend the discussion by having students address themes such as the value of life, "life is stronger than death," and the power of reaching out. What attitudes do students see and hear expressed in their families and communities and in the media? (American Association of School Librarians Standards 1.1.1, 1.1.2, 1.1.3, 1.1.6, 1.1.7, 1.1.9, 1.2.1, 1.2.2, 1.3.2, 1.3.4, 1.4.3, 2.1.1, 2.1.3, 2.1.5, 2.3.1, 2.4.3, 3.1.1, 3.1.2, 3.1.3, 3.1.5, 3.2.1, 3.2.2, 3.3.1, 3.3.2, 3.3.3, 3.3.5, 4.1.1, 4.1.7, 4.2.2, 4.2.3, 4.3.1, 4.3.3; English Language Arts Standards 4, 6, 11, 12; Social Studies Standards I)

3. Consider developing a social studies unit that examines how different cultures view death, i.e.: Ancient Egypt's emphasis on the afterlife, Buddhist and Hindu belief in reincarnation, Mexican celebration of the Day of the Dead, Asian respect for ancestors. Encourage students to read, research, and report their findings. (American Association of School Librarians Standards 1.1.1, 1.1.2, 1.1.3, 1.1.4, 1.1.5, 1.1.6, 1.1.7, 1.1.8, 1.1.9, 1.2.1, 1.2.2, 1.2.3, 1.2.4, 1.2.5, 1.2.6, 1.2.7, 1.2.1, 1.3.2, 1.3.3, 1.3.4, 1.3.5, 1.4.1, 1.4.2, 1.4.3, 1.4.4, 2.1.1, 2.1.2, 2.1.3, 2.1.4, 2.1.5, 2.1.6, 2.2.1, 2.2.4, 2.3.1, 2.3.2, 2.4.1, 2.4.2, 2.4.3, 3.1.1, 3.1.2, 3.1.3, 3.1.4, 3.1.5, 3.1.6, 3.2.1, 3.2.2, 3.2.3, 3.3.1, 3.3.2, 3.3.3, 3.3.4, 3.3.5, 3.3.6, 3.3.7, 4.1.1, 4.1.2, 4.1.3, 4.1.4, 4.1.5, 4.1.6, 4.1.7, 4.1.8, 4.2.1, 4.2.2, 4.2.3, 4.3.1, 4.4.4, 4.4.6; English Language Arts Standards 1, 2, 3, 4, 6, 7, 8, 11, 12; Social Studies Standards I)

Related Books

1. Banks, Kate. *Dillon Dillon*. New York: Farrar, Straus and Giroux, 2005. 160p. $5.95. ISBN 0-374-41715-6.

A pair of loons help ten-year-old Dillon when he learns that his first and last names are the same because his aunt and uncle adopted him when his parents died in a plane crash.

2. Gandolfi, Silvana (Translated by Lynne Sharon Schwartz). *Aladabra: The Tortoise Who Loved Shakespeare.* New York: Arthur A. Levine Books, 2004. 160p. $16.95. ISBN 439-49741-8.

Eliza visits her grandmother almost every day and sees her changing. Her grandmother tells Eliza, "The way to outsmart death . . . is to transform yourself."

3. Warfel, Elizabeth Stuart. *The Blue Pearls.* New York: Barefoot Books, 2001. 32p. Illustrated by Veronique Giarrusso. $16.99. ISBN 1-902-28378-3.

The story of the blue pearls that the angels must find to decorate the beautiful sapphire-blue dress that they are making for Elise was inspired by a dream that the author had shortly before her daughter died of cancer.

Funk, Cornelia. *Inkheart.* New York: Scholastic Inc., 2003. 563p. $9.99. ISBN 0-545-04626-2.

Author

Author Cornelia Funk was born, raised, and educated in Germany. She now lives in Los Angeles, CA. Her book *Igraine the Brave* was selected as an Outstanding International Book in 2008 by the United States Board on Books for Young People (USBBY).

📖 Fiction, Fantasy, Ages 9–12

Summary

In this gripping, action-packed fantasy, the first of a trilogy about books and a love for reading, readers meet eleven-year-old Meggie and her father Mo, a bookbinder. Mo has the power to read book characters and events right out of the pages of a book and into the real world. When Meggie was three years old, Mo "read" Dustfinger and several characters, including the evil Capricorn, out of the pages of the book, *Inkheart,* and into the real world. At the same time, Mo unwittingly "read" Meggie's mother Resa into the pages of *Inkheart,* where she remains trapped.

As the story begins, Dustfinger suddenly appears in the dark of night to warn Mo, also called Silvertongue, that Capricorn's henchmen are after him, and that Meggie is in danger. Mo and Meggie leave early the next morning for Italy, where they plan to stay with Meggie's Great-Aunt Elinor, who is a book collector. And so the chase begins, with Capricorn and his men trying to capture Mo, Meggie, Great-Aunt Elinor, and Dustfinger in order to force Mo to "read" another powerful and evil character out of the book and into the real world. At the same time Mo, Meggie, Great-Aunt

Elinor, and Dustfinger pursue Fenoglio, the author of *Inkheart,* in the hope that he will rewrite a new ending for *Inkheart.*

Readers who find *Inkheart* too long or too difficult to read might prefer *Inkheart: Movie Novelization,* or *Inkheart: Farid's Story,* both of which are based on the movie version of the book.

Curriculum Responses with Curriculum Standards

1. *Inkheart* has been made into a movie. Encourage children to read the book, see the movie, and then compare and contrast the two. (American Association of School Librarians Standards 1.1.6, 1.1.9, 1.3.4, 2.1.1, 2.1.5, 2.1.6, 3.2.3, 3.1.2, 3.1.3, 3.2.1, 3.2.2, 3.3.5, 4.1.1, 4.1.2, 4.1.3, 4.3.1; English Language Arts Standards 1, 2, 3, 8, 11, 12; Theater Content Standard 7)

2. Use *Inkheart: Farid's Story,* a picture book with limited text that retells a segment from the original book, as a model. Encourage children to form small groups, to select an episode or segment from the book, and to retell the episode or segment by creating a storyboard, illustrating and using simple text. Some groups might want to extend their retellings by acting them out. (American Association of School Librarians Standards 1.1.2, 1.1.6, 1.1.9, 1.2.3, 1.3.4, 2.1.2, 2.1.5, 2.1.6, 2.2.4, 3.1.2, 3.1.3, 3.2.1, 3.2.2, 3.2.3, 3.3.4, 3.3.5, 4.1.2, 4.1.3, 4.1.7, 4.1.8, 4.3.1; English Language Arts Standards 1, 2, 3, 4, 5, 6, 11, 12; Theater Content Standards 1, 2, 4; Visual Arts Content Standard 1)

3. Have children take on the role of the author Fenoglio and change the course of events by rewriting events and the ending. (American Association of School Librarians Standards 1.2.2, 1.2.3, 1.3.4, 2.1.6, 2.2.4, 3.1.2, 3.1.3, 3.2.1, 3.3.5, 4.1.3, 4.1.8, 4.3.1; English Language Arts Standards 4, 5, 6, 11, 12)

Related Books

1. Funk, Cornelia. *Dragon Rider.* New York: Scholastic, Inc., 2004. 544p. $14.99. ISBN 0-349-45695-9.

Ben, an orphan boy, befriends the dragons, Firedrake and Sorrel, and helps them find their way as they search for the Rim of Heaven, where dragons can live in peace.

2. Funk, Cornelia. *Igraine the Brave.* New York: Scholastic, Inc., 2007. 224p. $16.99. ISBN 0-439-90379-3.

Eleven-year-old Igraine just might realize her dream to become a knight as she tries to stop Osmond the Greedy from capturing the castle and her parents.

3. Funk, Cornelia. *Inkdeath.* New York: Scholastic, Inc., 2008. 656p. $24.99. ISBN 0-439-86628-6.

In this final book of the *Inkheart Trilogy,* only Meggie's father can write a new ending to save the children from a life of slavery in Adderhead's silver mines.

4. Funk, Cornelia. *Inkspell.* New York: Scholastic, Inc., 2005. 656p. $22.99. ISBN 0-429-55400-4.

In this sequel to *Inkheart,* Farid, Dustfinger's protégé, and Meggie read their way into Inkworld, where the battle between the book world and the real world continues.

5. Funk, Cornelia. *The Thief Lord.* New York: Scholastic, Inc., 2002. (Translated by Oliver Latsch) $19.99. ISBN 0-439-40437-1.

Set in Venice, this book tells of Victor Getz, an American detective, who searches for twelve-year-old Prosper and five-year-old Bo, who have run away from their aunt and uncle and are hiding with a gang of children led by the Thief Lord.

Gundisch, Karin. *How I Became an American.* Chicago: Cricket Books, 2002. 120p. Translated by James Skofield. $15.95. ISBN 0-88186-4875-7.

Author

Author Karin Gundisch was born in Romania and immigrated to Germany. *How I Became an American,* which is based on American immigrants' letters written from 1902 to 1986, received the Batchelder Award in 2002.

　📖　Historical Fiction, Ages 10–14

Summary

Mama said to write it down so that Peter, Regina, Emil, and I could remember. Eliss didn't have a gravestone because we had no money. I must write our story so we don't forget her. This is why Johann—"Johnny the American," his schoolmasters called him—wrote the story of his family's journey from Austria-Hungary to Rumania, back to Austria-Hungary, then through Germany and across the ocean to America, and finally, from New York to Youngstown, Ohio, where Johnny's father worked in the steel mills. In Youngstown, life was very different from life in Siebenburgen. And Johnny recorded it all in his notebook.

Curriculum Connections with Curriculum Standards

1. After reading, have students trace Johnny's journey from Austria-Hungary to Rumania, back to Austria-Hungary, then across Germany to the port of Bremerhaven, across the Atlantic to Ellis Island, then by train from New York to Youngstown, Ohio. Also have them locate California, where Johnny's brother went to become a farmer. (American Association of School Librarians Standards 1.1.6, 1.1.9, 1.3.4, 2.1.5, 2.3.1, 3.1.1, 3.1.2, 3.1.3, 3.2.1, 3.2.2, 3.2.3, 3.3.5, 4.1.1, 4.1.2, 4.3.1; English Language Arts Standards 1, 2, 3, 4, 6, 11, 12; Social Studies Standards III)

2. After reading, have students create a Venn diagram to compare and contrast the family's life in Siebenburgen with their life in Youngstown. (American Association of School Librarians Standards 1.1.6, 1.1.9, 1.3.4, 2.1.1, 2.1.2, 2.1.5, 2.2.4, 2.3.1, 3.1.1, 3.1.2, 3.1.3, 3.2.1, 3.2.2, 3.2.3, 3.3.1, 3.3.2, 3.3.3, 3.3.4, 3.3.5, 4.1.1, 4.1.2, 4.1.3, 4.1.6, 4.1.7, 4.3.1; English Language Arts Standards 1, 2, 3, 4, 5, 6, 11, 12; Social Studies Standards I, II, III, IV, VII)

3. After reading, engage students in a discussion of what Johnny and his family had to do to make a new life for themselves. (American Association of School Librarians Standards 1.1.6, 1.1.9, 1.3.4, 2.1.1, 2.1.3, 2.1.5, 3.1.1, 3.1.2, 3.1.3, 3.2.1, 3.2.2, 3.3.1, 3.3.2, 3.3.3, 3.3.5, 4.1.1)

Holub, Josef. *An Innocent Soldier.* Translated by Michael Hofmann. New York: Arthur A. Levine Books, 2005. 231p. $16.99. ISBN 0-439-62771-0.

Author and Translator

Author Josef Holub was born in Neuern, Bohemia. He is the recipient of the Peter Hartling Prize for Children's Literature and the Zurich Children's Book Prize. His books *The Robber and Me* and *An Innocent Soldier* received the Batchelder Award. *An Innocent Soldier* was also selected as an Outstanding International Book by the United States Board on Books for Young People (USBBY). Translator Michael Hofmann was born in West Germany and grew up in England. This story of Napoleon's campaign against Russia is set in Europe.

📖 Historical Fiction, Ages 10–14

Summary

Georg Bayh is the farmer's son. Adam is the farmhand, still a boy, too young for the army. Nevertheless, the farmer tells the conscription commission that Adam is his son George. The soldiers ignore Adam's protests, and Adam quickly discovers that he cannot run away. So Adam becomes Private Bayh, a new recruit in Napoleon's Grande Armee, marching from Germany to Russia and back in the War of 1812. Harassed by Sergeant Krauter, Adam is wet, cold, hungry, ragged, weary, and sick. He survives the long trek, only to return to Germany and march off to war again, hailed as a veteran of the Russian campaign.

Curriculum Responses with Curriculum Standards

1. After reading, have students use the map in the front of the book to trace the army's route from Wurttemburg, Germany, to Moscow and back. (American Association of School Librarians Standards 1.1.6, 2.1.1, 2.3.1, 3.3.5, 4.1.1, 4.1.2, 4.1.3, 4.3.1; English Language Arts Standards 1, 3, 4, 8, 11, 12; Social Studies Standards III)

2. Have students compare the map in the front of the book with a current map of the same area. How has the map changed? Why has it changed? (American Association of School Librarians 1.1.6, 1.1.8, 1.3.4, 2.1.1, 2.1.3, 2.1.4, 2.1.6, 2.2.3, 2.3.1, 2.3.2, 2.4.3, 3.1.1, 3.1.2, 3.1.3, 3.2.1, 3.2.2, 3.3.3, 3.3.5, 4.1.2, 4.1.4, 4.1.5, 4.1.7, 4.2.3, 4.3.1, 4.4.4; English Language Arts Standards 4, 6, 8, 11, 12; Social Studies Standards III, V, VI)

3. Have children research and report on the War of 1812. (American Association of School Librarians Standards 1.1.1, 1.1.3, 1.1.4, 1.1.5, 1.1.6, 1.1.8, 1.1.9, 1.2.2, 1.2.5, 1.2.6, 1.2.7, 1.3.1, 1.3.3, 1.3.4, 1.3.5, 1.4.1, 1.4.2, 1.4.3, 1.4.4, 2.1.1, 2.1.2, 2.1.4, 2.1.5, 2.1.6, 2.2.1, 2.2.3, 2.2.4, 2.3.2, 2.4.2, 2.4.3, 3.1.1, 3.1.2, 3.1.3, 3.1.4, 3.1.6, 3.2.1, 3.2.2, 3.3.1, 3.3.5, 3.4.1, 3.4.2, 4.1.2, 4.1.7, 4.3.1, 4.3.2; English Language Arts Standards 1, 2, 3, 5, 7, 8, 12; Social Studies Standards II, VI)

4. Adam changed from a young farmhand to a veteran of the Russian campaign. Encourage discussion. What personal qualities did he demonstrate, i.e.: bravery, loyalty, caring, and compassion? What roles did the farmer, the sergeant, and the lieutenant play in Adam's life? What effect did they have on Adam, and how did he respond to them? (American Association of School Librarians Standards 3.1.3, 3.2.1, 3.2.2, 3.3.1, 3.3.5, 4.1.2, 4.2.3, 4.3.1; English Language Arts Standards 3, 4, 6, 11, 12; Social Studies Standards IV, V)

5. Continue discussion by asking students how they would have felt and what they would have done had they been Adam. (American Association of School Librarians Standards 1.1.2, 1.1.3, 1.1.9, 1.3.4, 2.1.5, 2.3.1, 3.1.2, 3.1.3, 3.2.1, 3.2.2, 3.3.1, 3.3.2, 3.3.3, 3.3.5, 4.1.3, 4.3.1; English Language Arts Standards 4, 6, 11, 12; Social Studies Standards IV)

Related Books

Holub, Josef. *The Robber and Me.* New York: Yearling, 1999. 224p. Translated by Elizabeth D. Crawford. $12.80. ISBN 0-440-41540-3.

It is 1867 in a small village in Germany, where young Boniface Schroll, who only recently left the home of his stingy aunt to live with his stern uncle, befriends a robber's son, and thereby places his own tenuous comfort in jeopardy.

Jansson, Tove. *Moominvalley in November.* New York: Farrar, Straus, and Giroux, 2003. Translated by Kingsley Hart. 172p. $17.00. ISBN 0-374-35013-2.

Author

Author Tove Jansson is from Finland. She received the Hans Christian Andersen Prize in 1966.

📖   Fiction, Fantasy, Ages 8–12

Summary

Moominmamma and Moominpappa are gone. Snufkin, Toft, Fillyjonk, Hemulen, Mymble, and Grandpa-Grumble return to Moominvalley and are at a loss. They have depended on Moominmamma and Moominpappa for their happiness and well-being. Now they must learn to live with each other, to depend on themselves, and on each other.

Curriculum Responses with Curriculum Standards

1. Have students read, create puppets of the characters, design and construct cardboard background settings, write scripts, and act out episodes from the story. (American Association of School Librarians Standards 1.1.6, 1.2.3, 2.1.6, 2.3.4, 3.1.2, 3.1.3, 3.2.1, 3.2.2, 3.2.3, 4.1.1, 4.1.3, 4.1.8; English Language Arts Standards 1, 3, 4, 5, 6, 11, 12; Theater Content Standards 1, 2, 3, 4; Visual Arts Content Standards 1, 2, 6)

2. After reading, have students create shoebox dioramas of descriptive scenes, then explain their scenes to their classmates. (American Association of School Librarians Standards 1.1.6, 1.2.2, 1.2.3, 1.3.4, 2.1.6, 2.2.4, 3.1.3, 3.2.1, 3.2.2, 3.3.5, 4.1.1, 4.1.3, 4.1.8, 4.3.1; English Language Arts Standards 1, 3, 4, 6, 11, 12; Visual Arts Content Standards 1, 2, 3)

3. After reading, have students create a board game with game board and written questions and answers based on the story. Encourage

students to play the game. (American Association of School Librarians Standards 1.1.6, 1.1.9, 1.2.2, 1.2.3, 1.3.4, 1.4.4, 2.1.5, 2.1.6, 2.2.4, 3.1.2, 3.1.3, 3.2.1, 3.2.2, 3.2.3, 3.3.5, 4.1.1, 4.1.3, 4.1.8, 4.3.1; English Language Arts Standards 1, 3, 4, 5, 6, 11, 12; Visual Arts Content Standards 1, 2, 3)

Related Books

1. Jansson, Tove. *Comet in Moominland.* 1991. New York: Farrar, Straus, and Giroux, 1991. 192p. Translated by Elizabeth Portch. $6.95. ISBN 0-374-41331-2.

Moomintroll must save his home from destruction by a comet.

2. Jansson. Tove. *Finn Family Moomintroll.* 1990. New York: Farrar, Straus, and Giroux, 1990. Translated by Elizabeth Portch. $6.95. ISBN 0-374-42307-5.

Loosely connected stories told in short chapters introduce the Moominfamily—Moominpapa, Moominmama, and Moomintroll, their extended family, and neighbors as they meet the threatening Hobgoblin.

3. Jansson, Tove. *The Complete Tove Jansson Comic Strip: Book One.* Montreal, Quebec: Drawn and Quarterly, 2006. 96p. $19.95. ISBN 1-894-93780-5.

This collection of comic strips drawn for a London newspaper in the 1950s is the first of a five-volume set.

Meyer, Kai. *Pirate Wars.* New York: Margaret K. McElderry Books, 2008. 375p. Translated by Elizabeth D. Crawford. $16.99. ISBN 1-4169-2476-0.

Author and Translator

Author Kai Meyer is German and lives in Germany. Translator Elizabeth D. Crawford lives in the United States and has translated two Batchelder Award winning books.

📖 Fiction, Fantasy, Ages 10–14

Summary

Pirate Wars is the third book in *The Wave Walkers Trilogy.* This is a complex, action-packed, fast-moving fantasy series set in the Caribbean, with a cast of polliwogs, pirates, ghosts, and fantasy creatures. Be sure to read the series in sequence in order to keep track of the characters, action, and plot. As the final book unfolds, fourteen-year-old Jolly realizes that it is she who must save the entire Caribbean fantasy world from the evil Maelstrom. She no longer knows whom she can trust and is puzzled by the beautiful Aina, a polliwog from ancient times.

Curriculum Responses with Curriculum Standards

1. As students read, have them create a character web by identifying characters, describing attributes of each character, and then linking characters together, showing their relationships to each other. (American Association of School Librarians Standards 1.1.6, 1.1.9, 1.2.2, 1.3.4, 2.1.2, 2.1.5, 2.1.6, 2.2.4, 3.1.2, 3.1.3, 3.2.1, 3.2.2, 3.2.3, 3.3.4, 3.3.5, 4.1.3, 4.1.6, 4.3.1; English Language Arts Standards 1, 3, 4, 5, 6, 11, 12)

2. Extend the character webs by having students select a character and write blogs that the character might write about self, activities, and relationships. (American Association of School Librarians Standards 2.1.6, 2.2.4, 2.3.1, 3.1.3, 3.3.4, 4.1.3, 4.1.8; English Language Arts Standards 3, 4, 5, 6, 11, 12)

3. After reading, have students create collages about the book, the setting, the characters, and the events. (American Association of School Librarians Standards 1.1.6, 1.2.3, 2.1.6, 2.2.4, 4.1.1, 4.1.3, 4.1.8; English Language Arts Standards 1, 3, 4; Visual Arts Standards 1, 2)

Related Books

1. Meyer, Kai. *Pirate Curse.* New York: Aladdin, 2007. 320p. Translated by Elizabeth D. Crawford. $5.99. ISBN 1-416-92473-6.

In Book One of *The Wave Walkers Trilogy,* which is set in a Caribbean fantasy world, fourteen-year-old Jolly meets Munk, another polliwog, and together they have adventures with a monster, with the ghost crew of a pirate ship, and with the evil Maelstrom.

2. Meyer, Kai. *Pirate Emperor.* New York: Aladdin, 2008. 320p. Translated by Elizabeth D. Crawford. $5.99. ISBN 1-416-92475-2.

In Book Two of *The Wave Walkers Trilogy,* Jolly and Munk must dive deep into the Caribbean waters to prevent the gate to an evil world from opening.

3. Meyer, Kai. *The Glass Word.* New York: Simon Pulse, 2008. 288p. Translated by Elizabeth D. Crawford. $8.99. ISBN 0-689-87792-6.

In Book Three of *The Dark Reflections Trilogy,* Merle and her friends have escaped from Hell and must now find the Iron Eye in order to save the world as they know it.

4. Meyer, Kai. *The Stone Light.* New York: Simon Pulse, 2007. 384p. Translated by Elizabeth D. Crawford. $8.99. ISBN 0-689-87790-0.

In Book Two of *The Dark Reflections Trilogy,* Merle travels to Hell to enlist the aid of Lucifer against the Egyptian Pharoah in her attempt to save the city of Venice.

5. Meyer, Kai. *The Water Mirror.* New York: Simon Pulse, 2007. 384p. Translated by Elizabeth D. Crawford. $8.99. ISBN 0-689-87790-2.

In Book One of *The Dark Reflections Trilogy,* fourteen-year-old Merle must save the city of Venice from the invading Egyptian army.

Reiche, Dietlof. *Ghost Ship.* New York: Scholastic Press, 2005. 313p. Translated by John Brownjohn. $16.95. ISBN 0-439-59704-8.

Author and Translator

Author Dietlof Reiche lives in Hamburg, Germany. Translator John Brownjohn lives in Dorset, England, and has translated more than one hundred books for children and adults. This book is set in New England.

📖 Fiction, Mystery, Ages 10–14

Summary

The Storm Goddess sailed the seas in 1772. Two hundred thirty years later, the ship mysteriously appears in the dried up-bay in Vicki's New England town. Vicki thinks she will spend her summer vacation just helping her father by waiting tables in his seaside café. But the glass eyes of the figure-head of the lost ship, a packet of letters, and the lure of gold draw her into the mystery of the dried-up bay and the ship that is lodged there. Vicki realizes that she is the one who must solve the mystery of the ship and release the ghost crew from the curse that binds them.

Curriculum Responses with Curriculum Standards

1. At the end of each chapter, ask students to predict what will happen next. Invite them to share their predictions with substantiating clues. Then have them read to confirm their predictions. (American Association of School Librarians Standards 2.2.2, 2.2.3, 3.1.2, 3.1.3, 3.2.1, 3.2.2, 3.3.5, 4.2.3, 4.3.1; English Language Arts Standards 1, 3, 4, 6, 11, 12)
2. After reading, encourage students who are interested to generate questions, and then research more information about pirates, ship-wrecks, and sunken treasures off the New England coast. Provide opportunities for them to report their findings in oral, written, or visual forms to their classmates. (American Association of School Librarians Standards 1.1.1, 1.1.2, 1.1.3, 1.1.4, 1.1.5, 1.1.6, 1.1.7, 1.1.8, 1.1.9, 1.2.1, 1.2.2, 1.2.3, 1.2.4, 1.2.5, 1.2.6, 1.2.7, 1.3.1, 1.3.2, 1.3.3, 1.3.4, 1.3.5, 1.4.1, 1.4.2, 1.4.3, 1.4.4, 2.1.1, 2. .2, 2.1.6, 2.2.1, 2.2.2, 2.2.4, 2.4.1, 2.4.3, 3.1.1, 3.1.2, 3.1.3, 3.2.1, 3.2.2, 3.3.5, 4.1.1, 4.1.4, 4.1.5, 4.2.1, 4.2.2, 4.3.1, 4.3.2, 4.4.1; English Language Arts Standards 1, 3, 4, 5, 6, 7, 11, 12)

3. Discuss with students how the Storm Goddess hanging on the wall of the Seashell Room might have looked. Encourage them to make a papier-mâché figurehead of the Storm Goddess. (American Association of School Librarians Standards 1.1.2, 1.1.9, 1.2.1, 1.3.4, 2.1.5, 2.1.6, 2.3.4, 3.1.2, 3.2.1, 3.2.2, 3.3.5, 4.1.3, 4.1.8; English Language Arts Standards 3, 4, 6, 11, 12, Visual Arts Content Standards 1, 2, 3)

Related Books

1. Reich, Dietlof. *Freddy's Final Quest.* New York: Scholastic Paperbacks, 2008. 304p. $5.99. ISBN 0-439-87415-7.

In Book Five of the Golden Hamster Saga, Freddy and his friends must save Enrico and Caruso from the Crusaders.

2. Reich, Dietlof. *Freddy in Peril.* New York: Scholastic Paperbacks, 2006. 208p. Illustrated by Joe Cepeda. $5.99. ISBN 0-439-53156-X.

In this second book about Freddy, Freddy's friends—two guinea pigs, a car, and a family of sewer rats—save him from Professor Fleischkopf.

3. Reich, Dietlof. *Freddy to the Rescue.* New York: Scholastic Paperbacks, 2006. 240p. ISBN 0-439-53158-0.

In the third book about Freddy, it is Freddy's turn to save a colony of endangered hamsters.

4. Reiche, Dietlof. *I, Freddy.* New York: Scholastic Paperbacks, 2005. 208p. Illustrated by Joe Cepeda. $5.99. ISBN 0-439-28357-4.

Meet Freddy in the first of five humorous books about the hamster who teaches himself to read and use the computer.

5. Reich, Dietlof. *The Haunting of Freddy.* New York: Scholastic Paperbacks, 2007. 320p. $5.99. ISBN 0-439-53160-8.

Book four of the Golden Hamster Saga finds Freddy and his friends at Templeton Castle in England trying to unravel a series of mysterious events.

Sis, Peter. *The Wall: Growing Up behind the Iron Curtain.* New York: Farrar, Straus, and Giroux, 2007. Unpaged. $18.00. ISBN 0-374-34701-8.

Author and Illustrator

Author and Illustrator Peter Sis was born in Czechoslovakia, grew up in Prague, was educated in London, and now lives in the United States. In

2004, he received the BolognaRagazzi Award for nonfiction for his book *The Tree of Life.*

   📖 Nonfiction, Autobiography, Nontraditional Picture Book, Ages 9–12

Summary

Richly detailed illustrations, readable text, sidebars, journal entries, Introduction, and Afterword tell the story of the author's life and his love of drawing. As a very young child, Peter drew freely and spontaneously. When he entered school under the Communist regime, he drew what he was told to draw and thought what he was told to think. His journal entries from 1954 to 1977 record the restrictions of the Stalin era, the seeping in of Western influences behind the Iron Curtain, and a lingering hope for a freer environment, which was finally realized with the collapse of the Berlin Wall in 1989.

Curriculum Responses with Curriculum Standards

1. Read the Introduction. Look at the map, which is the frontispiece. Find Czechoslovakia and the city of Prague. Find Germany and the city of Berlin. Find the countries that comprised the Soviet Union and the Eastern Bloc on a world map. Ask children whether they have family members, neighbors, or friends who came to the United States from any of these countries. When and why did they come to the United States? Do they have stories to tell? Provide an opportunity for students to share their findings with their classmates. (American Association of School Librarians Standards 1.1.4, 1.1.6, 1.2.1, 1.2.2, 1.3.4, 2.1.1, 2.1.2, 2.1.3, 2.1.5, 2.3.1, 3.1.1, 3.1.2, 3.1.3, 3.1.5, 3.2.1, 3.2.2, 3.3.1, 3.3.2, 3.3.3, 3.3.5, 4.1.2, 4.1.3, 4.1.4, 4.1.7, 4.2.2, 4.3.1; English Language Arts Standards 1, 2, 7, 11, 12; Social Studies Strands I, II, III, V)

2. Look carefully at the illustrations. Take note of Peter Sis's use of color, i.e., black, white, and grey, with bits of red; the pink two-page spread, soft colors in small drawings, the brilliantly colored two-page spread, and the last two two-page spreads. What does the use of color tell the reader? (American Association of School Librarians Standards 1.1.1, 1.1.2, 1.1.3, 1.1.6, 1.3.4, 2.1.1, 2.1.3, 3.1.1, 3.1.2, 3.1.3, 3.2.1, 3.2.2, 3.3.1, 3.3.2, 3.3.3, 3.3.5, 4.1.3, 4.1.4, 4.3.1; English Language Arts Standards 3, 4, 6, 11, 12; Visual Arts Content Standards 1, 3, 5)

3. Consider selecting Peter Sis as an author/illustrator to study. Have students read more of his books paying particular attention to his use of graphics. Identity and discuss the many ways he uses graphics, layout, and illustrations. (American Association of School Librarian Standards 1.1.1, 1.1.2, 1.1.3, 1.1.4, 1.1.6, 1.1.9, 2.1.2.1, 1.2.2, 1.3.4,

2.1.1, 2.1.3, 3.1.1, 3.1.2, 3.1.3, 3.2.1, 3.2.2, 3.3.1, 3.3.2, 3.3.3, 3.3.5, 4.1.1, 4.1.2, 4.1.3, 4.2.4, 4.3.1, 4.4.1; English Language Arts Standards 1, Visual Arts Content Standards 1, 3, 5)

Related Books

1. Sis, Peter. *Madlenka.* New York: Frances Foster Books, 2000. Unpaged. $17.00. ISBN 0-374-39969-7.

Introduce students to Peter Sis's complex use of graphics, layout, and illustrations with this book for younger readers in which Madlenka walks around the block in New York City to tell her French, Indian, Italian, German, South American, Egyptian, and Asian neighbors that her tooth is loose!

2. Sis, Peter. *Madlenka's Dog.* New York: Farrar, Straus, Giroux, 2002. Unpaged. $17.00. ISBN 0-374-34699-2.

Madlenka takes another walk around the block—this time to show her neighbors her imaginary dog.

3. Sis, Peter. *Starry Messenger: Galileo Galilei.* New York: Farrar, Straus, Giroux, 2000. Unpaged. $5.95. ISBN 0-374-47027-8.

People believed that the Earth was the center of the universe until Galileo, a scientist, mathematician, astronomer, philosopher, and physicist, studied the sky and demonstrated with his observations and maps that the Earth revolves around the Sun.

4. Sis, Peter. *Tibet through the Red Box.* New York: Farrar, Straus, Giroux, 1998. 64p. $25.00. ISBN 0-374-37552-6.

Drawing on his father's diaries and childhood memories of his father's stories, Peter Sis invites readers to visit Tibet, "the roof of the world."

5. Sis, Peter. *The Tree of Life.* New York: Farrar, Straus, Giroux, 2003. Unpaged. $18.00. ISBN 0-374-45628-3.

Meet Charles Darwin, the nineteenth-century naturalist, whose detailed descriptions of his observations of the natural world provide the basis for his theory of evolution.

Verne, Jules. *Around the World in 80 Days.* New York: Aladdin Paperbacks, 2007. 320p. $5.99. ISBN 1-4169-3936-9.

Author

Author Jules Verne is a French writer, born in Paris, and credited as the father of science fiction writing. In his novels he predicted future modern technology and conveniences such as skyscrapers, nuclear submarines, atomic power, travel by rocket to the moon, helicopters, and airplanes. This book is his most successful novel, an adventure story reflecting social developments of the mid-to-late nineteenth century, in which the characters travel around the world.

📖 Science Fiction, All Ages

Summary

It is 1872. Phineas Fogg bets 20,000 pounds with members of his Reform Club that he can travel around the world in eighty days or less. He enters into discussion of the wager at ten minutes after six. At a quarter to nine, Phineas Fogg and his servant Passepartout leave London on the train for Dover. They are due back at the Reform Club on December twenty-first, by a quarter to nine. So their adventure begins. Traveling by train, steamboat, and hot-air balloon to Egypt, India, Hong Kong, Japan, San Francisco, and New York, Phineas Fogg and Passepartout arrive back in London just in the nick of time! A Reading Group Guide with discussion questions and activities completes the book.

Curriculum Responses with Curriculum Standards

1. Using a globe or world map, have students trace the route that Phineas Fogg traveled around the world. What modes of transportation did he use? If he were to make the trip today, what modes of transportation might he use? How have transportation and communication changed since Phineas Fogg traveled around the world? (American Association of School Librarians Standards 1.3.4, 2.1.1, 2.1.3, 2.2.2, 2.3.1, 2.3.2, 3.1.2, 3.1.3, 3.2.1, 3.2.2, 3.3.1, 3.3.2, 3.3.5, 4.1.2, 4.1.3, 4.2.3, 4.3.1; English Language Arts Standards 8, 12; Social Studies Standards II, III, VIII)

2. Have the students retell the story of Phineas Fogg's travels by creating a storyboard. (American Association of School Librarians Standards 1.1.9, 1.2.3, 1.3.4, 2.1.1, 2.1.2, 2.1.3, 2.1.6, 2.3.4, 3.1.2, 3.1.3, 3.1.4, 3.2.1, 3.2.2, 3.2.3, 3.3.5, 3.4.2, 4.1.3, 4.1.6, 4.1.8; English Language Arts Standards 3, 5, 12)

3. Encourage children to plan their own route around the world, including means of transportation. Have them create maps showing their routes and estimate how long their trips will take. (American Association of School Librarians Standards 1.1.1, 1.1.2, 1.1.3, 1.1.4, 1.1.5, 1.1.6, 1.1.8, 1.1.9, 1.2.1, 1.2.2, 1.2.3, 1.2.5, 1.2.6, 1.2.7, 1.3.4, 1.4.1, 1.4.2, 1.4.3, 1.4.4, 2.1.1, 2.1.2, 2.1.3, 2.1.4, 2.1.5, 2.1.6, 2.2.1, 2.2.2, 2.2.4, 2.3.1, 2.3.2, 2.4.1, 2.4.2, 3.1.1, 3.1.2, 3.1.3, 3.1.4, 3.2.1, 3.2.2, 3.2.3, 3.3.1, 3.3.2, 3.3.4, 3.3.5, 3.4.1, 3.4.2; 4.1.3, 4.1.7, 4.1.8, 4.3.1; English Language Arts Standards 8, 12; Social Studies Standards II, III)

4. Show the movie and encourage students to compare and contrast the movie with the book. (American Association of School Librarians Standards 1.1.6, 1.3.4, 2.1.1, 2.1.3, 2.2.3, 4.1.1, 4.1.5; Theater Content Standard 7)

5. Engage students in Discussion Questions and Activities suggested in the Reading Group Guide in the back of the book. (American Association of School Librarians Standards 1.1.1, 1.1.2, 1.1.3, 1.1.4, 1.1.6, 1.1.9, 1.2.2, 1.2.3, 1.2.4, 1.3.4, 2.1.1, 2.1.3, 2.1.5, 3.1.1, 3.1.2, 3.1.3, 3.2.1, 3.2.2, 3.3.1, 3.3.2, 3.3.3, 3.3.5, 4.1.1, 4.1.5, 4.3.1 ; English Language Arts Standards 1, 3, 4, 6, 11, 12)

Related Books

1. Verne, Jules. *Around the World in Eighty Days.* New York: HarperCollins, 2000. Illustrated by Barry Moser. This is an illustrated edition of the book.

2. Verne, Jules. *Journey to the Center of the Earth.* New York: Sterling Publishing Company, 2007. 256p. ISBN 1-402-74337-8.

Professor Liedenbrock follows the directions in a coded note to reach the core of the earth.

3. Verne, Jules. *Michael Strogoff: A Courier of the Czar.* New York: Atheneum Books for Young Readers, 1997. 416p. Illustrated by N. C. Wyeth. $25.99. ISBN 0-689-81096-2.

Michael Strogoff must warn the Governor-General of Siberia that Feofar-Khan and his men are stirring up rebellion in Siberia.

4. Verne, Jules. *20,000 Leagues under the Sea.* New York: HarperCollins, 2000. Illustrated by Leo and Diane Dillon. $21.95. ISBN 0-688-10535-1.

Dive deep below the waves aboard the submarine Nautilus with Captain Nemo and his crew, as they search for treasure, explore the lost city of Atlantis, and battle the giant octopus.

5. Verne, Jules. *The Mysterious Island.* New York: Atheneum Books for Young Readers, 1988. 508p. Illustrated by N. C. Wyeth. $28.00. ISBN 0-684-18957-7.

Cyrus, Pencroft, Herbert, Neb, and Gideon escape from a Civil War prison in a balloon, land on a volcanic island, then, like the Swiss Family Robinson, survive by creating a new home on the island.

GREENLAND, ICELAND, ARCTIC, AND ANTARCTIC

Richard Farr's nonfiction book about Apsley Cherry-Garrard's expedition to the South Pole with Captain Robert Falcon Scott, and related nonfiction books provide readers with information about the earth's polar regions.

Rune Michaels's realistic fiction about a young girl and her family sensitively addresses the topic not only of death, but of suicide, and of the process of grief, mourning, denial, and finally acceptance. Curriculum Responses include map work, research, discussion, and other activities.

Farr, Richard. *Emperors of the Ice: A True Story of Disaster and Survival in the Antarctic, 1910-13.* New York: Farrar, Straus and Giroux, 2008. 215p. $19.95. ISBN 0-374-31975-8.

Author

Author Richard Farr grew up in England and now lives in the United States. The Antarctic is the setting of the book.

📖 Nonfiction, Ages 11 and Up

Summary

Richard Farr draws on Apsley Cherry-Garrard's book, *The Worst Journey in the World,* to retell the account of Captain Robert Falcon Scott's 1910 expedition to reach the South Pole and the scientific expedition that Cherry and two others made to recover Emperor Penguin eggs from the cliffs of Cape Crozier. Photographs, journal entries, maps, and charts supplement the narrative that is told through the eyes of Apsley Cherry-Garrard, and Farr frequently uses Cherry's own words. The rigors and hardships of the journey and the courage, determination, and spirit of the men leave a lasting impression on the reader.

Curriculum Responses with Curriculum Standards

1. Have students find Antarctica on a world map. On a world map or map of Antarctic, have students find the Ross Sea, McMurdo Sound, the Ross Ice Shelf, Mt. Erebus, the Beardmore Glacier, and the South Pole. Use the map on page 25 as a guide, have students retrace the voyage of the Terra Nova on the world map. Using the map on page 25, have students compare the route of Scott with the route of Amundsen. (American Association of School Librarians Standards 1.1.1, 1.1.6, 1.1.8, 1.2.1, 1.3.4, 2.1.1, 2.1.3, 2.1.4, 2.3.1, 2.4.3, 3.1.2, 3.2.2, 3.2.3, 3.3.5, 4.1.4, 4.1.7, 4.2.1, 4.3.1; English Language Arts Standards 1, 4, 6, 11, 12; Social Studies Standards III)
2. After reading the book, consider showing your students one of several films cited by the author in Sources: *Scott of the Antarctic, 90 South, or Shackleton.* Have students discuss the likenesses and differences between print and film versions of a similar experience. (American Association of School Librarians Standards 1.1.6, 1.1.7, 1.1.9, 1.2.1,

1.3.3, 1.3.4, 2.1.1, 2.1.3, 2.1.4, 2.1.5, 3.1.3, 3.2.1, 3.2.2, 3.3.1, 3.3.2, 3.2.3, 3.3.5, 4.1.1, 4.1.3, 4.1.4, 4.1.5, 4.3.1; English Language Arts Standards 1, 3, 4, 6, 11, 12; Social Studies Standards III; Theater Content Standards 6, 7)

3. Encourage students to research and share with their classmates information about Roald Amundsen, who reached the South Pole before Scott, and about Ernest Shackleton, the explorer who made several expeditions to Antarctica. (American Association of School Librarians Standards 1.1.1, 1.1.2, 1.1.3, 1.1.4, 1.1.5, 1.1.6, 1.1.7, 1.1.8, 1.1.9, 1.2.1, 1.2.2, 1.2.3, 1.2.4, 1.2.5, 1.2.6, 1.2.7, 1.3.1, 1.3.2, 1.3.3, 1.3.4, 1.3.5, 1.4.1, 1.4.2, 1.4.3, 1.4.4, 2.1.1, 2.1.2, 2.1.3, 2.1.4, 2.1.5, 2.2.1, 2.4.3, 3.1.1, 3.1.2, 3.1.3, 3.1.6, 3.2.1, 3.2.2, 3.2.3, 3.3.2, 3.3.3, 3.3.5, 3.4.1, 3.4.2, 4.1.1, 4.1.2, 4.1.3, 4.1.4, 4.1.7. , 4.2.1, 4.3.1, 4.3.2, 4.4.2; English Language Arts Standards 1, 3, 4, 6, 7, 8, 11, 12; Social Studies Standards II)

4. After reading, the book, discuss with your students the personal qualities that enabled the men to survive the rigors and hardships of their journey, i.e.: persistence, perseverance, dedication, sense of purpose or mission, problem solving, using available resources, active decision-making, and others. Extend the activity by gathering news stories and biographic accounts of survival. Consider and discuss the following questions: What was the effect of the survival experience on the persons involved? Was healing necessary? Did change occur? (American Association of School Librarians Standards 1.1.1, 1.1.3, 1.1.6, 1.1.9, 1.2.1, 1.3.1, 2.1.1, 2.1.3, 2.1.5, 2.3.1, 3.1.1, 3.1.2, 3.1.3, 3.1.5, 3.2.1, 3.2.2, 3.3.2, 3.3.3, 3.3.5, 4.1.2, 4.1.4, 4.2.2, 4.3.1; English Language Arts Standards 4, 6, 7, 11, 12; Social Studies Standards IV)

5. Discuss with students the role of technology in the Antarctic expedition, i.e., motorized sleds, the use of horses and dogs for pulling, clothing, boots, sleeping bags, and foods (pemmican, biscuits, tea vs. cocoa). How did the choices Amundsen made give him an advantage over Scott? What might today's explorers use? (American Association of School Librarians Standards 1.1.1, 1.1.4, 1.1.6, 1.3.4, 2.1.1, 2.1.3, 2.1.5, 2.2.2, 2.2.3, 2.3.1, 3.1.4, 3.1.2, 3.1.3, 3.2.1, 3.2.2, 3.3.1, 3.3.2, 3.3.3, 3.3.5, 4.3.1; English Language Arts Standards 4, 6, 11, 12; Social Studies Standards VIII)

Related Books

1. Apte, Sunita. *Polar Regions: Surviving in Antarctica (X-Treme Places)*. New York: Bearport Publishing, 2005. 32p. $15.27. ISBN 1-597-16088-1.

This is an account of the 2001 attempt by Liv Arneson and Anne Bancroft to ski across Antarctica.

2. DK Children. *Atlas of Exploration.* New York: D.K. Publishing, Inc., 2008. 96p. $19.99. ISBN 0-756-63380-X.

This comprehensive guide to explorations of the continents, oceans, and space includes explorations to the North and South Poles.

3. Green, Jen. *You Wouldn't Want to be a Polar Explorer? An Expedition You'd Rather Not Go On.* Danbury, CT: Children's Press, 2000. 32p. Illustrated by David Antram. $9.95. ISBN 0-531-16207-9.

Cartoon-like illustrations and light-hearted text recount the1912 polar expedition of Ernest Shackleton.

4. Scott, Elaine. *Poles Apart: Why Penguins and Polar Bears Will Never Be Neighbors.* New York: Viking Juvenile, 2004. 64p. $17.99. ISBN 0-670-05925-0.

Black and white photos and informative text tell of the origins, seasons, animals, explorations, and more about the North and South Poles.

5. Snowden, Maxine. *Polar Explorers for Kids: Historic Expeditions to the Arctic and Antarctica with 21 Activities (For Kids Series).* Chicago Review Press, 2003. 160p. $16.05. ISBN 1-556-52500-1.

Biographic and factual information about explorations of the Arctic and Antarctic regions begins with Erik the Red in 981 and ends with scientific expeditions in 1994.

Michaels, Rune. *The Reminder.* New York: Atheneum Books for Young Readers, 2008. 182p. $16.95. ISBN 1-4169-4131-2.

Author

Author Rune Michaels lives in Reykjavik, Iceland.

📖 Realistic Fiction, Ages 12 and Up

Summary

Daze, that's short for Daisy, still misses her mom. It's been two years now since Mom died. Five-year-old Ryan doesn't really remember her anymore. Daze told her friend Lori all about her mother's illness, how she held Mom's hand as she died of cancer. But that's not the way it was. Mom committed suicide, and it was Daze who found her. The author addresses the topic of death, grief, denial, and suicide with gentleness and sensitivity. Resolution finally lies in acceptance of what happened, without trying to understand, but in loving and remembering the love of the mother who died.

Curriculum Responses with Curriculum Standards

1. Be sure to read and digest the entire book before introducing it to students. (American Association of School Librarians Standards 1.1.6, 4.1.1, 4.1.2; Standards for the English Language Arts 1, 2)
2. Be prepared to discuss with students their experiences of death, the grieving process, and the topic of suicide before reading the book. (American Association of School Librarians Standards 1.1.2, 1.1.3, 1.1.9, 1.3.4, 2.1.5, 2.3.1, 3.1.2, 3.1.3, 3.2.2, 3.3.1, 3.3.2, 3.3.5, 4.1.5, 4.3.1; Standards for the English Language Arts 4, 6, 11, 12; Social Studies Standards IV)
3. Again discuss with students their experiences of death, the grieving process, and the topic of suicide while they are reading and when they finish reading. Ask students whether their thoughts or understandings changed as a result of reading the book. (American Association of School Librarians Standards 1.1.2, 1.1.3, 1.1.9, 1.1.6, 1.3.4, 2.1.5, 2.3.1, 3.1.2, 3.1.3, 3.2.2, 3.3.1. 3.3.2, 3.3.5, 4.1.1, 4.1.2, 4.1.3, 4.1.4, 4.1.5, 4.3.1; Standards for the English Language Arts 1, 2, 3, 4, 6, 11, 12; Social Studies Standards IV)

Related Books

Michael, Rune. *Genesis Alpha.* New York: Atheneum Books for Young Readers, 2007. 208p. $14.99. ISBN 1-416-91886-8.

This is a thought-provoking story for older readers. It is about Josh, who was born to provide the stem cells needed to save the life of his older brother, Max, who as a young adult murdered a college girl.

INDIA, PAKISTAN, AND AFGHANISTAN

Readers will sample three very different perspectives in the following realistic fiction, fantasy, and literary folk tale selections from India, Pakistan, and Afghanistan. Francesco D'Adamo's *Iqbal* is a fictionalized account of a young boy's efforts to free the Pakistani children bound in servitude to the carpet factories of Pakistan. Uma Krishhnaswami tells the story of a young girl who returns to India with her mother, of the girl's efforts to reconcile her American identity with her family's Indian culture, and of her efforts to reconcile the tensions she experiences in her relationship with her mother, and the tensions of her parents' divorce.

Suzanne Fisher Staples tells the story of a young Afghan girl who finds refuge with an American woman teaching and living in Pakistan with her Afghan husband's family. Chitra Banerjee Divakaruni's fantasy series about *The Conch Bearers* introduces readers to the richness of India's culture and heritage. Finally, Rudyard Kipling, the first Englishman to receive the Nobel Prize for literature, delights readers with the lyrical language of his literary folktales. Curriculum Responses include discussion of social and economic conditions, research, writing, puppetry, creation of board games, readers' theater scripts, roll movies, and others.

D'Adamo, Francesco. *Iqbal.* New York: Atheneum Books for Young Readers, 2003. 120p. Translated by Ann Leonori. $15.95. ISBN 0-689-85445-5.

Author and Translator

Author Francesco D'Adamo is Italian. Translator Ann Leonori is American and has lived in Italy for over forty years. The book is set in Pakistan.

  📖   Realistic Fiction, Ages 8–12

Summary

This is a fictionalized story about thirteen-year-old Iqbal Masih, who died in 1995 trying to free the Pakistani children bound in servitude. Iqbal tells the children at the carpet factory that his older brother is sick and needs medicine. His father has no one to help him in the fields. The grain his father harvests belongs to the master. A man offered his father a lot of money ($26.00) to buy food until the next harvest. At first Iqbal's father said no to the money, but Iqbal's brother didn't get better, and Iqbal's mother cried. Iqbal's father accepted the money and told Iqbal that he will have to work in the carpet factory to pay off the debt. All of the children at the carpet factory have similar stories to tell. Iqbal and the children work, but their families' debts do not get smaller. Iqbal decides to do something to free himself and the other children.

Curriculum Responses with Curriculum Standards

1. Discuss the social and economic conditions that led families to place their children in servitude, What were the conditions that prevented the children from reducing their families' debts? (American Association of School Librarians Standards 1.1.3, 1.1.6, 1.1.9, 1.2.1, 1.3.4, 2.1.1, 2.1.5, 2.2.2, 2.2.3, 2.3.1, 2.4.1, 2.4.3, 3.1.3, 3.2.1, 3.2.2, 3.3.1, 3.3.5, 4.3.1, 4.4.4; English Language Arts Standards 3, 4, 11; Social Studies Standards I, V, VI, VII, IX, X)

2. Encourage children to learn more and to report about Iqbal and child labor laws by visiting the following Web sites listed in the back of the book: http://www.childrensworld.org/engiqbal/index.asp; http://www.mirrorimage.com/iqbal/index.html; http://www.freethechildren.org/campaigns/cl_realstories_iqbal.html. (American Association of School Librarians Standards 1.1.1, 1.1.2, 1.1.3, 1.1.4, 1.1.5, 1.1.6, 1.1.7, 1.1.8, 1.1.9, 1.2.1, 1.2.2, 1.2.3, 1.2.4, 1.2.5, 1.2.6, 1.2.7, 1.3.1, 1.3.2, 1.3.3, 1.3.4, 1.3.5, 1.4.1, 1.4.2, 1.4.3, 1.4.4, 2.1.1, 2.1.2, 2.1.3, 2.1.4, 2.1.5, 2.2.1, 2.2.2, 2.2.3, 2.3.1, 2.3.2, 2.4.1, 2.4.2, 2.4.3, 3.1.1, 3.1.2, 3.1.3, 3.1.4, 3.1.5, 3.1.6, 3.2.1, 3.2.2, 3.3.1, 3.3.2, 3.3.5, 3.3.6, 3.4.1, 3.4.2, 4.1.2, 4.1.4, 4.1.7, 4.2.3, 4.3.1, 4.3.2, 4.4.4; English Language Arts Standards 1, 7, 8; Social Studies Standards I, V, VI, VII, IX)

3. Have students use print and nonprint resources to research and report on child labor laws in their own communities. (American Association of School Librarians Standards 1.1.1, 1.1.3, 1.1.4, 1.1.5, 1.1.6, 1.1.7, 1.1.8, 1.1.9, 1.2.1, 1.2.2, 1.2.3, 1.2.4, 1.2.5, 1.2.6, 1.2.7, 1.3.2, 1.3.3, 1.3.1, 1.3.3, 1.3.4, 1.3.5, 1.4.1, 1.4.2, 1.4.3, 1.4.4, 2.1.1, 2.1.2, 2.1.3, 2.1.4, 2.1.5, 2.1.6, 2.2.1, 2.2.2, 2.2.3, 2.2.4, 2.3.1, 2.4.1, 2.4.2, 2.4.3, 3.1.1, 3.1.2, 3.1.3, 3.1.4, 3.1.5, 3.1.6, 3.2.1, 3.2.2, 3.2.3, 3.3.5, 3.4.1, 3.4.2, 4.1.2, 4.1.7, 4.3.2; English Language Arts Standards 1, 4, 7, 8, 11; Social Studies Standards V, VI, VII, X)

Divakaruni, Chitra Banerjee. *The Mirror of Fire and Dreaming.* New York: Aladdin Paperbacks, 2007. 329p. $6.99. ISBN 978-1-4169-1768-7.

Author

Author Chitra Banerjee Divakaruni was born in Calcutta, India, and now lives in the United States. This book is set in India.

📖 Fiction, Fantasy, Ages 8–12

Summary

In this sequel to *The Conch Bearers,* which is Book II of the Brotherhood of the Conch, twelve-year-old Anand breaks the rules of the Brotherhood to rescue the Master Healer, Abhaydatta. Nisha and the conch accompany Anand as he travels across India and back in time to the rule of the Moghuls. A magical mirror, a spirit devouring jinn, an ailing ruler, the ruler's weak son, and a beautiful princess complicate Anand's rescue of Abhaydatta. Finally, Anand must resist and overcome an evil sorcerer who tries to gain control of the ailing ruler and his kingdom.

Curriculum Responses with Curriculum Standards

1. After reading, encourage students to create book-based board games with written questions that incorporate travel across time and space, colorful characters, and adventure. (American Association of School Librarians Standards 1.1.2, 1.1.6, 1.1.9, ; 1.2.2, 1.2.3, 1.3.4, 2.1.6, 2.2.4, 3.1.2, 3.1.3, 3.2.1, 3.2.2, 3.2.3, 3.3.5, 4.1.1, 4.1.3, 4.1.8; English Language Arts Standards 1, 3, 4, 6, 11, 12; Visual Arts Content Standards 1, 2, 3)

2. After reading, encourage students to select episodes from the book and create reader's theater scripts to enact for their classmates. (American Association of School Librarians Standards 1.1.6, 1.1.9, 1.2.2, 1.2.3, 1.3.4, 2.1.5, 2.1.6, 2.3.4, 3.1.2, 3.1.3, 3.2.1, 3.2.2, 3.2.3, 3.3.5, 4.1.1, 4.1.3, 4.1.8, 4.3.1; English Language Arts Standards 1, 3, 4, 5, 6, 11, 12)

3. After reading, encourage students to select, block, and sequence scenes with characters and dialogues to create a roll movie of the book. (American Association of School Librarians Standards 1.1.6, 1.1.9, 1.2.2, 1.2.3, 1.3.4, 2.1.5, 2.1.6, 2.3.4, 3.1.2, 3.1.3, 3.2.1, 3.2.2, 3.2.3, 3.3.1, 3.3.2, 3.3.5, 4.1.1, 4.1.3, 4.1.8, 4.3.1; English Language Arts Standards 1, 3, 4, 5, 11, 12; Visual Arts Content Standards 1, 2, 3)

Related Books

1. Divakaruni, Chitra Banerjee. *The Conch Bearer.* New York: Aladdin Paperbacks, 2005. 272p. $5.99. ISBN 0-689-87242-9.

In the first book of the Brotherhood of the Conch Series, twelve-year-old Anand's life changes dramatically, and his adventures begin when he befriends the old man Abhaydatta, a healer who must retrieve a magical conch shell and return it to the Brotherhood of Healers, high in the mountains.

2. Divakaruni, Chitra Banerjee. *Neela: Victory Song.* New York: American Girl, 2002. 198p. $3.95. Illustrated by Troy Howell. ISBN 1-584-85521-5.

Twelve-year-old Neela runs away from home to find her father, who disappeared after joining Mohandas Gandhi's peaceful protest against two hundred years of British rule in India.

3. Divakaruni, Chitra Banerjee. *Shadowland.* New York: Roaring Brook Press, 2009. 240p. $17.50. ISBN 1-596-43153-9.

In this final book of the Brotherhood of the Conch Series, Anand, now fifteen years old, must again leave his studies with the Brotherhood to search for the conch and return it to Silver Valley.

Kipling, Rudyard. *Just So Stories.* New York: Aladdin Classics, 2002. 180p. $5.99. ISBN 0-689-85125-1.

Author and Illustrator

Author and illustrator Rudyard Kipling was born in India to British Colonial Parents. He was educated in England, traveled the world, married an American, lived in America for awhile, and, after the death of his daughter, returned to England. Rudyard Kipling was the first Englishman to receive the Nobel Prize for Literature. India is the setting for these stories.

📖　Fiction, Literary Folk Tales, All Ages

Summary

This is a complete and unabridged collection of the twelve "why" stories that the author originally told to his young daughter, Josephine, the Taffy addressed as "best beloved" in the stories. "How the Whale got his Throat," "The Beginning of the Armadillos," "The Elephant's Child," and others are frequently referred to as creation stories, stories about how things came to be, also known as pourquoi (why?) stories. The rich literary language, with its lyrical cadence is language to be heard as well as to read. Remember, these are oral stories that the author told to his beloved young daughter. It was years later before he wrote them down. A Foreword and Reading Group Guide complete the book.

Curriculum Responses with Curriculum Standards

1. Provide a listening experience by selecting a story to read aloud. Encourage children to listen to the story and to the the language Kipling uses. Practice reading aloud before you read to your students, so that you can do justice to the language, which is unique to Kipling, and which does not roll easily off the tongue. (American Association of School Librarians Standards 1.1.6, 4.1.1; English Language Arts Standards 9)
2. Encourage students to write their own "why" stories. (American Association of School Librarians Standards 1.1.2, 2.1.6, 2.2.4, 3.1.3, 4.1.3, 4.1.8; English Language Arts Standards 4, 5, 6, 12)
3. Consider developing a unit about pourquoi (creation) stories across cultures (African, Native American, Central and South American) Be sure to include family stories and local legends about how something came to be. (American Association of School Librarians Standards 1.1.2, 1.1.3, 1.1.4, 1.1.5, 1.1.6, 1.1.7, 1.2.2, 1.3.2, 1.4.1, 2.3.2, 4.1.2, 4.2.4, 4.3.3, 4.4.1, 4.4.4; English Language Arts Standards 1, Social Studies Standards 1)

4. Encourage students to retell stories by creating puppets and a puppet stage, by writing a script, rehearsing, and putting on a puppet show. (American Association of School Librarians Standards 1.1.6, 1.1.9, 1.2.3, 2.1.6, 2.2.4, 3.1.3, 3.2.3, 4.1.1, 4.1.3, 4.1.8; English Language Arts Standards 1, 3, 4, 5, 6, 11, 12; Theater Content Standards 1, 2, 3, 4; Visual Arts Content Standards 1, 2, 3)

5. See the Reading Group Guide for possible discussion questions. (American Association of School Librarians Standards 1.1.2, 1.1.9, 1.2.1, 1.3.4, 2.1.3, 2.1.5, 2.2.3, 3.1.2, 3.1.3, 3.2.1, 3.2.2, 3.2.3, 3.3.1, 3.3.2, 3.3.5, 4.3.1; English Language Arts Standards 11, 12)

Related Books

1. Kipling, Rudyard. *If: A Father's Advice to His Son.* New York: Atheneum Books for Young Readers. 2007. Unpaged. Photos by Charles R. Smith Jr. $14.99. ISBN 0-689-87799-4.

Photos from the lives of contemporary young people enhance Kipling's inspiring poem, written particularly for boys.

2. Kipling, Rudyard. *The Jungle Book.* New York: Sterling Publishing Company, 2007. 352p. Illustrated by Scott McKowen. $9.95. ISBN 1-402-74340-8.

This is a complete and unabridged edition of the stories of Mowgli, Rikki Tikki Tavi, Toomai, and Quiquern, as originally told in Books One and Two of the Jungle Book.

Krishnaswami, Uma. *Naming Maya.* New York: Farrar Straus Giroux, 2004. 178p. $16.00. ISBN 0-374-35485-5.

Author

Author Uma Krishnaswami was born in New Delhi, India, and now lives in New Mexico. This book is set in Southern India.

📖 Realistic Fiction, Ages 10–14

Summary

Maya's grandfather died. Maya and her mother travel from New Jersey to India to sell his house. Kamala Mami suggests that Maya's mother return to live in India, now that she and Maya's father are divorced. Maya's return visit to India is like stepping into another world with another family. Memories and a rush of feelings pour in, including memories of her father. The tension between Maya and her mother is always there. Why did her parents divorce? Does the divorce have something to do with Maya, with her name? Maya sorts through her many questions and feelings with the help of her cousin Sumati and with the help of Kamala Mami. Author's Note and Glossary of Tamil words complete the book.

Curriculum Responses with Curriculum Standards

1. Maya reconciles two worlds: her world, life, and family in New Jersey, with her world, life, and family in India. After reading, have students make a Venn diagram to compare and contrast Maya's two worlds. (American Association of School Librarians Standards 1.1.6, 1.3.4, 2.1.1, 2.1.2, 2.1.5, 2.1.6, 2.2.4, 2.4.3, 3.1.2, 3.1.3, 3.2.1, 3.2.2, 3.2.3, 3.3.1, 3.3.2, 3.3.5, 4.1.1, 4.1.2, 4.1.3, 4.1.6, 4.3.1; English Language Arts Standards 1, 3, 4, 5, 6, 11, 12; Social Studies Standards I, II, IV)

2. After reading, engage your students in discussion. Encourage them to use a journal to write their thoughts before and after discussion. Encourage students to relate Maya's experiences to their own experiences. Possible discussion topics might be: (1) Maya develops insight into what happened between her parents. (2) Maya develops insight into the tensions that she experiences with her mother. (3) Maya discovers from the changes around her that she can choose the memories and feelings to keep and the ones to discard. (American Association of School Librarians Standards 1.1.6, 1.3.4, 2.1.2, 2.1.5, 2.1.6, 2.3.1, 2.4.3, 3.1.2, 3.1.3, 3.2.2, 3.3.1, 3.3.2, 3.3.5, 4.1.1, 4.1.2, 4.1.3, 4.1.4, 4.1.5, 4.3.1; English Language Arts Standards 1, 3, 4, 5, 6, 11, 12; Social Studies Standards II, IV)

3. After reading, have students discuss how Sumati and Kamala Mami helped Maya. Encourage students to relate the help that Sumati and Kamala Mami gave Maya to similar help that they may have received from someone. (American Association of School Librarians Standards 1.1.6, 1.3.4, 2.1.5, 2.3.1, 2.4.3, 3.1.2, 3.1.3, 3.2.2, 3.3.1, 3.3.2, 3.3.5, 4.1.1, 4.1.2, 4.1.3, 4.1.4, 4.1.5, 4.3.1; English Language Arts Standards 1, 3, 4, 5, 6, 11, 12; Social Studies Standards II, IV)

Related Books

1. Khan, Rukhsana, Uma Krishnaswami, and Elisa Carbonne. *Many Windows.* Toronto, Canada: Napoleon and Company, 2008. 88p. $12.95. ISBN 1-894-91756-1.

Seven stories tell about six children (two white boys, a black girl, a Chinese girl, an Indian girl, and a Pakistani boy) who observe five different religious faiths (Buddhism, Islam, Christianity, Judaism, and Hinduism) and attend the same school.

2. Krishnaswami, Uma. *Shower of Gold: Women and Girls in the Stories of India.* North Haven, CT: Linnet Books, 1999. 125p. Illustrated by Maniam Selven. $22.99. ISBN 0-208-02484-0.

Retellings of eighteen traditional Indian tales from Hindu and Buddhist mythology, folktales, and legends feature women and girls.

3. Krishnaswami, Uma. *The Broken Tusk: Stories of the Hindu God Ganesha.* August House. 129p. $16.95. ISBN 0-874-83806-1.

Introduce students to Indian mythology and culture with these seventeen retellings of Hindu myths about Ganesha, who is recognized by his elephant head.

Staples, Suzanne Fisher. *Under the Persimmon Tree.* New York: Frances Foster Books, 2005. 275p. $17.00. ISBN 0-374-38025-2.

Author

Author Suzanne Fisher Staples is an American who served as a news reporter in Afghanistan, Pakistan, India, and Hong Kong. She also worked on a women's literacy project sponsored by the U.S. Agency for International Development in the same area. Afghanistan and Pakistan are the settings for this book.

📖 Realistic Fiction, Ages 12 and Up

Summary

Set in Afghanistan in 2001–2002, shortly after the fall of the twin towers in New York, the stories of Najmah, a young Afghan girl, and Elaine, a young American woman, unfold. When the Taliban kidnap Najmah's father and brother and kill her mother and infant brother, Najmah makes her way from her home in Kunduz Province, Afghanistan, to a refugee camp in Peshawar, Pakistan. Even in Peshawar, Najmah is not safe until she finds a home with Elaine. Elaine, whose Islamic name is Nusrat, operates a school for Afghan refugee children while she awaits the return of her Afghan husband from a medical clinic in Mazar-i-Sharif, Afghanistan, where he serves as a physician. Author's Note, Map, and Glossary complete the book.

Curriculum Responses with Curriculum Standards

1. After reading, use a world map to locate Afghanistan, Pakistan, and neighboring countries. Locate the places mentioned in the book: Kunduz Province and Mazar-i-Sharif in Afghanistan, and Peshawar in Pakistan. Trace Najmal's journey from her home in Kunduz Province to Peshawar. (American Association of School Librarians Standards 1.1.1, 1.1.6, 2.1.1, 2.1.3, 2.3.1, 3.1.4, 4.1.3; English Language Arts Standards 1, 2, 3, 11, 12; Social Studies Standards III)

2. After reading, engage students in a discussion. Why did Elaine convert to Islam? (See Chapter 12.) Compare the book's portrayal of Islam (see chapters 12 and 20) with the media's portrayal of Islam. (American Association of School Librarians Standards 1.1.1, 1.1.6, 1.3.2, 1.3.4, 2.1.1, 2.1.5, 2.3.1, 2.3.2, 2.4.3, 3.1.3, 3.2.1, 3.2.2, 3.3.1, 3.3.2, 3.3.5, 4.1.1, 4.1.2, 4.1.3; English Language Arts Standards 1, 2, 3, 4, 11, 12; Social Studies Standards I, II)

3. After reading, encourage students to discuss the last two lines on page 269. "There are few happy endings, . . . but there are good endings. . . ." (American Association of School Librarians Standards 1.1.6, 1.1.9, 1.3.2, 1.3.4, 2.1.5, 2.3.2, 2.4.3, 3.1.2, 3.1.3, 3.2.1, 3.2.2, 3.3.1, 3.3.2, 3.3.5, 4.1.1, 4.1.2, 4.1.3, 4.3.1; English Language Arts Standards 1, 2, 3, 4, 11, 12; Social Studies Standards II, IV, V)

Related Books

1. Ellis, Deborah. *Breadwinner.* Toronto: Groundwood Books, 2001. 170p. $8.95. ISBN 0-888-99416-8.

When the Taliban imprison her father in Kabul, Afghanistan, eleven-year-old Parvana disguises herself as a boy so that she can become the breadwinner to support her mother, younger sisters, and brother.

2. Staples, Suzanne Fisher. *Haveli.* New York: Laurel Leaf, 1995. 336p. $6.99. ISBN 0- 679-86569-1.

In the sequel to *Shabanu: Daughter of the Wind,* teen-aged Shabanu and her five-year-old daughter Mumtaz find sanctuary in the home of her sister-in-law, where Shabanu falls in love with her husband's young nephew.

3. Staples, Suzanne Fisher. *Shabanu: Daughter of the Wind.* New York: Laurel Leaf, 2003. 288p. $6.99. ISBN 0-440-23856-0.

Set in modern Pakistan, in the Cholistan desert, the story tells of twelve-year-old Shababu, the daughter of camel-herding nomads, who must marry a man old enough to be her father.

4. Staples, Suzanne Fisher. *Shiva's Fire.* New York: Farrar, Straus & Giroux, 2000. 276p. $17.00. ISBN 0-374-36824-4.

Parvati is born with a gift for dancing and must choose between her love of dancing and her love for the Maharaja's son.

5. Staples, Suzanne Fisher. *The House of Djinn.* New York: Farrar, Straus & Giroux, 2008. 224p. $16.95. ISBN 0-374-39936-0.

The third book continues the story of Shabanu's daughter Mumtaz, now fifteen years old, and her American cousin, Jameel, also fifteen years old, who must become the new tribal leader when his grandfather dies.

MEXICO, LATIN AND SOUTH AMERICA, AND THE CARIBBEAN

Mexico, Latin and South America, and the Caribbean are all represented in the following selections. Children in crisis is the theme of two books. In *Colibri,* Rosa helps Uncle beg, even though he's not her uncle, until she can safely get away from him. In *Sacred Leaf,* twelve-year-old Diego escapes from an illegal cocaine operation, only to get caught up in a protest against Bolivian government officials. Francisco Jiminez continues his autobiography by telling of his teen years as a Mexican migrant worker in California. Edwidge Danticat tells the story of the young Anacaona, a woman ruler of Hispaniola at the time of Columbus and the Spanish conquest. *Sacred Leaf* was selected as an Outstanding International Book for Young People in 2008 by the United States Board on Books for Young People (USBBY). Curriculum Responses include research, electronic messages, art, and other activities.

Cameron, Ann. *Colibri.* New York: Farrar Straus Giroux, 2003. 227p. $17.00. ISBN 0-376-31519-1.

Author

Author Ann Cameron is an American who has lived in Guatemala for the past twenty years. Guatemala is the setting for this book.

  📖 Realistic Fiction, Ages 10 and Up

Summary

Rosa's job is to help Uncle beg. But she doesn't do it very well. Her mother taught her to be honest. Uncle isn't blind, nor is he her uncle. Rosa is afraid to make Uncle angry. He is her only protector. Then Rosa meets the Day-Keeper. The Day-Keeper is kind. When Uncle and Raimundo decide to steal the statue from the church, Rosa knows that she can no longer help them. Might she be safe with the Day-Keeper? She has to find out.

Curriculum Responses with Curriculum Standards

1. In Chapter 14, Colibri talks about having a "divided heart." Engage students in a discussion of what it means to have a "divided heart." Ask if any of them has had a "divided heart." (American Association

of School Librarians Standards 1.1.2, 1.1.3, 1.1.6, 1.1.9, 1.3.4, 2.1.5, 2.3.1, 3.1.2, 3.1.3, 3.2.1, 3.2.2, 3.3.1, 3.3.2, 3.3.5, 4.1.1, 4.1.2, 4.1.5, 4.3.1; English Language Arts Standards 1, 2, 3, 4, 6, 11, 12; Social Studies Standards IV)

2. Colibri treasures the broken cup that the woman gave her. To Colibri it is beautiful. She says "A person can't live without something beautiful." Ask students whether they have something that they treasure and think is beautiful. (American Association of School Librarians Standards 1.1.2, 1.1.3, 1.1.6, 1.1.9, 1.3.4, 2.1.5, 2.3.1, 3.1.3, 3.2.1, 3.2.2, 3.3.1, 3.3.2, 3.3.5, 4.1.1, 4.1.2, 4.1.5, 4.3.1; English Language Arts Standards 1, 2, 3, 4, 6, 11, 12)

3. Encourage students to select thought-provoking lines such as "some people . . . have kind of a shine to them." Record them as Philosophical Gems. Share with classmates, and explain what the lines mean to them. (American Association of School Librarians Standards 1.1.2, 1.1.6, 1.1.9, 1.2.2, 1.2.3, 1.3.4, 2.1.2, 2.1.6, 2.3.4, 2.3.1, 3.1.3, 3.2.1, 3.2.2, 3.3.1, 3.3.2, 3.3.5, 4.1.1, 4.1.2, 4.1.3, 4.1.5, 4.1.6, 4.1.7, 4.1.8, 4.3.1; English Language Arts Standards 1, 2, 3, 4, 5, 6, 11, 12)

Danticat, Edwidge. *Anacaona: Golden Flower.* New York: Scholastic Inc., 2005. 186p. $10.95. ISBN 0-439-49906-2.

Author

Author Edwidge Danticat was born in Port-au-Prince, Haiti. Her mother was born in Leogane, the Haitian town in the area where Anacaona ruled. The story of Anacaona is set in Hispaniola (Haiti) from 1490 to 1492.

📖 Historical Fiction, Ages 8–14

Summary

The story of Anacaona, one of the last and most powerful Taino leaders, is a book in the *Royal Diary Series*. Although the Tainos had no written language, this is a fictionalized version of the dairy that Anacaona might have kept of her thoughts, feelings, and experiences as a young woman. Anacaona's uncle is the chief of their people. Anacaona and her brother are next in line to rule. Her love for Chief Caonabo is so great that she willingly forfeits her right to rule her own people in order to become his wife, return to his lands, and rule as his queen. The arrival of Columbus and the Spaniards bring fighting and death to Caonabo, to Anacaona, and even to the Taino people. An Epilogue, a Historical Note describing life in Haiti, Anacaona's family tree, photos, a map, and a glossary of Taino words complete the book.

Curriculum Responses with Curriculum Standards

1. Encourage students to generate questions and research and share with their classmates more information about the Taino people. (American Association of School Librarians Standards 1.1.1, 1.1.3, 1.1.4, 1.1.5, 1.1.6, 1.1.7, 1.1.8, 1.1.9, 1.2.1, 1.2.2, 1.2.3, 1.2.4, 1.2.5, 1.2.6, 1.2.7, 1.3.2, 1.3.3, 1.3.4, 1.3.5, 1.4.1, 1.4.2, 1.4.3, 1.4.4, 2.1.1, 2.1.2, 2.1.3, 2.1.4, 2.1.5, 2.1.6, 2.2.1, 2.2.4, 2.3.1, 2.4.1, 2.4.3, 3.1.1, 3.1.2, 3.1.3, 3.1.4, 3.2.1, 3.2.2, 3.2.3, 3.3.3, 3.3.5, 3.4.1, 4.1.2, 4.1.3, 4.1.6, 4.1.7, 4.2.2, 4.3.1, 4.3.1, 4.4.3; English Language Arts Standards 7, 8, 11, 12; Social Studies Standards III)

2. After reading, have students select descriptive passages and create pictures of Anacaona's environment, plants, and wildlife. Allow students to use media of their choice. Mount a display of "Anacaona's World." (American Association of School Librarians Standards 1.1.6, 1.3.4, 2.1.6, 2.3.4, 3.3.5, 4.1.1, 4.1.2, 4.1.3, 4.1.8; English Language Arts Standards 1, 2, 3, 4, 6, 11, 12; Social Studies Standards III; Visual Arts Content Standards 1, 2, 3)

3. Have students find Haiti and the Dominican Republic on a map and locate Xaragua in the Southwest part of Haiti. (American Association of School Librarians Standards 1.1.6, 1.1.9, 1.3.4, 2.3.1, 2.4.3, 3.1.2, 3.1.3, 3.1.4, 3.2.1, 3.2.2, 4.1.2, 4.1.4, 4.1.7, 4.3.1; English Language Arts Standards 1, 2, 12; Social Studies Standards III)

Related Books

1. Alvarez, Julia. *How Tia Lola Came to (Visit) Stay.* New York: Yearling, 2002. 160p. $5.99. ISBN 0-440-41870-4.

Colorful, exotic Tia Lola from the Dominican Republic comes to visit, just when ten-year-old Miguel is trying to fit into his new home with new friends following his family's move from New York to Vermont.

2. Danticat, Edwidge. *Behind the Mountains.* New York: Scholastic Paperbacks, 2004. 166p. $20.60. ISBN 0-439-373000-X.

Thirteen-year-old Celiane Esperance records in her journal the journey she makes with her mother and brother from their home in the mountains of Haiti to the city of Port-au-Prince and then to New York City to join her father.

3. Ortiz Cofer, Judith. *Call Me Maria.* New York: Scholastic Paperbacks, 2006. 144p. $6.99. ISBN 0-439-38578-4.

Maria records her thoughts and feelings in poetry and prose as she tries to fit into her new home with her father in New York City, while her mother remains in Puerto Rico.

Ellis, Deborah. *Sacred Leaf.* Toronto: Groundwood Books, 2007. 206p. $16.95. ISBN 0-88899-751-5.

Author

Author Deborah Ellis is a Canadian writer, an antiwar activist, and a feminist. She writes about children in crisis in Afghanistan, Israel, Palestine, and South America. She traveled to Afghanistan and other countries to research her writing. She has received numerous awards, including the Governor General's Award, Sweden's Peter Pan Prize, the Ruth Schwartz Award, the Jane Addams Children's Book Award, and the Vicky Metcalf Award. *Sacred Leaf* was selected as a 2008 United States Board on Books for Young People (USBBY). Outstanding International Book for Young People. Bolivia is the setting for this book.

📖 Realistic Fiction, Ages 11–13

Summary

Twelve-year-old Diego finds refuge with the Ricardo family, poor Bolivian cocoa farmers (cocaleros), after escaping from an illegal cocaine operation. When government officials destroy the cocoa crops that the farmers depend on for their livelihood, the Ricardos and other cocaleros protest by occupying the bridge leading into and out of their village. Diego gets caught up in the protest out of loyalty to the Ricardos while other cocaleros are organizing and protesting across the country in a similar manner.

Curriculum Responses with Curriculum Standards

1. After reading, have students read the Author's Note at the end of the book. Encourage them to research more information about Bolivia: the protests of the cocaleros, the election of 2005, when a union leader was elected president of Bolivia, and the new constitution that was written as a result of the protests. Provide students with opportunities to report their findings to their classmates. (American Association of School Librarians Standards 1.1.1, 1.1.3, 1.1.4, 1.1.5, 1.1.6, 1.1.7, 1.1.8, 1.2.1, 1.2.2, 1.2.4, 1.2.5, 1.2.6, 1.2.7, 1.3.1, 1.3.2, 1.3.3,1.3.4, 1.3.5, 1.4.1, 1.4.2, 1.4.3, 1.4.4, 2.1.1, 2.1.2, 2.1.3, 2.1.4, 2.1.5, 2.1.6, 2.2.3, 2.2.3, 2.2.4, 2.3.1, 2.3.3, 2.4.1, 2.4.2, 2.4.3, 3.1.1, 3.1.2, 3.1.3, 3.1.4, 3.1.6, 3.2.1, 3.2.2, 3.2.3, 3.3.1, 3.3.2, 3.3.3, 3.3.4, 3.3.5, 3.3.7, 3.4.1, 3.4.2, 4.1.1, 4.1.2, 4.1.4, 4.1.7, 4.1.8, 4.2.1, 4.2.2, 4.2.3, 4.3.1, 4.3.2, 4.3.4, 4.4.1, 4.4.3, 4.4.4; English Language Arts Standards 1, 2, 3, 4, 6, 7, 8, 11, 12; Social Studies Standards V, VI)
2. While reading, encourage students to create text messages that the cocaleros might have sent to each other while they were building the

barricade on the bridge. Have students discuss how the ability to send text messages might have made a difference to the cocaleros' experiences of building and defending the barricade. Extend the activity by encouraging students to rewrite episodes to reflect the changes that sending text messages might have made. (American Association of School Librarians Standards 1.1.1, 1.1.2, 1.1.3, 1.1.6, 1.1.8, 1.1.9, 1.2.1, 1.2.2, 1.3.2, 1.3.4, 2.1.1, 2.1.3, 2.1.5, 2.1.6, 2.2.3, 2.2.4, 2.3.1, 3.1.1, 3.1.2, 3.1.3, 3.2.1, 3.2.2, 3.2.3, 3.3.1, 3.3.2, 3.3.3, 3.3.4, 3.3.5, 4.1.1, 4.1.2, 4.1.3, 4.1.8, 4.3.1; English Language Arts Standards 1, 3, 4, 5, 6, 11, 12; Social Studies Standards IV, V, VIII)

3. After reading, have students create email messages that Diego might have sent to his parents. How might his parents have responded to Diego's messages? (American Association of School Librarians Standards 1.1.2, 1.1.6, 1.2.1, 1.2.2, 1.3.4, 2.1.5, 2.1.6, 2.2.4, 3.1.2, 3.1.3, 3.1.4, 3.2.1, 3.2.2, 3.3.1, 3.3.2, 3.3.3, 3.3.4, 3.3.5, 4.1.1, 4.1.3, 4.1.8, 4.3.1; English Language Arts Standards 1, 3, 4, 5, 6, 11, 12; Social Studies Standards IV, V)

Related Books

1. Ellis, Deborah. *I Am a Taxi.* Toronto: Groundwood Books, 2006. 208p. $8.95. ISBN 0-888-997736-1.

In the first of the two *Cocalero Novels,* Diego lives with his parents in the prison in Cochalamba, Bolivia, and hires out, only to become enslaved in a cocaine manufacturing ring in the jungle.

Jiminez, Francisco. *Breaking Through.* Boston, Houghton Mifflin Company, 2001. 195p. $15.00. ISBN 0-618-01173-0.

Author

Author Francisco Jimenez was born in Mexico, immigrated to California, and worked in the fields with his family. He now lives in Santa Clara, California, where he serves as Fay Boyle Professor of Modern Languages and Literatures, and he is also director of the ethnic studies program at Santa Clara University. He writes of his experiences as a Mexican migrant child in California. His book *The Circuit: Stories from the Life of a Migrant Child,* received the Jane Addams Book Award in 2000.

📖 Nonfiction, Autobiography, Ages 11 and Up

Summary

In the sequel to *The Circuit,* Francisco Jiminez continues his story of growing up as a Mexican migrant worker. After living and working in California for ten years, Francisco, his parents, and his brothers and sisters are sent back to Mexico by the Border Patrol. Papa has a green card; Trampito, Torito, Rorra, and Reuben are United States citizens because they were born in California. Only Mama, Roberto, and Francisco are illegal and have to return to Mexico. But Papa and Mama will not separate the family, so all return to Nogales where Mama, Roberto, and Francisco get visas. Roberto and Francisco return to Santa Maria, where they can go to school. The boys work in the fields until Roberto gets back his old job of cleaning at Main Street School. Mama, Papa, and the other children stay in Mexico with Aunt Chana until the rainy season ends, and they can get work in the fields again. The day finally comes when the family rejoins the boys in their barracks in Santa Maria. Each of the twenty-five chapters relates an episode from Francisco's teen years, i.e., graduating from junior high, learning to dance, learning to drive, becoming class president and others. The book culminates with Francisco's graduation from high school and his entrance into college.

Curriculum Responses with Curriculum Standards

1. The author tells of hard work, disappointments, poverty, his father's poor health and depression, all within the context of close family ties, with love and respect for self, family, and others. After reading, engage students in a discussion of the help and support that members of the author's family give to each other. Encourage students to think about their own families, difficulties they may face, and the ways in which family members help and support each other. (American Association of School Librarians Standards 1.1.2, 1.1.6, 1.1.9, 1.3.4, 2.3.1, 3.1.1, 3.1.2, 3.1.3, 3.2.1, 3.2.2, 3.3.1, 3.3.2, 3.3.3, 3.3.5, 4.1.1, 4.1.2, 4.1.3, 4.1.5, 4.3.1; English Language Arts Standards 1, 2, 3, 4, 6, 11, 12; Social Studies Standards IV)

2. The author loves school and loves to learn, in spite of many challenges. After reading, engage students in a discussion of the persistence and perseverance that the author demonstrates. Ask students to think of their own lives, of their family, and friends. Ask whether they or anyone they know has faced challenges that require persistence and perseverance to achieve something they want. (American Association of School Librarians Standards 1.1.2, 1.1.3, 1.1.6, 1.1.9, 1.2.1, 1.3.4, 2.1.1, 2.1.3, 2.1.5, 2.3.1, 3.1.1, 3.1.2, 3.1.3, 3.2.1, 3.2.2, 3.3.1, 3.3.2, 3.3.5, 4.1.1, 4.1.2, 4.1.3, 4.1.4, 4.1.5, 4.3.1; English Language Arts Standards 1, 2, 3, 4, 6, 11, 12; Social Studies Standards IV)

3. Using this book as a model, encourage students to write about a short episode from their lives. (American Association of School Librarians

Standards 1.1.2, 2.1.6, 2.2.4, 3.1.3, 3.3.4, 4.1.3, 4.1.5, 4.1.8; English Language Arts Standards 3, 4, 5, 6; Social Studies Standards IV)

Related Books

1. Carlson, Lori Marie (Ed.) *Voices in First Person: Reflections on Latino Identity.* New York, Atheneum Books for Young Readers, 2008. 84p. Photography by Manuel Rivera-Ortez. $16.99. ISBN 9-781416-90635-3.

Twenty-two fictional monologues written by Latino authors, many of whom were born in the United States, and some who were born in other countries, reflect the diverse experiences of Latino teens and preteens in today's society—experiences ranging from humor, love, and hope, to fear and anger, including abuse, teen suicide, pregnancy, and sexuality.

2. Calcines, Eduardo F. *Leaving Glorytown: One Boy's Struggle Under Castro.* New York: Farrar Straus Giroux, 2009. 221p. $17.97. ISBN 0-374-34394-2.

The author writes of his experiences growing up in Cuba under Castro from 1959 to 1969, until his family emigrates to the United States when he is thirteen years old.

3. Delacre, Lulu. *Salsa Stories.* New York: Scholastic Press, 2000. 112p. $15.95. ISBN 0-590-63118-7.

Carmen Teresa records in her new blank notebook, stories about celebrations and recipes that she gathers from family members.

4. Jimenez, Francisco. *The Circuit: Stories from the Life of a Migrant Child.* Boston: Houghton Mifflin Company, 1999. 128p. $15.00. ISBN 0-395-97902-1.

The author writes of his childhood in twelve chapters, each a self-contained episode.

5. Johnston, Tony. *Any Small Goodness: A Novel of the Barrio.* New York: Blue Sky Press, 2001. 128p. Illustrated by Raul Colon. $15.95. ISBN 0-439-18936-5.

Arturo's father tells him that he must create good if he does not find it, and it is the good extended to Arturo and his family that softens their hard life in the barrio of Los Angeles.

MIDDLE EAST

Realistic fiction, nonfiction, poetry, and folk stories reflect contemporary life and the traditional cultures of Israel, Palestine, Lebanon, and Iraq. Israeli authors Daniella Carmi and Uri Orlev tell two very different stories. Daniella Carmi writes of a Palestinian boy in a Jewish Hospital in Israel. Uri Orlev tells the story of a Jewish boy who spends the years of World War II running and hiding in the Polish countryside, and who eventually emigrates to Israel as a young adult. Naomi Shihab Nye, a Palestinian American who lived in Jordan and Jerusalem, compiled a collection of poems by Middle Eastern poets. Palestinian author Sonia Nimr retells nine short stories that introduce readers to the Palestinian story-telling tradition. Three related books by British author Elizabeth Laird reflect her experiences of living in Iraq and Lebanon.

Both Daniella Carmi and Uri Orlev are recipients of the Batchelder Award. Uri Orlev also received the Hans Christian Andersen Prize. Books by Sonia Nimr and Elizabeth Laird were selected by the United States Board on Books for Young People (USBBY). as Outstanding International Books in 2007 and 2009 respectively. Curriculum responses include reading aloud, taking on the persona of book characters, making a Venn diagram, and other activities.

Carmi, Daniella. *Samir and Yonatan.* New York: Scholastic Inc., 2000. 185p. Translated by Yael Lotan. $5.99. ISBN 0-439-13523-0.

Author

Author Daniella Carmi was born in Tel Aviv and now lives in Jerusalem. Translator Yael Lotan lives in Israel. *Samir and Yonatan* received the Batchelder Award in 2001. Related Book, *A Little Piece of Ground,* was selected by the United States Board of Books for Young People (USBBY) as an Outstanding International Book in 2007.

📖 Realistic Fiction, Ages 9–12

Summary

When Samir, a young Palestinian boy, crushes his kneecap in a bicycle accident, he is taken from the Occupied Territory to a Jewish Hospital in Israel, where he shares a hospital room with four Jewish children, Yonatan, Razia, Ludmilla, and Tzahi. There in the hospital room, stories unfold: the story of Samir's life and family in the Occupied Territory, the stories of the four Jewish children, and the story of life in the hospital and the growing bonds between the children.

Curriculum Responses with Curriculum Standards

1. After reading, have five students become the characters of the five children, tell their stories to their classmates, and be prepared to answer questions that their classmates may ask. Have the listeners prepare questions to ask about the five characters. (American Association of School Librarians Standards 1.1.3, 1.1.4, 1.1.6, 1.1.9, 1.2.1,

1.3.4, 1.4.2, 2.1.1, 2.1.2, 2.1.5, 3.1.2, 3.1.3, 3.2.1, 3.2.2, 3.2.3, 3.3.1, 3.3.5, 4.1.1, 4.1.2, 4.1.3, 4.1.6, 4.3.1, 4.3.1; English Language Arts Standards 1, 2, 3, 4, 5, 6, 11, 12)

2. After reading, have students set up a Web site for Samir similar to caringbridge.org. (Caringbridge.org is a hospice Web site where families can journal patients' progress, and friends can post messages to the families and patients.) Have some students post regular progress reports for Samir's family and friends in the Occupied Territory. Have other students send messages to Samir from his family and friends. (American Association of School Librarians 1.1.6, 1.1.9, 1.2.3, 1.3.4, 2.1.2, 2.1.4, 2.1.5, 2.1.6, 2.1.4, 3.1.2, 3.1.3, 3.1.4, 3.2.1, 3.2.2, 3.2.3, 3.3.4, 3.3.5, 4.1.1, 4.1.2, 4.1.3, 4.1.6, 4.3.1, English Language Arts Standards 1, 2, 3, 4, 5, 6, 8, 11, 12)

3. After reading, engage students in a discussion; then have them make a Venn diagram showing how Samir's life is similar to and different from their lives. (American Association of School Librarians Standards 1.1.6, 1.1.9, 1.2.1, 1.2.2, 1.3.4, 2.1.2, 2.1.5, 2.1.6, 2.1.4, 3.1.1, 3.1.2, 3.1.3, 3.2.1, 3.2.2, 3.2.3, 3.3.4, 3.3.5, 4.1.1, 4.1.2, 4.1.3, 4.1.6, 4.3.1; English Language Arts Standards 1, 2, 3, 4, 5, 11, 12; Social Studies Standards IV)

Related Books

1. Ellis, Deborah. *Three Wishes: Palestinian and Israeli Children Speak.* London: Frances Lincoln Children's Books, 2007. 112p. $8.64. ISBN 1-845-07743-1.

Mature readers might be interested in reading the accounts of twenty Israeli and Palestinian young people, ages 8–18, who talk about their experiences of war and how it has affected them.

2. Laird, Elizabeth and Sonia Namir. *A Little Piece of Ground.* Chicago: Haymarket Books, 2006. 240p. $9.95. ISBN 1-931-859-388.

Twelve-year-old Karim and two friends try to clear an empty lot for a soccer field in the occupied zone in Ramallah, Palestine.

3. Laird, Elizabeth. *Oranges in No Man's Land.* Chicago: Haymarket Books, 2008. 128p. $9.95. ISBN 1-931-85956-6.

Civil War is raging in Lebanon, Grandma is dying, and ten-year-old Ayesha must cross No Man's Land to find a doctor and medicine.

Nimr, Sonia. *Ghaddar the Ghoul and other Palestinian Stories.* Frances London: Lincoln Children's Books, 2007. 96p. Illustrated by Hannah Shaw. $14.95. ISBN 978-1-84507-771-6.

Author and Illustrator

Sonia Nimr is Palestinian and lives in Ramallah. Illustrator Hannah Shaw is British. Sonia Nimr's book *A Little Piece of Ground* was selected by the United States Board on Books for Young People (USBBY) as an Outstanding International Book in 2007.

📖 Fiction, Folk Stories, Ages 8–12

Summary

Nine stories, of which three are retellings from *The Thousand and One Nights,* and six are retellings from other Arabic sources, introduce readers to Palestinian storytelling. Readers will meet jinn and ghouls and learn why mosquitoes can't speak. They will read about Ahmad, who set out to retrieve three magic hairs from Ghaddar the Ghoul in order to marry the princess; about the girl who told impossible tales to make the prince laugh; and about stupid Salma, who wasn't so stupid after all.

Curriculum Responses and Curriculum Standards

1. After reading, have students select a story to retell, using the following storytelling format. Introduce the story by setting the scene and introducing the characters. Select and develop three episodes leading to the climax of the story. Following the story climax, wind down to the ending. Encourage students to visualize rather than memorize their stories. Produce opportunities for students to rehearse and then to tell their stories. (American Association of School Librarians Standards 1.1.6, 1.3.4, 2.2.4, 3.1.2, 3.1.3, 3.2.1, 4.1.1, 4.1.8, 4.3.1; English Language Arts Standards 1, 3, 4, 6, 11, 12)

2. As students read the story "Ghaddar the Ghoul," encourage them to predict why the golden apple tree is dying, why the stream has dried up, and why the fish are disappearing from the lake. Have students write their predictions, discuss, brainstorm, and then read to confirm. (American Association of School Librarians Standards 1.1.6, 1.3.4, 2.1.5, 3.1.2, 3.1.3, 3.2.1, 3.2.2, 3.3.1, 3.3.2, 3.3.5, 4.1.1, 4.3.1; English Language Arts Standards 1, 3, 4, 5, 6, 11, 12)

3. Repetition in threes is a frequent characteristic of folktales. Encourage students to look for and identify the pattern of three repetitions as they read. Provide opportunities for students to share and discuss the patterns that they find. (American Association of School Librarians Standards 1.1.6, 1.1.9, 1.3.4, 3.1.5, 3.1.2, 3.1.3, 3.2.1, 3.2.2, 3.3.1, 3.3.2, 3.3.3, 3.3.5, 4.1.1, 4.1.3, 4.3.1; English Language Arts Standards 1, 3, 4, 6, 11, 12)

Related Books

Laird, Elizabeth. *A Fistful of Pearls and Other Tales from Iraq.* New York: Frances Lincoln Limited, 2008. 90p. Illustrated by Shelley Fowles. $14.95. ISBN 978-1-84507-811-9.

The author writes about her experience of living in Iraq, briefly describes the land and the people, then presents nine short stories that reflect Iraq's folk and storytelling traditions.

Nye, Naomi Shihab (Ed.) *The Flag of Childhood: Poems from the Middle East.* New York: Aladdin Paperbacks, 2002. 99p. $3.99. ISBN 0-689-851712-3.

Author

Author Naomi Shihab Nye was born in the United States to a Palestinian father and American mother, lived in Jordan and Jerusalem for a number of years, and now lives in the United States.

📖 Poetry, Ages 8–12

Summary

Poems written by Middle Eastern poets from Syria, Turkey, Palestine, Lebanon, Iraq, Jordan, Morocco, Iran, Israel, Egypt, Saudi Arabia, Yemen, and Tunisia give voice to the loves, longings, and details of daily life in a land and culture known to young readers primarily through the media. Nye's book *Habibi* received the Jane Addams Book Award in 1998.

Curriculum Responses with Curriculum Standards

1. Introduce the book by reading aloud a poem such as "I Remember My Father's Hands." Encourage students to listen for and discuss statements that are universal, that could be descriptive of someone they know, and for statements that are specific to someone from the Middle East. (American Association of School Librarians Standards 1.1.1, 1.1.2, 1.1.6, 1.1.9, 1.2.1, 1.2.2, 1.2.4, 1.3.2, 1.3.4, 1.4.2, 2.1.1, 2.1.3, 2.1.5, 2.2.3, 2.3.1, 2.3.2, 3.1.1, 3.1.2, 3.1.3, 3.2.1, 3.2.2, 3.3.1, 3.3.2, 3.3.5, 4.1.1, 4.1.2, 4.1.3, 4.1.5, 4.3.1; English Language Arts Standards 1, 2, 3, 4, 6, 11, 12; Social Studies Standards IV)

2. Continue by reading aloud "A Day in the Life of Nablus." Encourage students to compare and contrast Nablus's day with a day in their own lives by creating a Venn diagram. (American Association of School Librarians Standards 1.1.1, 1.1.2, 1.1.3, 1.1.6, 1.1.9, 1.2.1, 1.2.2, 1.2.3, 1.2.4, 1.3.4, 2.1.1, 2.1.2, 2.1.3, 2.1.4, 2.1.5, 2.1.6, 2.2.3,

2.2.4, 2.3.1, 2.4.1, 3.1.1, 3.1.2, 3.1.3, 3.1.4, 3.2.1, 3.2.2, 3.2.3, 3.3.1, 3.3.2, 3.3.4, 3.3.5, 4.1.1, 4.1.2, 4.1.3, 4.1.5, 4.1.6, 4.1.7, 4.1.8, 4.3.1; English Language Arts Standards 1, 2, 3, 4, 5, 6, 11, 12, Social Studies Standards IV)

3. Encourage children to read poems of their own choosing and to use these poems as models for writing poetry about their own lives. Invite them to share their poems with their classmates. How are their experiences like the experiences of the Middle Eastern poets? How are they different? (American Association of School Librarians Standards 1.1.1, 1.1.2, 1.1.6, 1.2.2, 1.2.3, 1.3.4, 2.1.1, 2.1.2, 2.1.6, 2.2.4, 3.1.1, 3.1.2, 3.1.3, 3.1.4, 3.1.5, 3.2.1, 3.2.2, 3.2.3, 3.3.1, 3.3.2, 3.3.4, 3.3.5, 4.1.1, 4.1.2, 4.1.3, 4.1.4, 4.1.5, 4.1.6, 4.1.7, 4.1.8, 4.3.1; English Language Arts Standards 1, 2, 3, 4, 5, 6, 11, 12, Social Studies Standards IV)

Related Books

1. Nye, Naomi Shihab. *Habibi.* New York: Simon Pulse, 1999. 272p. $6.99. ISBN 0-689-825-234-0.

Fourteen-year-old Liyana's world and life change when she and her Arab American family move from St. Louis back to Jerusalem.

2. Nye, Naomi Shihab (Ed.) *This Same Sky: A Collection of Poems from Around the World.* New York: Aladdin, 1996. 208p. $9.99. ISBN 0-689-806-302-0.

One hundred twenty-five poems from 68 countries in the Middle East, Asia, Africa, India, South and Central America introduce readers to the universality and diversity of experiences in other cultures.

Orlev, Uri. *Run, Boy, Run.* Boston: Houghton Mifflin Co., 2003. 186p. Translated by Hillel Halkin. $15.00. ISBN 0-616-16465-0.

Author

Author Uri Orlev was born in Warsaw, Poland. As a young boy he spent two years in hiding in the Warsaw ghetto. When Uri was eleven years old, the Nazis killed his mother and sent Uri and his brother to Bergen-Belsen. When the war ended, Orlev went to Israel. He now lives in Jerusalem. Orlev received the Hans Christian Andersen Prize in 1996. Translator Hillel Halkin was born in New York and moved to Israel where he now lives. Three novels written by Uri Orlev and translated by Hillel Halkin received the Batchelder Award in 1985, 1992, and 1996. This book is set in Poland during World War II, and it provides historical perspective to the immigration of Jews to Israel.

📖 Historical Fiction, Ages 9–12

Summary

They are starving in the Ghetto, when nine-year-old Srulik and his parents cross through the opening in the wall, walk through the city to the edge of the countryside, then leap into the ditch to hide from the German soldiers. Srulik's father manages to run away when the soldiers take Srulik and his mother to the Gestapo. The Gestapo beat his mother and send her and Srulik back to the Ghetto. Soon after their return to the Ghetto, Srulik's mother disappears, and Srulik begins to run. Srulik runs until the war ends—sometimes begging and stealing with other orphan boys, sometimes hiding in the forests, sometimes living with a kind family on a farm or in a village. Srulik's father tells him that he must take another name, a good Polish name—Jurek Staniak, learn to cross himself and pray like a Christian, forget his family and who he is, but never forget that he is a Jew. Finally the Russians invade Poland, the war ends, and Srulik remembers only that he is now Jurek. The story ends with Jurek being taken to the Jewish Children's Home and his memory returning when he visits his village and hears the story of his family. The Epilogue continues the story of Srulik, who as an adult emigrated to Israel, where he was reunited with his sister and her family. This story is based on a true story told to the author.

Curriculum Responses with Curriculum Standards

1. As Jurek survives the war years, he meets many people—some kind, some cruel, others indifferent. After reading, engage students in a discussion about the difference that people made in Jurek's life. Ask students to think about their own experiences and to share the difference that kindness or cruelty has meant to them in their own lives. Ask them to think about ways they can extend kindness to others. (American Association of School Librarians Standards 1.1.2, 1.1.3, 1.1.6, 1.1.9, 1.3.4, 2.1.5, 2.3.1, 3.1.1, 3.1.2, 3.1.3, 3.2.1, 3.2.2, 3.3.1, 3.3.2, 3.3.5, 4.1.1, 4.1.2, 4.1.5, 4.3.1; English Language Arts Standards 1, 2, 3, 4, 6, 11, 12)

2. After reading, ask students to identify and discuss the personal qualities that enabled Jurek to survive the war years. Ask them how they might have felt and what they might have done had they been Jurek. (American Association of School Librarians Standards 1.1.2, 1.1.3, 1.1.6, 1.1.9, 1.3.4, 2.1.5, 2.3.1, 3.1.1, 3.1.2, 3.1.3, 3.2.1, 3.2.2, 3.3.1, 3.3.2, 3.3.5, 4.1.1, 4.1.2, 4.1.5; English Language Arts Standards 1, 2, 3, 4, 6, 11, 12)

3. After reading, ask students to discuss why Jurek was taken to the Jewish Children's Home rather than being allowed to continue living

with the Polish farmer and his family. (American Association of School Librarians Standards 1.1.2, 1.1.3, 1.1.6, 1.1.9, 1.3.4, 2.1.5, 2.3.1, 3.1.1, 3.1.2, 3.1.3, 3.2.1, 3.2.2, 3.3.1, 3.3.2, 3.3.5, 4.1.1, 4.1.12, 4.1.5; English Language Arts Standards 1, 2, 3, 4, 6, 11, 12)

UNITED KINGDOM OF GREAT BRITAIN AND IRELAND

Authors from the United Kingdom offer realistic fiction, classics, fantasy, and nonfiction. In Emma Barnes's humorous story of Jessica and her mother, a professional witch, Jessica learns that what people think really doesn't matter. Authors J. M. Barrie and Daniel Defoe present the classic stories of *Peter Pan* and *Robinson Crusoe.* Related books offer additional classic titles, such as *The Secret Garden, Treasure Island, Robin Hood,* and others. Neil Philip introduces readers to Jewish fairy tales and parables written by a seventeenth century rabbi. Jane Johnson's *The Shadow World* takes readers on an adventure into the Secret Country of Eidolon. Nonfiction books offer an abundance of information and specific facts. The *Ultimate Interactive Atlas of Space* and related books provide information about space and other topics such as pyramids, the Titanic, and robots. These nonfiction books are enhanced with pop-ups, pull-tabs, slide-outs, and other interactive features. Anna Claybourne identifies and offers survival tips about one hundred natural and human dangers. Her related books present detailed information about ancient Greece, the Renaissance, and the Titanic. Finally, Sally Jeffrie writes tips for girls with related books offering "how-to" suggestions for both boys and girls. Curriculum Responses include activities such as developing book-based games, interviewing book characters, dramatizations, and others.

Barnes, Emma. *Jessica Haggerthwaite: Witch Dispatcher.* New York: Walker & Co. 2001. 168p. Illustrated by Tim Archbold. $15.95. ISBN 0-8027-8794-0.

Author and Illustrator

Author Emma Barnes lives in England. Illustrator Tim Archbold lives in Scotland. This book is set in England.

📖 Humorous Fiction, Ages 8–12

Summary

When Jessica's mother decides to go into business as a professional witch, Jessica knows that she must do something to prevent her mother from embarrassing the family. As each of Jessica's plans backfires, her mother's witch business prospers, and family troubles escalate. When the opportunity finally comes for Jessica to put a stop to her mother's business, Jessica realizes that what people think doesn't matter.

Curriculum Responses with Curriculum Standards

1. After reading, engage students in a discussion. How did Jessica come to realize that what people think doesn't matter? What does matter to Jessica? Encourage students to relate Jessica's experiences to their own experiences. (American Association of School Librarians Standards 1.1.9, 1.3.4, 1.4.2, 2.1.1, 2.1.5, 2.3.1, 2.4.3, 3.1.2, 3.2.2, 3.3.2, 3.3.5, 4.1.2, 4.1.5, 4.3.1; English Language Arts Standards 1, 3, 4, 6, 11, 12; Social Studies Standards IV)

2. After reading, encourage students to "help" Jessica prevent her mother from embarrassing the family. Each of Jessica's plans backfires. Ask students what they would do. Have them suggest plans that Jessica might use. (American Association of School Librarians Standards 1.1.2, 1.1.6, 1.1.9, 1.2.2, 1.3.4, 2.1.5, 2.2.2, 3.1.2, 3.1.3, 3.2.1, 3.2.2, 3.3.1, 3.3.2, 3.3.5, 4.1.1, 4.1.3, 4.3.1; English Language Arts Standards 1, 3, 4, 6, 11, 12)

3. After reading, encourage students to select, write, and act out scenes from the book. Have students retell the story to another class or group of students by acting out their scenes for them. (American Association of School Librarians Standards 1.1.6, 2.1.6, 2.3.4, 3.1.3, 3.2.1, 3.2.2, 3.3.4, 4.1.1, 4.1.3, 4.1.8, 4.3.1; English Language Arts Standards 1, 3, 4, 6, 11, 12; Theater Content Standards 1, 2)

Related Books

1. Barnes, Emma. *Sam and the Griswalds.* UK: Bloomsbury, 2004. 320p. Illustrated by Tim Archbold. $12.99. ISBN 0-747-55906-6.

When the Griswalds move next door to Sam Harris, not only does Sam's life change; so does life in the entire town of Bellstone.

2. Lynch, Chris. *Cyberia.* New York: Scholastic Press, 2008. 158p. $16.99. ISBN 0-545-02793-4.

Zane, whose every move is monitored, pits himself against Dr. Gristle, the veterinarian who controls the animals and intends to control the world with electronic microchips.

Barrie, J. M. *Peter Pan.* New York: Aladdin Classics, 2003. 228p. $3.99. ISBN 0-689-86691-7.

Author

Author J. M. Barrie was a journalist and writer who was born in Scotland.

📖 Fantasy, Fiction, All Ages

Summary

Wendy, John, and Michael Darling meet Peter Pan, when he and Tinker Bell fly through the window and into their nursery looking for his shadow. Gentle Wendy sews the shadow back onto Peter, who teaches the children how to fly and takes them back to his home in Never-Never-Land. Wendy becomes a mother to Peter Pan and the Lost Boys, while she and her brothers join Peter's adventures with Captain Hook, his pirate crew, and the ticking crocodile.

Curriculum Responses with Curriculum Standards

1. If Wendy and her brothers had cell phones, what kind of text messages might they write to their parents and friends? What might their parents and friends write in reply? Have students discuss how today's technology would make a difference in the story of Peter Pan. Might Peter and the Darling children send text messages to Captain Hook, his pirates, and the Indians? Finally have students write text messages among the Darling children, their parents, and friends, and to other characters in the story. (American Association of School Librarians Standards 1.1.1, 1.1.2, 1.1.3, 1.1.6, 1.3.2, 1.3.4, 2.1.1, 2.1.6, 2.2.4, 2.4.3, 3.1.2, 3.1.3, 3.2.2, 3.2.2, 3.3.2, 3.3.5, 4.1.3, 4.3.1; English Language Arts Standards 3, 4, 5, 6, 11, 12; Social Studies Standards VIII)

2. Have each student select and become a character from the book, learn as much as possible about that character, develop interview questions about other characters, and interview each other. (American Association of School Librarians Standards 1.1.2, 1.1.3, 1.1.9, 1.2.1, 1.2.5, 1.3.4, 3.1.3, 3.2.1, 3.2.2, 3.2.3, 3.3.3, 3.3.5, 4.1.3, 4.2.2, 4.3.1; English Language Arts Standards 3, 4, 11, 12)

3. *Peter Pan* was first presented as a play. It easily lends itself to student retellings, such as script writing, the creation of stage settings, and dramatizations such as reader's theater, puppet shows, or a play. (American Association of School Librarians Standards 1.2.3, 2.1.6, 2.2.4, 3.1.2, 3.1.3, 3.2.2, 3.2.3, 3.3.5, 4.1.3, 4.1.8, 4.3.1; English Language Arts Standards 3, 4, 5, 6, 11, 12; Theater Content Standards 1, 2, 3)

4. Have children create shoebox dioramas showing episodes from the book, such as the mermaid lagoon, flying to Never-Never-Land, or Captain Hook's pirate ship. (American Association of School Librarians

Standards 1.2.3, 2.1.2, 2.1.6, 2.2.4, 3.2.1, 4.1.3, 4.1.6, 4.1.8; English Language Arts Standards 11, 12; Visual Arts Content Standards 1, 2, 3, 5.) Engage students in Discussion Questions and Activities suggested in the Reading Group Guide in the back of the book.

Related Books

1. Burnett, Frances Hodgson. *The Secret Garden.* New York: Aladdin Classics, 2008. 386p. $14.00. ISBN 1-439-52807-1.

As Mary Lennox, her sickly cousin Colin, and the chambermaid's brother Dickon reclaim the walled garden that Colin's deceased mother loved and tended, Colin regains his health.

2. Carroll, Lewis. *Alice's Adventures in Wonderland.* New York: Aladdin Paperbacks, 2000. 176p. $4.19. ISBN 0-689-83375-X.

Enter a curious fantasy world of nonsense verse and adventure with Alice as she follows the White Rabbit down a rabbit hole, eats foods that makes her grow very tall and then very small, and meets the Mad Hatter, the Duchess, and other memorable characters.

3. Grahame, Kenneth. *The Wind in the Willows.* New York: Aladdin Classics, 2008. 305p. Illustrated by Ernest H. Shepard. $14.99. ISBN 1-439-52806-3.

Mischievous Toad has a way of getting into trouble, but with the help of his friends Mole, Water Rat, and Badger, he manages to escape from the castle dungeon and find his way back home to Toad Hall.

4. Sewell, Anna. *Black Beauty.* New York: Aladdin Classics. 2008. 210p. $4.99. ISBN 1-439-52841-1.

Black Beauty, the black quarter horse with the white star on his forehead, tells his own story in his own voice from his days as a young colt with his mother, through many masters—some cruel, others kind—to the last years of his life in a comfortable pasture.

5. Stevenson, Robert Louis. *Treasure Island.* New York: Aladdin Paperbacks, 2000. 368p. Illustrated by N. C. Wyeth. $6.99. ISBN 0-689-83212-5.

Join young Jim Hawkins and Long John Silver with his pirate crew in their adventure on the high seas, as they follow the map in search for Captain Flint's treasure.

Claybourne, Anna. *100 Most Dangerous Things on the Planet: What to Do If It Happens to You.* New York: Scholastic Inc., 2008. 112p. $7.99. ISBN 0-545-06927-0.

Author

Author Anna Claybourne lives in Edinburgh, Scotland.

📖 Nonfiction, Ages 9–12

Summary

Clean water, modern medicine, and rescue services contribute greatly to the safety of people in today's world. However, dangers that occur in wild places or from natural disasters still exist. This book lists one hundred natural and human dangers. Natural dangers are classified as Natural Disasters, Dangerous Weather, Lost in the Wild, or Dangerous Animals, whereas human dangers are those caused by humans. Each page identifies a danger with an illustration, short bits of information, and survival tips. Risk and Survival Ratings are included for each danger. The Introduction strongly recommends that the best way to stay safe is to stay away from dangerous situations, use common sense, pay attention to warnings, and obey instructions.

Curriculum Responses with Curriculum Standards

1. Encourage students to read, with each one picking a danger to report on to the rest of the class. In their reports, have students include risk and survival ratings. Which dangers have the highest and lowest risk and survival ratings? Encourage discussion about dangers that they or someone they know may have experienced. Extend the activity by having students research to learn more and report on the danger which they experienced. (American Association of School Librarians Standards 1.1.3, 1.1.6, 1.3.4, 2.1.15, 2.3.1, 3.1.1, 3.1.2, 3.1.3, 3.1.5, 3.2.1, 3.2.2, 3.3.1, 3.3.2, 3.3.3, 3.3.5, 4.1.1, 4.1.2, 4.1.3, 4.1.5, 4.3.1; English Language Arts Standards 1, 3, 4, 6, 11, 12)

2. Encourage students to read the newspaper and newsmagazines to learn about currently occurring dangers. Have students bring the articles to class to share with students, and then post their articles on a bulletin board for all to see. Extend the activity by discussing safety precautions and emergency responses. (American Association of School Librarians Standards 1.1.2, 1.1.6, 1.1.9, 1.2.2, 1.2.3, 1.3.4, 2.1.2, 2.1.5, 2.1.6, 2.2.4, 2.3.1, 3.1.2, 3.1.3, 3.2.1, 3.2.2, 3.2.3, 3.3.2, 3.3.4, 3.3.5, 4.1.1, 4.1.2, 4.1.3, 4.1.4, 4.1.5, 4.1.7, 4.2.1, 4.3.1; English Language Arts Standards 1, 3, 4, 6, 11, 12)

3. After reading, have students pick a danger and then role-play the danger, precautions, and rescue responses. (American Association of School Librarians Standards 1.1.2, 1.1.5, 1.1.9, 1.3.4, 2.1.5, 2.2.4, 2.3.1, 3.1.2, 3.1.3, 3.2.1, 3.2.2, 3.2.3, 3.3.4, 3.3.5, 4.1.1, 4.1.2, 4.1.3,

4.1.8, 4.3.1; English Language Arts Standards 1, 3, 4, 6, 11, 12; Theater Content Standards 2)

Related Books

1. Claybourne, Anna. *Ancient Greece.* London: Hodder Wayland, 2002. 48p. $16.32. ISBN 0-50-23908-5.

Maps, diagrams, artwork, photographs, timeline, glossary, and index provide information about ancient Greece, with each two-page spread addressing separate topics such as education, medicine, ships and trading, and others.

2. Claybourne, Anna. *Time Travel Guide: The Renaissance.* NY: Raintree/Pearson Education, 2008. $8.95. ISBN 1-410-93295-8.

This readable, illustrated, and informative travel guide takes students back in time to the Renaissance.

3. Claybourne, Anna, and Katie Daynes. *Titanic.* London: Usborne Books, 2006. 64p. Illustrated by Ian McNee. $8.99. ISBN 0-794-51269-0.

Photos and information tell the story of the Titanic.

Defoe. Daniel. *Robinson Crusoe.* New York: Atheneum Books for Young Readers, 2003. 52p. Illustrated by N. C. Wyeth. $18.95. ISBN 0-689-85104-9.

Author and Illustrator

Author Daniel Defoe is English and lived from 1660 to 1731. Illustrator N. C. Wyeth is American, lived from 1882 to 1945, and illustrated over one hundred books, including most of the Scribner Illustrated Classics series.

Summary

Vibrant and realistic illustrations enliven this abridged version of the story of Robinson Crusoe, who spent over twenty-eight years shipwrecked on a deserted island off the coast of Brazil before being rescued and returning to his home in England. This is a classic survival tale of learning to create shelter, explore a new environment, live off the land, and withstand loneliness. Robinson Crusoe's loneliness is eased by the appearance and companionship of Friday, until the two return to England together.

Curriculum Responses with Curriculum Standards

1. Have students trace the route of Robinson Crusoe's travels on a map. (American Association of School Librarians Standards 2.1.2, 2.1.4,

2.3.1, 3.1.4, 4.1.3, 4.1.4; English Language Arts Standards 3, 11, 12; Social Studies Standards III)

2. Robinson Crusoe was captured by pirates and was on the lookout for pirates when at sea. Suggest that students generate questions, research, and learn more about pirates during the seventeenth century. Provide opportunities for them to share their findings with their classmates. (American Association of School Librarians Standards 1.1.1, 1.1.2, 1.1.3, 1.1.4, 1.1.5, 1.1.6, 1.1.7, 1.1.8, 1.1.9, 1.2.1, 1.2.2, 1.2.3, 1.2.4, 1.2.5, 1.2.6, 1.2.7, 1.3.1, 1.3.2, 1.3.3, 1.3.4, 1.3.5, 1.4.1, 1.4.2, 1.4.3, 1.4.4, 2.1.1, 2.1.2, 2.1.3, 2.1.4, 2.1.5, 2.1.6, 2.2.1, 2.2.2, 2.2.3, 2.2.4, 2.3.1, 2.4.3, 3.1.1, 3.1.2, 3.1.3, 3.1.4, 3.1.6, 3.2.1, 3.2.2, 3.2.3, 3.3.3, 3.3.5, 4.1.1, 4.1.2, 4.1.5, 4.1.6, 4.1.7, 4.2.2, 4.2.4, 4.3.1, 4.3.2, 4.3.4; English Language Arts Standards 1, 7, 8, 11, 12; Social Studies Standards II)

3. The story of Robinson Crusoe is considered to be one of the greatest survival stories. Have students discuss why that might be. Do they know of any other survival stories? How do those stories compare to this story? (American Association of School Librarians Standards 1.1.2, 1.1.9, 1.2.1, 1.3.4, 2.1.5, 3.1.2, 3.1.3, 3.2.2, 3.3.1, 3.3.2, 3.3.3, 3.3.5, 4.1.3, 4.1.5, 4.3.1; English Language Arts Standards 3, 4, 6, 11, 12)

Related Books

1. Creswick, Paul. *Robin Hood.* New York: Atheneum Books for Young Readers, 2004. 52p. Illustrated by N. C. Wyeth. $18.95. ISBN 0-689-85467-6.

This abridged and illustrated retelling of the legend of Robin Hood introduces readers to the adventures of Robin Hood, Friar Tuck, Little John, and others who opposed the tyranny of the English Prince John, while his brother Richard the Lionheart led a crusade to free Jerusalem from the Turks.

2. Defoe, Daniel. *Robinson Crusoe.* New York: Aladdin Classics, 2001. 486p. $3.99. ISBN 0-689-84408-5.

This unabridged version may appeal to mature readers who want to know more about Robinson Crusoe's adventures.

3. Kimmel, Eric A. *The Hero Beowulf.* New York: Farrar, Straus and Giroux, 2005. Unpaged. Illustrated by Leonard Everett Fisher. $16.00. ISBN 0-374-30671-0.

This story of how Beowulf slew the monstrous creature, Grendel, is an illustrated and adapted retelling of the oldest surviving epic poem in English literature, a story that was retold orally for two hundred years, until it was written in Anglo-Saxon.

4. Malcolmson, Anne. *Song of Robin Hood.* New York: Houghton Mifflin, 1975. 1947. 123p. Illustrated by Virginia Lee Burton. Music Arranged by Gracee Castagnetta. $20.00. ISBN 0-618-07185-5.

With its exquisite illustrations, authentic verse, and music, this remains the definitive edition of the legend of Robin Hood, a story originally sung as a ballad throughout England during the thirteenth and fourteenth centuries.

5. Stevenson, Robert Louis. *Kidnapped.* New York: Atheneum Books for Young Readers, 2004. 64p. Illustrated by N. C. Wyeth. $18.95. ISBN 0-689-86542-2.

David's father is dead, and not only will his uncle not give him his inheritance, but he has David kidnapped and sold into slavery in North Carolina.

Jeffrie, Sally. *The Girls' Book of Glamour: A Guide to Being a Goddess.* New York: Scholastic Inc., 2008. 126p. Illustrated by Nellie Ryan. $9.99. ISBN 0-545- 08537-3.

Author and Illustrator

Biographical information about author Sally Jeffrie was not available. Illustrator Nellie Ryan was born, raised, and educated in New Zealand, and he now lives in England.

📖 Nonfiction, Ages 8–12

Summary

One hundred three tips for making and doing things, for improving appearance and behavior, and for handling social situations make for quick, informative, and entertaining reading. How to hail a taxi, apply eye shadow, walk in high heels, cry at a wedding, and make a skirt out of jeans are only a few. A Note to Readers in the beginning of the book urges readers to use common sense and to be considerate of others all of the time.

Curriculum Responses with Curriculum Standards

1. While the girls read this book, encourage boys to read their companion survival book listed in related books. After reading, have girls share with girls, and boys share with boys, tips and survival strategies that were of interest. Allow girls to read the boys' book and share survival strategies if they wish. (Boys are not likely to be interested in the glamour tips for girls.) (American Association of School Librarians Standards 1.1.6, 1.3.4, 2.1.5, 3.1.2, 3.1.3, 3.2.1,

3.2.2, 3.2.1, 3.2.2, 3.3.1, 3.3.2, 3.3.3, 3.3.5, 4.1.1, 4.1.2, 4.1.3, 4.3.1; English Language Arts Standards 1, 3, 4, 6, 11, 12)

2. Encourage boys and girls to demonstrate for their classmates how to do something that they read about, such as survive falling off a horse or walking with confidence. (American Association of School Librarians Standards 1.1.6, 1.3.4, 2.3.1, 3.1.2, 3.1.3, 3.2.1, 3.2.2, 3.3.1, 3.3.2, 3.3.5, 4.1.1, 4.1.2, 4.1.3, 4.1.8, 4.3.1; English Language Arts Standards 1, 2, 3, 4, 6, 11, 12)

3. Encourage boys and girls to make something that they read about, such as a dugout canoe or a button-and-bead charm bracelet, and to set up a display of their products for their classmates and other students. (American Association of School Librarians Standards 1.1.6, 1.1.9, 1.3.4, 2.1.5, 2.1.6, 2.2.4, 2.3.1, 3.1.2, 3.1.3, 3.2.1, 3.2.2, 3.2.3, 3.3.1, 3.3.2, 3.3.4, 3.3.5, 4.1.1, 4.1.2, 4.1.3, 4.1.5, 4.1.8, 4.3.1; English Language Arts Standards 1, 3, 4, 6, 11, 12; Visual Arts Content Standards 1, 2)

Related Books

1. Campbell, Guy. *The Boys' Book of Survival: How to Survive Anything, Anywhere.* New York: Scholastic Inc. 2008. 125p. Illustrated by Simon Ecob. $9.99. ISBN 0-545-08536-5.

One-to-three-page illustrated instructions for surviving emergencies such as "How to Survive a Duel," How to Gut a Fish," and "How to Survive Your Teachers," plus fifty-seven others that are equally useful, or useless, make for quick, informative, and entertaining reading.

2. Enright, Dominique, Guy MacDonald, and Nikalas Catlow. *The Boys' Book: How to Be the Best at Everything.* New York: Scholastic Press, 2007. 126p. $9.99. ISBN 0-545-01628-2.

Fun ideas and helpful information for activities such as making a water bomb, hypnotizing a chicken, escaping from quicksand, and others will entertain boys and girls too.

3. Foster, Juliana. *The Girls' Book: How to be the Best at Everything.* New York: Scholastic Press, 2007. 128p. $9.99. ISBN 0-545-01629-0.

A girls' companion book to the boys' book offers tips, suggestions, and directions for designing your own clothes, creating a dance routine, making a crystal, and other activities.

Johnson, Jane. *The Shadow World.* New York: Simon & Schuster Books for Young Readers, 2007. 277p. $15.99. ISBN 1-4169-1783-7.

Author

Author Jane Johnson lives in London and Morocco.

📖 Fantasy, Ages 8–12

Summary

In this second book of the *Eidolon Chronicles,* Ben Arnold's mother, Queen of Eidolon, returns to her home to save it from the evil Dodman. Queen Isadora takes baby Alice and the cat Iggy with her to Eidolon. She assures her husband, son Ben, and daughter Ellie that she will return soon. When Ellie disappears, Ben realizes that she has followed their mother into the Secret Country. Knowing that Ellie will be in danger, Ben and his father quickly follow Ellie. Now the entire Arnold family is in Eidolon, separated from one another, and in danger. In the ensuing battle between good and evil, Ellie must be rescued from the Dodman's dungeon, and only the Arnold children can save Eidolon.

Curriculum Responses with Curriculum Standards

1. Have children create a map or salt-dough model of Eidolon. (American Association of School Librarians Standards 1.1.2, 1.1.9, 1.2.2, 1.2.3, 1.3.4, 2.1.2, 2.1.6, 2.3.4, 3.1.2, 3.2.3, 3.3.4, 4.1.3, 4.1.6, 4.1.8, 4.3.1; English Language Arts Standards 3, 4, 6, 11, 12; Visual Arts Content Standards 1, 2, 3, 6)
2. Some children may want to create and play a board game with written questions drawn from the book. (American Association of School Librarians Standards 1.1.2, 1.1.9, 1.2.3, 1.3.4, 2.1.2, 2.1.5, 2.1.6, 2.2.4, 3.1.2, 3.1.3, 3.2.1, 3.2.2, 3.2.3, 3.3.5, 4.1.3, 4.1.6, 4.1.8, 4.3.1; English Language Arts Standards 3, 4, 5, 6, 11, 12; Visual Arts Content Standards 1, 2, 3, 6)
3. Have children create masks, write scripts, and act out scenes from the book. (American Association of School Librarians Standards 1.1.9, 1.2.2, 1.2.3, 1.3.4, 2.1.2, 2.1.5, 2.1.6, 2.2.3, 2.2.4, 3.1.2, 3.31.3, 3.2.1, 3.2.2, 3.2.3, 3.3.4, 3.3.5, 4,1.3, 4.1.8, 4.3.1; English Language Arts Content Standards 3, 4, 5, 6, 11, 12; Theater Content Standards 1, 2, 3, 4; Visual Arts Content Standards 1, 2, 3, 6)

Related Books

1. Johnson, Jane. *Dragon's Fire.* New York: Simon & Schuster Books for Young Readers 320p. $8.73. ISBN 1-416-92590-2.

In this third book of the Eidolon Chronicles, Isadora returns to Eidolon, and it is baby Alice who conquers the evil Dodman and secures the throne for her mother.

2. Johnson, Jane. *The Secret Country.* New York: Simon & Schuster Books for Young
   Readers, ISBN 1-4169-3815-X.

In this first book of the *Eidolon Chronicles,* Ben finds the cat Iggy in a
pet shop, listens to his story about a magical place called Eidolon, and even
travels there with him.

Philip, Neil. *The Pirate Princess and Other Fairy Tales.* New York: Arthur A. Levine Books, 2005. 88p. Illustrated by Mark Weber. $19.99. ISBN 0-590-10855-7.

Author and Illustrator

Author Neil Philip is British. Illustrator Mark Weber is American. This
book was selected by the United States Board on Books for Young People
(USBBY) as an Outstanding International Book in 2005.

📖 Fairy Tales, Picture Book, Ages 8–12

Summary

Introduction, Notes on the Stories, and Further Reading elaborate on the
four original fairy tales and three parables adapted for children from the
writings of Rabbi Nahman of Bratslav, a seventeenth-century religious
leader, teacher, and mystic. Stories about the princess who became a pirate
in order to search for her lost love, the poor man who found treasure in his
own house, the prince who thought he was a turkey, and others are rooted
in the Yiddish and Slavic folktale traditions, contain elements of universal
fairytales, and will appeal to both boys and girls.

Curriculum Responses with Curriculum Standards

1. Introduce this book to students by selecting a simple story such
   as "The Treasure." After reading, encourage discussion by asking
   students why they think the poor man had to travel to Vienna to
   discover the treasure in his own house. What might have happened
   had the poor man not listened to and believed the soldier's dream?
   (American Association of School Librarians Standards 1.1.2, 1.1.3,
   1.1.6, 1.1.9, 1.3.4, 2.1.5, 2.3.1, 3.1.2, 3.1.3, 3.2.1, 3.2.2, 3.3.1, 3.3.2,
   3.3.5, 4.1.1, 4.1.2, 4.1.3, 4.3.1; English Language Arts Standards 1,
   3, 4, 6, 11, 12)

2. "The Fixer" is a story about a happy man. Encourage discussion
   by asking students how The Fixer remained happy as circum-
   stances changed. Ask what the king learned about being happy.
   Then ask students whether they can learn something about being
   happy in their own lives from this story. (American Association of

School Librarians Standards 1.1.2, 1.1.3, 1.1.6, 1.1.9, 1.3.4, 2.1.5, 2.3.1, 3.1.2, 3.1.3, 3.2.1, 3.2.2, 3.3.1, 3.3.2, 3.3.3, 3.3.5, 4.1.1, 4.1.2, 4.1.3, 4.1.5, 4.3.1; English Language Arts Standards 1, 3, 4, 6, 11, 12)

3. Encourage students to select and read a story of their own choice. Encourage them to retell the story to their classmates, share their thoughts, and raise questions about the story. (American Association of School Librarians Standards 1.1.6, 1.3.4, 3.1.3, 3.2.1, 3.2.2, 3.3.5, 4.1.1, 4.1.13, 4.3.1; English Language Arts Standards 1, 3, 4, 6, 11, 12)

Related Books

1. Colum, Padraic. *The Children's Homer: The Adventures of Odysseus and the Tale of Troy.* New York: Aladdin Books, 2004. 256p. Illustrated by Willy Pogany. $9.95. ISBN 1-604-50024-7.

Originally published in 1918, Padraic Colum's retelling of Homer's epic tales with lyrical, sophisticated language and complex sentence structure is still regarded as the finest version for young people.

2. Datlow, Ellen and Terri Windling (Eds.) New York: Simon and Schuster Books for Young Readers. 2003. 165p. $16.95. ISBN 0-689-84613-4.

Jane Yolen, Tanith Lee, and eleven other authors write contemporary versions of fairytales such as "Sleeping Beauty" and "Rapunzel."

3. Philip, Neil. *Illustrated Book of Myths.* DK Children, 2007. 192p. Illustrated by Nilesh Mistry. $7.79. ISBN 0-756-62223-9.

Short retellings of myths of the world from Middle Eastern, Asian, Persian, Native American, Scandinavian, Celtic, Anglo-Saxon, Welsh, Irish, Serbian, Greek, Roman, Egyptian, Australian, Polynesian, Indonesian, and Indian cultures are organized around the themes of creation, beginnings, fertility and cultivation, gods and people, gods and animals, and visions of the end.

Scagell, Robin. New York: Scholastic, 2008. *The Ultimate Interactive Atlas of Space.* 50p. Illustrated by KJA Artists. $17.95. ISBN 0-545-07456-8.

Author and Illustrator

Author Robin Scagell is a British space writer and broadcaster for BBC News.

📖 Nonfiction, Ages 8 and Up

Summary

This interactive atlas with pull-tabs, wheels, flaps, pop-ups, and a 3-D solar system is an excellent resource for information about space and space travel. Three chapters entitled Our Solar System: Its Planets and the Earth's Moon; Other Celestial Objects, and Discovering the Universe, provide photos, illustrations, diagrams, and factual information about the planets, galaxies, northern and southern skies, space travel, and other topics. Each two-page spread features its own topic.

Curriculum Responses and Curriculum Standards

1. Encourage children to use the star wheels and maps to identify stars, planets, and constellations that they see in the sky. (American Association of School Librarians Standards 1.1.6, 1.2.3, 1.4.4, 2.2.1, 2.4.1, 3.2.3, 4.1.7, 4.3.2; English Language Arts Standards 1; Life Science Standards)

2. Encourage students to use this book as a resource when studying the solar system, space, or astronomy. For more information, contact the National Aeronautics and Space Administration (NASA) at http://www.nasa.gov for teacher and student resources and materials about space, space flights, career opportunities, and other related topics. (American Association of School Librarians Standards 1.1.4, 1.1.6, 1.1.8, 1.2.3, 1.3.1, 1.3.3, 1.3.5, 1.4.1, 2.2.1, 4.1.2, 4.1.4, 4.1.5, 4.1.7, 4.3.2; English Language Arts Standards 1, 9; Life Science Standards)

3. Encourage children to use information in this book to create quiz games, such as Trivial Pursuit, Wheel of Fortune, Jeopardy, or others. (American Association of School Librarians Standards 1.3.1, 1.3.3, 1.3.4, 1.4.3, 2.1.2, 2.1.6, 2.2.4, 3.1.2, 3.1.3, 3.2.1, 3.2.3, 3.3.1, 3.3.2, 3.3.4, 3.3.5, 3.4.2, 4.1.3, 4.1.6, 4.1.7, 4.1.8, 4.3.1; English Language Arts Standards 3; Life Science Standards)

Related Books

1. Bolton, Anne. *Pyramids and Mummies.* New York: Simon & Schuster Books for Young Readers. 2007. Unpaged. $21.99. ISBN 1-4169-5873-8.

Timeline, flaps, fold-ups, pull-outs, pop-ups, and the board game "Asps and Ladders" add to text and illustrations on each two-page spread of this triangular (pyramid-shaped) book about ancient Egypt, preparation of mummies for the afterlife, grave robbers, spells and stories, and the curse of Tutankhamen.

2. Crosbie, Duncan. *Titanic: The Ship of Dreams.* New York: Orchard Books, 2007. Unpaged. Illustrated by Bob Moulder, Peter Kent, and Tim Hutchinson. $18.99. ISBN 0-439-89995-8.

Photographs, letters, journals, pop-ups, pull-tabs, slide outs, fold-out maps, and booklets enliven this documentary of the ship, its passengers, the voyage, and the tragic sinking of the Titanic.

3. Gifford, Clive. *Robots.* New York: Atheneum Books for Young Readers, 2008. Unpaged. Art Director Russell Porter. $21.95. ISBN 1-4169-6414-2.

Flaps, pull-tabs, pop-ups, pull-outs, and time-line augment fact-filled text, photos, drawings, and illustrations that depict and explain what robots are, robot history, and uses for robots in the workplace, in hazardous situations, in space, and in the field of medicine and other settings, along with future expectations.

4. Gifford, Clive. *Spies Revealed.* New York: Atheneum Books for Young Readers, 2008. Unpaged. $21.99. ISBN 1-4169-7113-0.

Flaps and pullouts, photos, maps, drawings, cartoon-like illustrations, text boxes, and fact-filled narrative fill each two-page spread that addresses topics related to spying, such as new identity, equipment, danger, and other things.

5. Jackson, Elaine. *The Ultimate Interactive Atlas of the World.* New York: Scholastic Inc., 2007. 50p. Illustrated by Julian Baker and Sebastian Quigley. $17.99. ISBN 0-439-90340-8.

Pull-tabs, sliders, flaps, pop-ups, and a two-dimensional map that curls into a three-dimensional globe supplement informative text, photos, illustrations, and diagrams about maps, time, formation of the earth, climate, countries, and regions around the world.

Appendix

NATIONAL STANDARDS FOR ARTS EDUCATION

National Standards for Arts Education were developed by the Consortium of National Arts Education Associations, through a grant administered by MENC: The National Association for Music Education. The associations are the National Art Education Association, the National Dance Association, the American Alliance for Theatre Education, and the MENC: The National Association for Music Education. The information for music, dance, and theater content standards is from *National Standards for Arts Education,* Copyright ©1994 by MENC: The National Association for Music Education, and is used with permission. The National Dance Association is the official author of the dance section within these National Arts Standards.

Dance Content Standards

Content Standard: 1: Identifying and demonstrating movement elements and skills in performing dance

Content Standard: 5: Demonstrating and understanding dance in various cultures and historical periods

Music Content Standards

Content Standard: 1: Singing, alone and with others, a varied repertoire of music

Content Standard: 3: Improvising melodies, variations, and accompaniments

Content Standard: 4: Composing and arranging music within specified guidelines

Theater Content Standards

Content Standard: 1: Script writing by planning and recording improvisations based on personal experience and heritage, imagination, literature, and history

Content Standard: 2: Acting by assuming roles and interacting in improvisations

Content Standard: 3: Designing by visualizing and arranging environments for classroom dramatizations

Content Standard: 4: Directing by planning classroom dramatizations
Content Standard: 5: Researching by finding information to support classroom dramatizations

National Visual Arts Standards

The National Visual Arts Standards were developed by The National Art Education Association (NAEA). For more information, see www.arteducators.org. Reprinted with permission from *The National Visual Arts Standards,* Copyright 1994, National Art Education Association.

Content Standard: 1: Understanding and applying media, techniques, and processes
Content Standard: 2: Using knowledge of structures and function
Content Standard: 3: Choosing and evaluating a range of subject matter, symbols, and ideas
Content Standard: 4: Understanding the visual arts in relation to history and cultures
Content Standard: 5: Reflecting upon and assessing the characteristics and merits of their work and the work of others
Content Standard: 6: Making connections between visual arts and other disciplines

STANDARDS FOR THE ENGLISH LANGUAGE ARTS

The Standards for the English Language Arts were published in 1996 by the International Reading Association and the National Council of Teachers of English and can be downloaded from http://www.ncte.org/standards. *Standards for the English Language Arts,* by the International Reading Association and the National Council of Teachers of English, Copyright 1996 by the International reading Association and the National Council of Teachers of English. Reprinted with permission.

1. Students read a wide range of print and nonprint texts to build an understanding of texts, of themselves, and of the cultures of the United States and the world; to acquire new information; to respond to the needs and demands of society and the workplace; and for personal fulfillment. Among these texts are fiction and nonfiction, and classic and contemporary works.
2. Students read a wide range of literature from many periods in many genres to build an understanding of the many dimensions (e.g., philosophical, ethical, aesthetic) of human experience.
3. Students apply a wide range of strategies to comprehend, interpret, evaluate, and appreciate texts. They draw on their prior experience,

their interactions with other readers and writers, their knowledge of word meaning and of other texts, their word identification strategies, and their understanding of textual features (e.g., sound-letter correspondence, sentence structure, context, and graphics).

4. Students adjust their use of spoken, written, and visual language (e.g., conventions, style, vocabulary) to communicate effectively with a variety of audiences and for different purposes.

5. Students employ a wide range of strategies as they write and use different writing process elements appropriately to communicate with different audiences for a variety of purposes.

6. Students apply knowledge of language structure, language conventions (e.g., spelling and punctuation), media techniques, figurative language, and genre to create, critique, and discuss print and nonprint texts.

8. Students use a variety of technological and information resources (e.g., libraries, databases, computer networks, video) to gather and synthesize information and to create and communicate knowledge.

9. Students develop an understanding of and respect for diversity in language use, patterns, and dialects across cultures, ethnic groups, geographic regions, and social roles.

12. Students use spoken, written, and visual language to accomplish their own purposes (e.g., for learning, enjoyment, persuasion, and the exchange of information).

NATIONAL SCIENCE EDUCATION STANDARDS

National Science Education Standards were developed as one component of the comprehensive vision of science education presented in the *National Science Education Standards* and can be downloaded at http://www.nap.edu/catalog-php?record id=4962. Reprinted with permission from List of Content Standards, *National Science Education Standards, 1996*, by the National Academy of Sciences, courtesy of the National Academies Press, Washington, D.C.

1. Unifying Concepts and Processes
2. Science as Inquiry
3. Physical Science
4. Life Science
5. Earth and Space Science
6. Science and Technology
7. Science in Personal and Social Perspectives
8. History and Nature of Science

NATIONAL COUNCIL FOR THE SOCIAL STUDIES

Curriculum Standards for Social Studies were developed by a Task Force of the National Council for the Social Studies (NCSS) and approved by the NCSS Board of Directors in April 1994. The opening chapters can be downloaded from the NCSS Web site. Reprinted with permission from the National Council for the Social Studies (NCSS), *Expectations of Excellence: Curriculum Standards for Social Studies* (Washington, DC: NCSS, 1994). The NCSS Web site is at www.socialstudies.org.

Thematic Strand I: Culture— Social studies programs should include experiences that provide for the study of culture and cultural diversity.

Thematic Strand II: Time, Continuity, and Change—Social studies programs should include experiences that provide for the study of the ways human beings view themselves in and over time.

Thematic Strand III: People, Places, and Environments—Social studies programs should include experiences that provide for the study of people, places, and environments.

Thematic Strand IV: Individual Development and Identity —Social studies programs should include experiences that provide for the study of individual development and identity.

Thematic Strand V: Individuals, Groups, and Institutions—Social studies programs should include experiences that provide for the study of interactions among individuals, groups, and institutions.

Thematic Strand VI: Power, Authority and Governance—Social studies programs should include experiences that provide for the study of how people create and change structures of power, authority, and governance.

Thematic Strand VII: Production, Distribution, and Consumption— Social studies programs should include experiences that provide for the study of how people organize for the production, distribution, and consumption of goods and services.

Thematic Strand VIII: Science, Technology, and Society—Social studies programs should include experiences that provide for the study of relationships among science, technology, and society.

Thematic Strand IX: Global Connections—Social studies programs should include experiences that provide for the study of global connections and interdependence.

Thematic Strand X: Civic Ideals and Practices—Social studies programs should include experiences that provide for the study of the ideals, principles, and practices of citizenship in a democratic republic.

Index

C

F

G

H

N

About the Author

ROSANNE J. BLASS, EdD, is a retired professor of education who taught at the University of South Florida College of Education, St. Petersburg, Florida. Her published works include Libraries Unlimited's *Celebrate with Books: Booktalks for Holidays and Other Occasions; Booktalks, Bookwalks, and Read-Alouds: Promoting the Best New Children's Literature across the Elementary Curriculum; Cultivating a Child's Imagination through Gardening; Beyond the Bean Seed: Gardening Activities for Grades K-6;* and *Responding to Literature: Activities for Grades 6, 7, 8.*